# Signaling Student Success

## Thematic Learning Stations and Integrated Units for Middle Level Classrooms

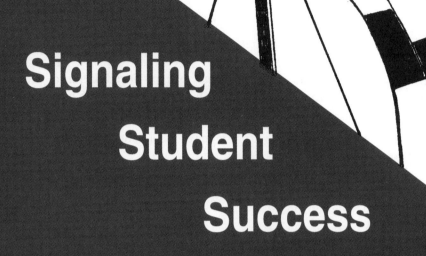

# Signaling
# Student
# Success

## Thematic Learning Stations
## and Integrated Units
## for Middle Level Classrooms

*by*
*Sandra Schurr*
*Sharen Lewis*
*Kathy LaMorte*
*Kathy Shewey*

National Middle School Association
Columbus, Ohio

**National Middle School Association**
**2600 Corporate Exchange Drive, Suite 370**
**Columbus, Ohio 43231**
**Telephone (800) 528-NMSA**

Printed in the United States of America

ISBN: 1-56090-112-8    NMSA Stock Number:  1236




**Library of Congress Cataloging-in-Publication Data**

Signaling student success: thematic learning stations and integrated
 units for middle level clasrooms/by Sandra Schurr ... (et al.).
    p.    cm.
 Includes bibliographical references.
 ISBN: 1-56090-112-8 (pbk.)
 1.  Classroom learning centers--United States--Curricula--Handbooks, manuals,
 etc.  2.  Middle schools--United States--Curricula--Handbooks,
 manuals, etc.  3.  Interdisciplinary approach in education--United
 States--Handbooks, manuals, etc.  4.  Activity programs in education-
 -United States--Handbooks, manuals, etc.    I.  Schurr, Sandra.
 LB3044.82.S54    1996                                    96-35190
 373.13'078--dc20                                         CIP

# Dedication

We dedicate this book to the "grand dame" of learning stations, IMOGENE FORTE, with great love, thanks, and affection from her fans and friends – Sandra Schurr, Kathy Shewey, Sharen Lewis, and Kathy LaMorte.

# About the Authors

**Sandra L. Schurr** is the Director of the National Resource Center for Middle Grades/High School Education located at the University of South Florida. A former classroom teacher and administrator, Dr. Schurr, known internationally for her dynamic workshops, is the author of many NMSA publications widely acclaimed by classroom teachers for their imaginative and practical instructional activities.

**Sharen Lewis** is a language arts teacher on a seventh grade team in the Venice Area Middle School, Venice, Florida. She has also served as a full-time consultant for the National Resource Center. A highly successful teacher at all levels, Sharen conducts interactive workshops that combine humor and practical strategies. She has presented at conferences in the United States, Panama, Korea, and in several European countries.

**Kathy LaMorte**, a social studies teacher on a sixth grade team in the Venice Area Middle School in Venice, Florida, also was a full-time consultant with the USF Resource Center for many years. Her workshops combine experiential philosophy and techniques with innovative activities and have been presented throughout the United States, Europe, Japan, and other countries.

**Kathy Shewey** is the Curriculum Resource Teacher at Kanapaha Middle School in Gainesville, Florida. Kathy has extensive experience as a team leader and has conducted staff development activities for the National Resource Center. She is on the Florida League of Middle Schools Executive Board and is co-author with Paul George of NMSA's publication *New Evidence for the Middle School.*

# Contents

Dear Middle Level Colleague:

Reviewing *Signaling Student Success* brought back memories of my middle school teaching days. During those years I worked (and struggled) to develop a variety of teaching strategies in order to meet the diverse needs of my students. I utilized interdisciplinary units of study, learning centers or stations, student choice opportunities, small group inquiry projects, and simulations to actively engage young adolescents in the learning process. I learned two important things during the development and implementation of these strategies. First, I never had as much time as I needed or wanted to locate and organize the material necessary to implement these approaches to learning. Second, although some resources were helpful, they always required considerable teacher adaptations to make them appropriate for use.

As I reviewed this new publication I was reminded of those lessons from my own experiences in the classroom and kept saying to myself, "Where was this book when I needed it?" Believe me, I would have jumped for joy had I discovered such a resource while I was teaching middle school language arts and social studies in Colorado. A resource like this would have maximized the time I had available to develop learning stations and interdisciplinary units.

Beginning with the "How to Use This Resource" section and continuing through the eleven independent thematic learning modules, this is truly a one-of-a-kind publication. It provides teacher support and student-ready materials and strategies geared to engage students actively in learning tasks as well as challenge them appropriately throughout the learning process. A real strength of this resource will evolve with its use over time, for it will serve as a strong foundation for the further development of these thematic modules to match the needs and interests of the students with whom you will work in the future. I learned new ways to stretch my learning centers and to improve my interdisciplinary units of study every year I used them. "Learning through doing" was just as important for me – the teacher – as it was for my students. This treasury of imaginative ideas and activities will have continuing use as a source to draw on, adapt from, and add to.

*Signaling Student Success* is a pioneering example of the type of instructional material that is needed to engage our diverse students adequately in the learning process. This kind of resource will enable teachers to implement middle level schools that are truly developmentally responsive. The need to produce varied teaching and learning approaches is addressed in NMSA's important position paper *This We Believe.*

Teaching techniques should enhance and accommodate the diverse skills, abilities, and knowledge of young adolescents, cultivate multiple intelligences, and capitalize on students' individual learning styles. Students should acquire diverse ways of posing and solving questions and engage in learning activities wherein basic skills can be taught in functional contexts. New concepts should be built on the knowledge students already possess (p. 24).

In my opinion, *Signaling Student Success* will make it possible for middle level teachers to create learning environments that match these ideals.

I encourage you to review this book carefully, consider the many possibilities it presents for use in your own classroom, and select one module to implement ASAP. If you haven't utilized learning stations, interdisciplinary units of study, student contracts, or cooperative learning strategies – now is the time to give them a try! Take advantage of the time this resource gives you to be creative in responding to the needs of your students. They deserve your best efforts.


Sincerely,

*Sue Swaim*

Sue Swaim
Executive Director, NMSA

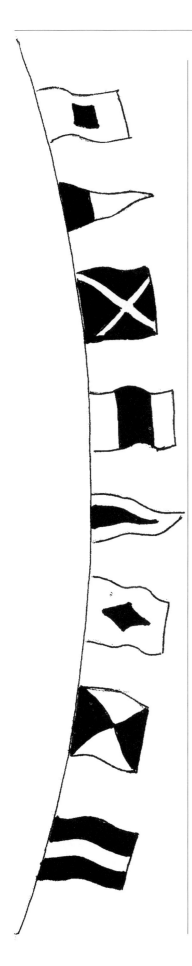

# HOW TO USE THIS RESOURCE

**Each of these eleven independent modules includes:**

- **Introduction of theme and guiding questions.**
- **Overview of topics and tasks.**
- **Ten to fifteen interdisciplinary activities.**
- **Concise directions for student and/or teacher.**
- **Student rubric and response sheet.**

These modules can be used in different ways. Although the focus of this special publication is on the use of these modules as learning stations, they can be used readily and successfully in other formats. Specifically, teachers can use these materials as the basis for cooperative learning group tasks, for interdisciplinary units, and for independent student contracts. The modules would require little, if any, modification when using them in any of these or other learning contexts.

The following pages will provide the reader with "How-To" guidelines for implementing eleven interesting, thematic modules for use in any delivery system or combination of systems.

The learning stations described here are designed around several different models for infusing creative and critical thinking skills throughout the prescribed tasks. One will find considerable use of Bloom's Taxonomy for teaching critical thinking skills, Williams' Taxonomy for teaching creative thinking skills, and Gardner's Multiple Intelligences for teaching varied thinking modes. Another important dimension incorporated in these learning station themes deals with the scheduling of students so that they *all accomplish the same basic outcomes but that they do so through alternative time frames, differentiated activities, and student-selected choices*. Some teachers, for example, may prefer to have all students rotate through every station on a predetermined schedule. While this method is efficient, it does not allow for individual differences in interests, learning styles, or abilities. A preferable system of scheduling would be to have more stations than groups of students so that individuals or groups who finish at one station can move on to another station with an available opening. In this type of schedule, some stations are required while others are optional according to student interests and aptitudes. Furthermore, this type of rotation schedule allows teachers to do a better job of prescribing instruction for individual or special student needs.

Technology is another key component of the learning stations presented in this package. The involvement of technologies in classroom instruction is invaluable because teachers can shift their attention from whole class to small group instruction, from passive to active learning experiences, from competition to collaboration among students, from teacher as dispenser of knowledge to teacher as coach, and from everybody doing the same thing at the same time to different kids doing different things at different times.

In short, the learning stations/thematic units included in this resource have been developed to reflect a wide range of student needs, middle school curricula, alternative delivery systems, and societal issues.

**What is a learning station?**

A learning station is a place in or near the classroom where students can go to participate in activities designed to introduce, reinforce, and/or extend their knowledge or skill base as it relates to a particular topic, concept, or interest.

Learning stations allow teachers and students to engage in a new educational paradigm where learning is the product, students are workers, and teachers are the managers. Such a classroom organizational structure is more developmentally responsive to the needs and characteristics of young adolescents who work and learn best in collaborative, small group settings and with varied instructional materials that promote active learning practices.

**What are the key characteristics of a learning station?**

1. **Learning stations entice students to work in them** because they:

   — cater to student interests, aptitudes, and abilities.
   — offer student choices and opportunities for involvement in decision-making tasks.
   — provide experiences for student interaction and cooperation.

2. **Learning stations help teachers differentiate instruction** because they encourage alternative delivery systems that capitalize on student strengths. Sample station activities that accommodate different types of learners include the following:

| Auditory | Visual | Kinesthetic |
|---|---|---|
| listening | reading | manipulating |
| brainstorming | journaling | role playing |
| speaking | researching | demonstrating |
| rapping | note taking | writing |
| discussing | mapping | building |
| watching TV | drawing | performing |
| rhyming | watching TV | experimenting |
| interviewing | graphing | discovering |
| presenting | imagining | inventing |
| explaining | illustrating | making |

3. **Learning stations offer students the chance to practice, apply, reinforce, or enrich specific curriculum objectives** because they focus on process skills that include:

| | | |
|---|---|---|
| vocabulary development | computing | writing |
| problem solving | communicating | researching |
| drawing conclusions | classifying | measuring |
| comparing/contrasting | thinking | reading |
| following directions | defining | identifying |
| locating | summarizing | concluding |
| converting | estimating | preparing |
| demonstrating | solving | judging |
| applying | analyzing | creating |
| experimenting | examining | study skills |
| decision making | organizing | questioning |
| goal setting | observing | ordering |
| encoding | recalling | predicting |
| identifying relationships | inferring | verifying |
| elaborating | restructuring | |

4. **Learning stations motivate students** because they are rich in diverse materials and resources that include:

| | |
|---|---|
| textbooks | posters |
| newspapers | games |
| videos | magazines |
| pamphlets | CD ROMs |
| maps | laser disks |
| literature selections | pictures |
| computers | puzzles |
| filmstrips | |

## What are the advantages of learning stations?

1. Learning stations are developed around student needs and characteristics.

2. Learning stations empower students to assume responsibility for their own learning.

3. Learning stations expand student "time on task" to allow for acquisition and application of important knowledge and skills.

4. Learning stations provide connections for students between/among varied subject areas.

## Where does one put learning stations?

Some possible options for locating learning stations are:

| | | |
|---|---|---|
| counter tops | windows | walls |
| tables | clotheslines | boxes |
| file cabinets | shelves | doors |
| student desks | bookcases | easels |
| cabinets | bulletin boards | |
| desk tops | display boards | |

## How does one set up a learning station program?

Decide how to set up your classroom around these designated locations choosing the locations most suitable in your classroom. Consider these possibilities:

- using the perimeter of the room to maximize space.
- placing a table or row of desks in front of a bulletin board.
- grouping student desks around a TV/VCR in a corner of the room.
- placing chairs around one or more computers in a corner or along an outside wall.
- sectioning off bookshelves, cupboards, or cabinets.
- putting stations outside the classroom (such as in the media center or portable ones in the hallways) to gain additional space and resources.

The following four diagrams suggest various ways to set up a typical classroom for a learning station program.

Figure A is best suited for the teacher who wants to spend part of the period with direct instruction in a traditional classroom setting with students using the learning stations only part of the time. Students might move to the learning stations as other work is completed, or the teacher may schedule part of the class into the stations at a time.

**Figure A**

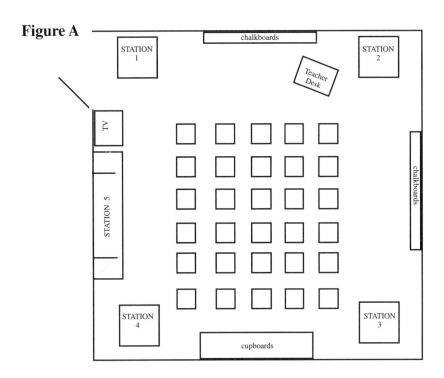

To provide for small group instruction, a classroom may be set up for half direct instruction and half learning stations as represented in Figure B. The teacher can differentiate instruction by grouping some of the students within the class for skill instruction and by setting up learning stations for practice, remediation, and/or extension to accommodate the other students.

**Figure B**

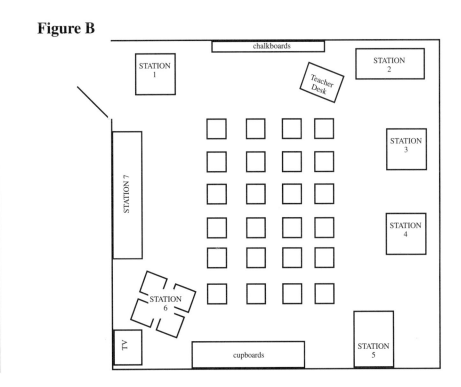

The teacher may choose to set up the room with all learning stations for a particular unit or segment of time. In this situation, the entire room is used for station work.

**Figure C**

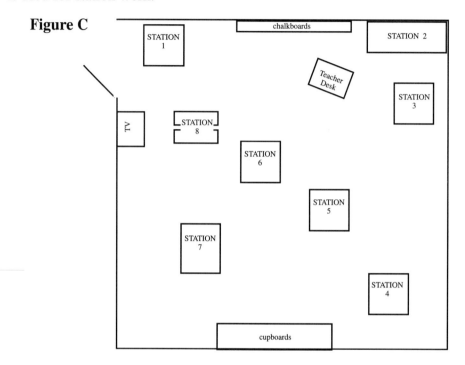

The teacher who uses learning stations on a regular basis might wish to set up a classroom that can function for either individual station work or for collaborative station work while still making provisions for total group instruction.

**Figure D**

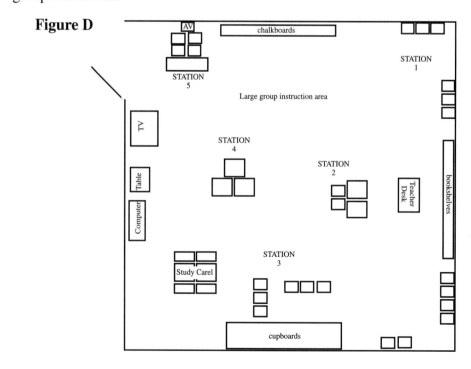

**How does one manage a learning station program?**

The two major ways for managing learning stations are (1) through the use of a scheduled rotation plan or (2) through the use of an open rotation plan. The factors that determine the best format for a given teacher are: time constraints, number of stations, number of students to be housed at a station, length of time for completing activities at a station, and the teacher's comfort zone in using stations.

When implementing a scheduled rotation format, there is a set amount of time for each station which can range from one class period to an entire week. The learning activities at each station in this situation should vary in scope and number of student options, but the actual time spent at each station is standard and inflexible. A scheduled rotation plan is often a good way for teachers and students to begin a learning station program. A rotation schedule for six separate learning stations might look like the following chart. Note that the stations are numbered and the rotating groups identified with letters.

| Station # | Day 1 | Day 2 | Day 3 | Day 4 | Day 5 | Day 6 |
|-----------|-------|-------|-------|-------|-------|-------|
| **One** | A | B | C | D | E | F |
| **Two** | F | A | B | C | D | E |
| **Three** | E | F | A | B | C | D |
| **Four** | D | E | F | A | B | C |
| **Five** | C | D | E | F | A | B |
| **Six** | B | C | D | E | F | A |

The open schedule plan is often preferred by experienced learning station users. In this model, there are more stations than there are groups of students. Students are assigned by the teacher to the first station only. From then on, as a student or a group of students finishes one station, they move to any other station that has available space. With this open schedule, more emphasis can be placed on student interests, needs, abilities, and choices. For example, in the rotational schedule, all students would attend the same stations, but in the open schedule, it would be open to student choices.

**How does one assess student progress in a learning station program?**

Learning stations should be managed by students as much as possible. This is an opportunity for them to take responsibility for their own learning.

1.  Learning logs can be maintained by students with daily entries which include the date, learning station(s) attended, tasks completed, and personal reflections.

2.  At some stations, students may have access to an answer key. The student might check his or her own work, or a designated "checker" might get the key from the teacher and check the papers of students as they finish the station task(s).

3.  Each student may maintain a working portfolio of his/her station work. A checklist, recording sheet, or rubric for the stations can help to keep track of student progress.

4.  The teacher may record observations of students working at the learning stations. Often this takes the form of observable social skills such as "stays on task," "works well with others," or "uses time and materials well." Specific content skills might also be observed. Some teachers make up a simple observation checklist with students' names along the side and observables along the top. New barcode and computer technology (Apple Newton with Learner Profile software) make observations of content and social skills easy to manage.

**How does one use the learning stations in this book?**

The modules in this book are designed to be used around one theme at a time. Each module contains 10 to 15 different learning stations, and each of these includes several different activities. Some of the activities are mandated as requirements, while others are designated as bonus choices for students. Teachers should feel free to adjust these requirements to meet individual student and curricular needs. The activities can be photocopied, mounted on card stock, and possibly laminated for durability. Teachers may wish to color-code the stations and reproduce the direction/task cards for the various stations on separate colors for easy identification. If one plans to set up a station for four students at a time, then one might make up extra sets of task cards for the station or for absent students.

Establishing a learning station program initially will require considerable time and effort to locate and gather materials needed, to make copies of activity cards and other items, and to physically organize and set up the centers. Once done, however, they are essentially self-sustaining and require little teacher preparation time. After completion, the set of stations can easily be stored for future use. Most activities require students to use their own notebook paper; however, some stations have reproducible student pages, which are marked accordingly. These pages should be provided for each student and made available at the appropriate station.

The theme for each set of learning stations is highlighted on the first page of the module along with guiding questions. An OVERVIEW of tasks and topics that gives the teacher a picture of what will be involved follows. Some of the themes have a total class INTRODUCTORY ACTIVITY as well. Each theme has a station RUBRIC (Recording Sheet) which lists the learning stations in the theme as well as possible points that can be awarded when earned. A grading scale can be determined by calculating the suggested percentages listed below against the points of the required activities. Bonus activity points may be figured in to raise a student's total point value.

| | |
|---|---|
| 94 - 100 | A |
| 85 - 93 | B |
| 75 - 84 | C |
| 65 - 74 | D |

Consider the following suggestions for using the RUBRIC/RECORDING SHEETS. If you plan to use the open rotation schedule, you might wish to prescribe certain stations for specific students in the class or you might want to make certain stations required for everyone with others designated as free choice stations. You can star or circle the station number(s) on the RUBRIC for those stations required. To help manage the record keeping, it is advisable for the teacher to evaluate and award points as students progress through the stations. This avoids a "paper crunch" at the end and lets students know their point status at any given time.

**What is cooperative learning?**

Cooperative learning is a structured form of group work. The students, usually in heterogeneous teams, work together to attain a common goal. The situation is structured for specific learning outcomes such as *brainstorming, shared learning, consensus building, communication*, and *team building*. Forte and Schurr (1993) further define cooperative learning as the following:

1. Mutual success through a collaborative effort

2. Individual accountability and responsibility requiring each group member to contribute to the group's work to successfully meet desired goals

3. Face-to-face interaction

4. Group processing through discussion and evaluation of direction and working relationships

5. Appropriate use of collaborative skills and social skills

**What are the key characteristics of cooperative learning?**

1. When students are placed in cooperative learning groups, each student in the group should have a specific role to perform to help the group accomplish its task. Roles are assigned based on the jobs needed to accomplish the goal. Roles should be rotated periodically so that students have the opportunity to experience each role. Some possible roles include the following:

   a. LEADER to keep the team on task

   b. CHECKER to check for group members' understanding or to use an answer key to check for accuracy

   c. RECORDER to write group responses

   d. ENCOURAGER to make sure everyone has input and provides positive feedback

   e. TIMER to keep track of time

   f. READER to read directions, problems, and resource materials to the group

   g. GO-FOR to pick up and return materials and run errands for the group

   h. A/V SPECIALIST to set up and operate equipment

   I. ARTIST to illustrate and display products

   j. QUIET CONTROLLER to reinforce the use of quiet voices

   k. OBSERVER to keep notes on group processing and social skills

2. A few simple guiding principles should be in place to provide for a classroom climate that is conducive to cooperative learning. Cooperative learning rules should be posted in the classroom and reviewed before each cooperative activity until they become routine. Possible rules include the following:

   a. Be responsible for your own behavior.
   b. Contribute to the assigned task.
   c. Help any group member who needs help.
   d. Ask your team for help before asking the teacher.
   e. Support one another; do not tolerate "put downs."

3. Teach social skills along with academic content. Select the targeted social skill from those you perceive as class weaknesses. Review the social skill that will be observed during the cooperative activity. Have students identify what the targeted social skill

"looks like" and "sounds like." Observe students practicing this skill during the cooperative activity and give feedback on your observations. Some social skills to work on in cooperative groups include the following:

| | |
|---|---|
| taking turns | encouraging participation |
| listening to the speaker | clarifying ideas |
| using time wisely | criticizing ideas not people |
| sharing ideas and resources | working quietly |
| expressing feelings | giving directions |

4. Share your observations of how the groups did on practicing the social skill and on completing the cooperative task. Engage students in group and/or individual processing. Use the processing outcomes for class, group, and individual goal setting for future cooperative activities. Processing questions for students to answer might include the following:

   a. How well did I perform my role? How could I improve next time?
   b. Was my team successful with the social skill? How could we improve next time?
   c. What was my major contribution to the task today? Did everyone contribute to the assignment?
   d. How could our team improve?

**How does one use the activities in this book for cooperative learning?**

The task card activities should be reproduced in sufficient numbers so that each team member has a copy. Consider copying the materials on colored card stock and laminating the task cards. Color-code the cards so that each set of cards in the Unit Theme is recognizable by color. Consider having different cooperative groups working on different activities within the UMBRELLA THEME. This will help with the sharing of resources. Activities can then be rotated among the groups. The reproducible pages and the Recording Sheet should be reproduced, one per group.

Establish your cooperative groups. Determine the appropriate group size for each set of learning activities: pairs, triads, or quads. Consider a heterogeneous mix of students with varying learning styles and ability levels. Determine which roles will be needed to complete each set of activities. If more roles are needed than you have students in the group, consider assigning more than one role to students.

**Where can one go for more information on cooperative learning?**

Forte, I., & Schurr, S. (1993). *The definitive middle school guide: A handbook for success.* Nashville, TN: Incentive Publications, Inc.

Forte, I., & Schurr, S. (1992). *The cooperative learning guide & planning pak for middle grades, thematic projects, and activities.* Nashville, TN: Incentive Publications, Inc.

Holt, Larry (1993). *Cooperative learning in action.* Columbus, OH: National Middle School Association

Johnson, D. W., Johnson, R. T., & Holubec, E. J. (1991). *Circles of learning: Cooperation in the classroom.* Rev. Ed. Edina, MN: Interaction Book Company.

Scearce, C. (1992). *100 ways to build teams.* Palatine, IL: IRI/Skylight Publishing.

Schurr, S. (1994). *Dynamite in the classroom: A how-to-book for teachers.* Columbus, OH: National Middle School Association.

**What is interdisciplinary instruction?**

Interdisciplinary instruction helps students make connections between and among different content areas. In interdisciplinary instruction, language and methodology from more than one discipline are used to examine a central theme, issue, problem, topic, or experience (Jacobs 1989). Integrating instruction is valuable for the following reasons:

- Interdisciplinary instruction reduces fragmentation.
- Interdisciplinary instruction helps students see the big picture.
- Interdisciplinary instruction models the real world where life is not divided into separate disciplines.
- Students learn and remember best when learning is integrated because skills and concepts are reinforced and applied in various situations.
- Interdisciplinary instruction saves instructional time as multiple objectives from different disciplines can be met at the same time.

**What are the key characteristics of interdisciplinary units?**

Good interdisciplinary units take the following criteria into consideration:

- Does the theme correlate to the curriculum?
- Does the theme provide for opportunities to compare and contrast?
- Is the theme broad enough? Too broad?
- Is the theme of interest to students? To teachers?

- Does the theme contribute to student outcomes?
- Does the theme focus on active learning experiences?
- Are resources available and accessible?

Commonly identified elements in a great interdisciplinary unit include.

1.  Relevant topics — those students perceive as having a direct relationship to their lives

2.  Clear goals and objectives — which, when conveyed to students, make learning meaningful

3.  Variety in topics, activities, grouping — including individual/small group/large group research, project construction, simulations, guest speakers, presentations, interviews, and surveys

4.  Choice in topics, projects, groupings — ample opportunities for student input and options

5.  Adequate time — to explore and incubate ideas, practice skills, and complete quality work

6.  Processes and/or products — for weaving skill development into the unit topic

7.  Field trips — which enable students to "experience" the topic beyond the school walls

8.  Group cooperation — including committee work, group projects, and tasks

9.  Sharing — which includes public performance such as inviting other classes or parents to view projects and share knowledge

10. Community involvement — using parents and other community members as resource people and aides helps to build bridges between school and community.

**What steps should one take to develop an interdisciplinary unit?**

STEP ONE: SELECT AN ORGANIZATIONAL CENTER

This can be a theme, a subject area, an event, a concept, an issue, or a problem. The organizational center often reveals itself after the team has completed a curriculum map/matrix (Forte & Schurr 1993). The theme should not be too general nor too narrow. It should be relevant and interesting to students. Students may suggest ideas for the organizational center.

## STEP TWO:  BRAINSTORM ASSOCIATIONS

It is important to generate many ideas about the theme and how to use it in one's classroom. The interdisciplinary planning wheel recommended by Heidi Jacobs (1989) is useful in brainstorming. Where appropriate, involve students in the brainstorming process.

## STEP THREE:  ESTABLISH GUIDING QUESTIONS

These serve as a scope and sequence for the unit. The guiding questions reflect the major focus of the unit and come from the brainstorming of the associations. Use the guiding questions to help eliminate any activities that are superfluous. Make sure that the guiding questions are cross-disciplinary in nature.

## STEP FOUR:  GATHER AND WRITE ACTIVITIES FOR IMPLEMENTATION

As you gather and write activities for the unit, you might consider using Bloom's or Williams' Taxonomies (Schurr 1994), Gardner's Multiple Intelligences, and students' learning styles, as you plan varied delivery.

**How does one use the activities in this book for interdisciplinary units?**

The activities in this book were designed to be interdisciplinary in nature. Each of the UMBRELLA THEMES has activities relating to the various content areas. GUIDING QUESTIONS and OBJECTIVES are found in the topic overview for each theme. Consider dividing the activities among the members of the interdisciplinary team. It is possible all team members may not spend the same amount of time on the unit, but an overall time frame should be decided. Consider launching the unit together as a team with a special activity, a related video or film, a guest speaker, or a field trip. Consider a culminating activity to bring closure to the unit. Consider project, portfolio, or performance assessments for the unit. Consider a unit evaluation form for teachers/students to complete as input for the next time the unit is considered.

**Where can one go for more information on interdisciplinary units?**

Beane, J. (1993). *A middle school curriculum: From rhetoric to reality*. 2nd ed. Columbus, OH: National Middle School Association.

Forte, I., & Schurr, S. (1993). *The definitive middle school guide: A handbook for success*. Nashville, TN: Incentive Publications, Inc.

Forte, I., & Schurr, S. (1994). *Interdisciplinary units and projects for thematic instruction for middle grades success.* Nashville, TN: Incentive Publications, Inc.

Jacobs, H. H., et al. (1989). *Interdisciplinary curriculum: Design and implementation.* Alexandria, VA: Association for Supervision and Curriculum Development.

Lounsbury, J. H. (Ed.) (1992). *Connecting the curriculum through interdisciplinary instruction.* Columbus, OH: National Middle School Association.

**What are independent learning contracts?**

An independent learning contract is an agreement between the student and the teacher in which the student commits to complete certain learning activities within a predetermined amount of time. Contracts can range from simple to complex, depending on the purpose and the desired outcomes. A contract describes specifically what a student is to do and offers specific criteria against which the student is to be judged.

Contracts are prepared by the teacher or teacher and student together and are designed to be self-directed so that students can complete them independently or with a minimum of teacher direction. There are several types of independent learning contracts, including the following:

1. **Interest contracts** which capitalize on students' hobbies and personal interests.

2. **Exploratory contracts** which allow students to learn more about contemporary issues, careers, or relevant hot topics.

3. **Skill development contracts** which provide students with hands-on practice activities.

4. **Reinforcement and remediation contracts** which provide for application of newly introduced or previously taught skills.

5. **Enrichment and extension contracts** which offer students a variety of experiences to extend, enrich, and synthesize their understanding of already-introduced curriculum.

16

**How does one use the activities in this book for independent learning contracts?**

Each UMBRELLA THEME in this book can be used as the basis of an independent learning contract. Consider creating a folder for each student working on an independent contract. (A folder with pockets would be best.) Duplicate the complete theme unit for each student assigned the contract. Consider stapling the unit together with the Recording Page on top. This can be kept on one side of the folder while work done on notebook paper can be kept on the other side. Direct students to head their notebook paper consistent with the activity title and to identify the various activities by number, in order to be consistent with the contract.

Circle those titles listed on the Recording Sheet which you are requiring of the student. Orient students to the goals, timelines, directions, and assessment procedures. Set up a structure for monitoring student progress. Consider using student conference, self-reports, and informal observations as an integral part of the contract process.

**Where can one go for more information on independent learning contracts?**

Forte, I., & Schurr, S. (1994). *Tools, treasures, and measures for middle grades success*. Nashville, TN: Incentive Publications, Inc.

Schurr, S. (1992). *The ABC's of evaluation: 26 alternative ways to assess student progress*. Columbus, OH: National Middle School Association.

Schurr, S. (1995). *Dynamite in the classroom: A how-to handbook for teachers*. 2nd ed. Columbus, OH: National Middle School Association.

Schurr, S., Thomason, J., & Thompson, M. (1995). *Teaching at the middle level: A professional's handbook*. Lexington: MA: Houghton Mifflin.

# Signaling
# Student
# Success

# CHANGE

- **Meeting with Change**
- **Changeless Ideas**
- **Changes in Language**
- **Character Changes**
- **Investigating Changes**
- **Changing Science Careers**

- **Changes in Science**
- **Trace the Change**
- **Change Agents**
- **Change**
- **Changing Numbers**
- **Money Exchange**

National Middle School Association

**An Introduction
to CHANGE**

What do you think of when you hear the word *change* – money, seasons, careers? Here are some things we change: our minds, our beds, our clothes, our directions, our habits, our voices, and our points of view. Can you think of others? We make change, watch or observe change, and use a change purse.

**Change** as a verb means *to make or become different; to alter; to take, put or use something in place of another; to exchange; to put fresh clothes on; to become deeper in tone.* **Change** as a noun is the *act or process of changing*; *a number of coins*; *money returned*; *a break in one's routine*.

Something that never changes is considered changeless. The weather can be changeable. When we move from one activity to another, it is called a changeover. Idiomatically, when something passes from one owner to another, it may be called changing hands.

---

### THE GUIDING QUESTIONS

1. How can change be both positive and negative?

2. How does change of any kind affect you?

3. What personal qualities enable us to accept change?

4. What kinds of changes do human beings experience?

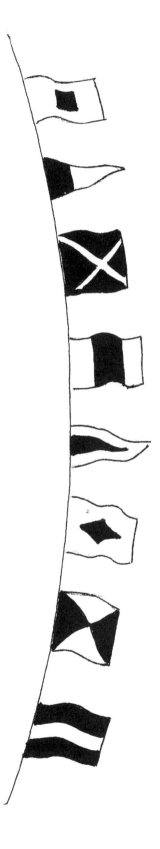

# At a glance — topics and tasks

- Create an orientation guide for students
- Explore various aspects of personal change
- Consider elements of change from different perspectives
- Review and practice basic grammar activities
- Rewrite the end of a story
- Design interview questions and perform an interview
- Consider character changes
- Investigate change as it relates to specific areas of science
- Consider current careers in the field of science
- Examine metamorphosis
- Examine changes in transportation and communication
- Investigate individuals from our history who were influential in making change
- Use coins in several ways
- Change Roman numerals into Arabic numbers; change Arabic numbers into Roman numerals
- Investigate several examples of foreign currency
- Change U.S. dollars into foreign currency

## Optional (full class) Activities

### PURPOSE
To create an orientation (survival) guide for students new to your school. (Note that the full class activities are not learning stations. Your teacher may assign points if needed.)

### SPECIAL MATERIALS NEEDED
Access to computer for word processing (if available) and/or construction paper; white paper; markers; scissors; magazines; school folder/handbook

### DIRECTIONS
Follow the steps and suggestions below in order.

## ACTIVITY

In cooperative groups created by your teacher, complete the following tasks after these roles have been assigned: *recorder*, *timer*, *encourager*, and *go-getter*.

Brainstorm a list of the changes you encountered as you entered middle school from elementary school. Consider classes, teachers, class size, campus, identity, lunch, administrators, recess, rules/regulations, and as many more as possible.

After your teacher has called "time" on the brainstorming period, discuss the list at length; add to it if more ideas occur.

Next, categorize the brainstormed list in some manner. For instance, Faculty and Staff, In the Classroom, Out on Campus, or something like this. Then rank order your list from most important (in your group's estimation) to least.

Keeping the above list in mind, decide on a title for an orientation guide for incoming fifth graders or for all incoming new students. Design a cover page with the title, school name, address, and telephone number, and some kind of illustration.

Now create a list of the most important questions you feel will be answered by your brainstormed changes. You may add items if necessary. Decide on a format for this guide; write the questions and the answers; include illustrations whenever you can. Try to keep it brief, concise (to the point), and helpful, as well as colorful and easy to read.

Present your group's orientation guide to the class.

21

## Change Rubric

Name _____ Class _____

Here is a list of the learning stations from which you may choose to work in order to earn your points. All activities must be done completely, accurately, and neatly to earn full point value. The grading scale is as follows:

| A | B | C | D |
|---|---|---|---|
| 1222-1415 pts. | 1221-1105 pts. | 1104-975 pts. | 974-845 pts. |

| Date Completed | Activity | Possible Points | Points Earned |
|---|---|---|---|
| _____ | Meeting with Change | 100-125 | _____ |
| _____ | Changeless Ideas (Bonus Station) | 25 | _____ |
| _____ | Changes in Language | 100-110 | _____ |
| _____ | Character Changes | 100-200 | _____ |
| _____ | Investigating Changes | 100 | _____ |
| _____ | Changing Science Careers | 100 | _____ |
| _____ | Changes in Science | 100-110 | _____ |
| _____ | Trace the Changes | 100 | _____ |
| _____ | Change Agents | 100 | _____ |
| _____ | Change | 200 | _____ |
| _____ | Changing Numbers | 100-120 | _____ |
| _____ | Money Exchange | 100-125 | _____ |
| | **TOTAL POINTS** | | _____ |
| | **GRADE** | | _____ |

## Meeting With Change

PURPOSE
To explore various aspects of personal change

SPECIAL MATERIALS NEEDED
None

DIRECTIONS  (100 points)
Complete Activity 1. Select three questions to respond to in Activity 2. Choose one of the two prompts in Activity 3. Are you interested in the bonus? Try it!

---

## ACTIVITY 1  (20 points - REQUIRED)

Describe how your life style might change in each of the following situations:
- a baby brother or sister is born
- you move to another city in another state
- a grandparent or close relative dies
- your parents divorce
- one of your parents remarries
- your parents win the state million dollar lottery
- your best friend moves to another state
- one of your parents becomes ill for an extended period of time
- you have a part-time job every weekend
- a grandparent moves in to live with you

---

## ACTIVITY 2  (60 points)

Select three questions; responses should be at least two paragraphs each.

1.  How might success or the lack of success in school change your future?

2.  What kinds of changes in families do you know about?

3.  What changes might you experience as a foreign exchange student? (Consider – climate, culture, customs, language, fashion, music . . .)

4.  Why do careers change? Give five examples.

5.  Have you changed your behavior in any way either at home or at school? Why or why not?

6.  What do you do to help your parents change their minds? How do changes affect each family member?

## ACTIVITY 3 (20 points)

Choose one.

1.  Think about your life at the present time. Decide on at least 10 things in your life right now that you don't ever want to change. List these things and then rank order them from most to least important. Explain your top two and your last choices.

2.  Determine in what way these traits will enable you to accept change as a normal, natural process as you grow and mature:

    sense of humor

    persistence or determination

    positive attitude

    objective outlook (able to see pros and cons of a situation)

    What other attributes or traits would you add to this list? Why?

## BONUS (25 points)

(**Note:** You may need parental assistance with this one.)

How have you changed since you started school in kindergarten or first grade?

Find a kindergarten or first grade picture and some kind of picture for each year up to the present time (if possible). Post these on large light colored construction paper or posterboard with your name at the top. Below each picture list your age, grade, favorite food, best friend, family pet, and favorite song, TV show, and hobby/ activity at that time.

In three or four paragraphs, describe the physical changes you have experienced as shown in the pictures. Draw some conclusions about your "favorites." (Ask your teacher what format you should use for this portion of the assignment.)

## Changeless Ideas

PURPOSE
To consider elements of change from different perspectives

SPECIAL MATERIALS NEEDED
None

DIRECTIONS  (25 points)

This is a BONUS learning station. Select five of the quotations. Write them in order, beginning with the one you like the best.

Then, in your own words, explain what you think each of the five means.

## BONUS ACTIVITY

*There is nothing permanent except change.*
— Heraclitus

*Just because everything is different doesn't mean anything has changed.*
— Irene Peter

*Progress is a nice word. But change is its motivator and change has its enemies.*
— Robert F. Kennedy

*Most of us are willing to change, not because we see the light, but because we feel the heat.*— Anonymous

*If you want to make enemies, try to change something.*
— Woodrow Wilson

*The wheel of change moves on, and those who were down go up and those who were up go down.* — Jawaharlal Nehru

*Some things, of course, you can't change. Pretending that you have is like painting stripes on a horse and hollering 'Zebra!'* — Eddie Cantor

*When I accept myself as I am, I change, and when I accept others as they are, they change.*— Carl Rogers

*There is nothing wrong with change, if it is in the right direction.* — Winston Churchill

*All change is not growth, as all movement is not forward* — Ellen Glasgow

*To grow is to change, and to have changed often is to have grown much.*
— John Henry Newman

*When you're through changing, you're through.* — Bruce Barton

*Change your thoughts and you change your world.* — Anonymous

## Changes in Language

PURPOSE
To review and practicesome basic grammar constructs

SPECIAL MATERIALS NEEDED
Grammar/composition text to use as reference

DIRECTIONS (100 points)
Complete the activities in order.

## ACTIVITY 1 (20 points)

Add a prefix or suffix to change ten of these words. Then use each word in an original sentence.

| | | |
|---|---|---|
| annual | exist | circle |
| change | active | town |
| call | large | child |
| month | enjoy | friend |
| finish | act | freeze |

## ACTIVITY 2 (20 points)

Change the spelling as you make each singular noun plural.

Example:  man - men
tax - taxes

| | | | | |
|---|---|---|---|---|
| body | lady | calf | leaf | child |
| mouse | city | potato | die | speech |
| echo | tooth | foot | veto | glass |
| waltz | goose | wolf | knife | woman |

## ACTIVITY 3 (20 points)

Change these common nouns to two proper nouns of your choice.

Example:  teacher - Mr. Jordan - Mrs. Atkinson

| soda | restaurant | girl | team | county |
|------|-----------|------|------|--------|
| friend | boy | relative | town | state |

## ACTIVITY 4 (20 points)

Change each of the present tense verbs to past tense and past participle.

Example:  Present (today);  Past (yesterday);  Past Participle (have, has, had)

| ride | rode | ridden |
|------|------|--------|
| learn | learned | learned |

Remember, this is the present tense list:

| sing | write | run | ring | bring |
|------|-------|-----|------|-------|
| drive | tell | watch | cry | see |

## ACTIVITY 5 (20 points)

Change each pair or set of words into correctly spelled contractions.

Example:  could not = couldn't

| they have | do not | I will | she is |
|-----------|--------|--------|--------|
| you have | of the clock | he would | |
| will not | we are | should not | |

Now think of five more pairs of words; write them and their correctly spelled contractions.

## BONUS  (10 points)

Design a "word find" or a crossword puzzle using the answers from the completed work at this station. Be sure to give it a name, include clear directions, and make an answer key.

# Character Changes

PURPOSES
To rewrite the ending of a story; to interview an older relative or friend; to consider character changes

SPECIAL MATERIALS NEEDED
Literature book or short story anthology and Reproducible Student Page

DIRECTIONS  (100 points)
Complete the activities below in any order you wish.

## ACTIVITY 1 (30 points)

Select one of the short stories suggested by your teacher (from your literature book or short story anthology). Read the story carefully, making note of the setting, the plot, the characterization, the theme (author's message), and the ending. Use your notes and your personal reaction to the story to change the ending.

Rewrite the ending in at least two well-developed paragraphs OR change the ending by adding at least two more paragraphs to extend what you read.

In another paragraph (as a kind of aside), justify your reasons for the changes you made.

## ACTIVITY 2  (40 points)

Plan an interview. Decide on your subject, someone such as a grandparent, older family friend, or older neighbor. Your interview questions should relate to the changes this person has seen in his/her lifetime. These might be personal physical changes, social changes, transportation and communication changes, etc. Ask what life was like when he/she was your age. How is it different today? What are some positive changes seen or experienced? negative changes?

Plan your interview questions using the suggestions above; add others to extend the information you derive from the interview.

Request permission to complete the interview. Set up day and time. Be sure to explain your reasons for the interview.

On the day of the interview, dress nicely, be prompt, and be very courteous. Take your questions (one each on 3 X 5 cards or typed with space in between for you to write responses). You might want to consider a tape recorder if this is all right with your subject.

ACTIVITY 2  (con't.)

When the interview is over, be sure to thank your subject and leave promptly.

Make an appointment with your teacher to discuss how you can share what you learned about this person and the changes he/she witnessed.

## ACTIVITY 3 (30 points)

Write a five-paragraph review of a novel or movie about someone who has experienced a major change. Trace the emotional, physical, social, and/or intellectual changes in the main character. Be sure to include your personal reaction to the novel or movie.

## BONUS (100 points)

Read "Flowers for Algernon," a short story by Daniel Keyes. In this story, Charlie's intelligence is changed and therefore his life changes. After you have completed your reading, you will note the major changes in Charlie and his life on the *Reproducible Page* provided at this station.

Complete the chart.

Answer these questions honestly.

1.  If you could double your intelligence, would you? Why or why not?

2.  Do you agree with human experimentation, such as the kind Charlie experienced? Explain.

3.  Think carefully and then explain the significance of the title of this story.

4.  What kinds of changes did you see in Charlie's spelling, grammar, and writing skills?

5.  Why did Charlie have to leave his job at the factory?

6.  How did Charlie's feelings change during the story?

7.  What do you think will ultimately happen to Charlie? Why do you think as you do?

# "Flowers for Algernon"

| (Note the changes as you complete this page.) | Before the Operation (March 5 - March 10) | After the Operation (March 15 - June 4) | As Charlie and Algernon Regress (June 5 - July 28) |
|---|---|---|---|
| Charlie's personality traits | | | |
| His intelligence | | | |
| How he is treated by co-workers, doctors, Miss Kinnian | | | |

## Investigating Changes

PURPOSE
To investigate change as it relates to specific areas of science

SPECIAL MATERIALS NEEDED
Science textbooks; reference material; posterboard; markers; colored pencils; blackline world map (one per student); access to science equipment and materials

DIRECTIONS  (100 points)
Select five activities to complete for 100 points.

### ACTIVITY 1 (20 points)

Investigate a baby's physical changes from birth to 15 months. Find out about muscle development, reflex actions, sitting up, crawling, walking, talking, teeth, types of food, and more. This can be a written report of three to five paragraphs or a chart. Illustrations will be helpful.

### ACTIVITY 2  (20 points)

Investigate the three states of matter – solids, liquids, and gases. How can they change from one state to another? What are particles? Why is energy needed? What is subliming? Explain melting, freezing, condensing, and evaporating. Plan a lesson to teach about "change of state" to a fourth grade class.

### ACTIVITY 3 (20 points)

Investigate Fahrenheit and Celsius temperature scales. When was each developed and by whom? Which is used more widely? Discover the boiling point and melting point of water on each scale. Draw and label a thermometer which shows both temperature scales. Design two problems to be solved relating to these two scales. Include answers.

## ACTIVITY 4 (20 points)

Investigate a chemical reaction (change). What happens? Why does a chemical reaction take place? Describe a chemical reaction in your body. What are compounds? What are reactions? Write this information in paragraph form and draw at least one illustration.

## ACTIVITY 5 (20 points)

Investigate to discover what plate boundaries, volcanoes, and earthquakes have in common as they relate to changes in the earth's surface. Define plate tectonics, volcano, and earthquake. Discover the three types of regions where volcanoes occur. Where are areas of high earthquake activity? Identify high earthquake and volcano activity areas on the world map. Use two different colors. Explain the relationship and what changes occur when earthquakes and volcanoes occur.

## ACTIVITY 6 (20 points)

Investigate the four seasons of the year. In two or three paragraphs, explain what causes them to change. Key terms to include: axis, rotation, revolution, ellipse, horizon. What occurs in each season with regard to the length of the day and the behavior of animals and plants? Name the seasons. What is "midnight sun"?

# Changing Science Careers

PURPOSE
To consider current careers in the field of science

SPECIAL MATERIALS NEEDED
Access to reference materials, either in the classroom or in the media center

DIRECTIONS  (100 points)
Read through the following list and proceed with the numbered items.

## Activity

CURRENT SCIENCE CAREERS

| | |
|---|---|
| agronomist | environmental scientist |
| forensic chemist | immunologist |
| nurse-midwife | volcanologist |
| acoustical physicist | medical researcher |
| urban forester | dietician |
| economic geologist | food chemist |
| metallurgist | water quality engineer |
| astronaut | robot engineer |
| holographer | hydroponic farmer |
| MRI (Magnetic Resonance | oncologist |
| Imaging)  technician | bionic specialist |

Because of changes in all aspects of life today, new careers are needed to continue our progress and our survival.

1.  Select ten careers from the above list that you would like to know more about.
2.  Find and write a working definition of each. Include an example if possible.
3.  Determine if any of your ten selections were in existence in any form fifty years ago. Explain.
4.  Discover the reasons that each of the ten careers you selected is necessary today.
5.  Investigate each to discover the following:

    - schooling requirements
    - apprenticeship length
    - starting salary
    - percent of demand/section of country or part of world

6.  Which one of the 10 careers you selected is the most interesting to you? Why?

<table>

| **Changes in Science** |
| --- |

PURPOSE
To examine metamorphosis

SPECIAL MATERIALS NEEDED
Science textbooks; dictionary; access to reference materials; plain white paper; colored pencils; markers; posterboard

DIRECTIONS  (100 points)
Complete all four activities. Consider doing the bonus.

## ACTIVITY 1 (30 points)

The changes in form that organisms undergo in their life cycles are called META-MORPHOSIS.

Research to find the stages of metamorphosis that occur during the growth of a frog, a fruit fly, and a butterfly. Draw, label, and explain the stages in order for all three.

## ACTIVITY 2  (10 points)

Find a butterfly that interests you. Discover at least 10 facts about this butterfly. Create a "Magazine Report" to turn in to your teacher. Steps to follow:

1. Write each of your facts in a complete sentence.

2. Find or draw an illustration for each fact.

3. Use three sheets of 12 X 18 construction paper for your report. Fold in half (to regular paper size).

4. Design a title page (front cover).

5. Next, place one fact and at least one illustration on each page.

6. On the last page (the back), tell us "About the Author." Include your name, age, birthdate, interest/hobbies, and a pictureor sketch if possible.

## ACTIVITY 3

Discover why a grasshopper undergoes incomplete metamorphosis. Draw, label, and explain its stages in order.

## ACTIVITY FOUR (25 points)

Many times the names of grown/adult animals change from when they were young. For instance, a young tadpole becomes a frog; a kitten becomes a cat, etc. Discover the "young" names of the following animals.

1. kangaroo
2. swan
3. bear
4. dog
5. deer
6. lion
7. penguin
8. elephant
9. goat
10. rabbit
11. seal
12. sheep
13. whale
14. goose
15. pigeon

On your answer sheet, star (*) the ones which were unknown to you before this exercise. Find five more to add to this list.

## BONUS (10 points)

Find pictures of at least five pairs of animals (young and adult) from above. Cut out or draw, arrange, and label on posterboard.

## Trace the Changes

**PURPOSE**
To examine changes in transportation and communication

**SPECIAL MATERIALS NEEDED**
Access to reference materials either in the classroom or media center

**DIRECTIONS** (100 points)
Read the list and make your selection.

## ACTIVITY

### TRANSPORTATION AND COMMUNICATION

Ships
Flight
Railways
Automobiles
Photography
Telecommunications
Computers and Robots
Paper and Printing

Select one item from the list of transportation and communication topics below. You will become the "expert" on your choice. Your assignment is to trace the changes which have occurred from its beginning to present day. Include dates, major changes in form and function, reasons for those changes, and illustrations.

Use the reference material available in your classroom or request a pass to the media center to gather your information and make your notes. Your teacher will determine the amount of time necessary for this.

Your final product may be a written report, including illustrations; an oral report with notes and illustrations; or a time line which includes all required information and illustrations. Because this is a comprehensive assignment, your teacher may allow you to work in pairs or triads.

## Change Agents

**PURPOSE**
To investigate individuals from our history who were influential in making change

**SPECIAL MATERIALS NEEDED**
Access to reference material either in the classroom or in the media center

**DIRECTIONS** (100 points)
Make your selections from the list provided.

## ACTIVITY

Susan B. Anthony
Franklin D. Roosevelt
Eli Whitney
Winston Churchill
Thomas Jefferson
Elizabeth Cady Stanton
Harriet Tubman
Martin Luther King, Jr.

Alexander G. Bell
Neil Armstrong
John F. Kennedy
Rachel Carson
George Washington Carver
Thomas Edison
Harriet Beecher Stowe

Investigate 10 of the individuals listed above to discover . . .

1. Who the person is.

2. When the person lived.

3. For what was the person best known?

4. In what way did this person bring about change in the world?

Example:  Harriet Tubman, 1821 (circa) - 1913

"Conductor" on the Underground Railroad (an organization that helped escaped slaves from the South to get to Canada).

She helped slaves to gain their freedom. As an abolitionist she helped to prepare the way for emancipation by helping to change northern attitudes toward slavery.

After you have investigated your choices, select the one person you feel made the most important changes in the world. Design an award to celebrate this person's achievements.

# ¢hange

PURPOSE
To use coins in several different ways

SPECIAL MATERIALS NEEDED
Suggested coins in a plastic bag: 4 quarters, 3 dimes, 3 nickels, 7 pennies; access to reference materials; ruler and construction paper; assorted small cardboard boxes and plastic containers

DIRECTIONS  (200 points)
Select two activities from each level listed. Your total points will be 200. Use your own paper or an answer sheet provided by your teacher

## ACTIVITY 1 (5 points)

Knowledge Level - Choose two.
1. Count the change in the plastic bag at this station.
2. List the name and value of each different kind of coin.
3. Trace and label each kind of coin.
4. Define: alloy, ingot, mint (v.), motto, commemorate.

## ACTIVITY 2  (10 points)

Comprehension Level - Choose two.
1. Convert the amount of change to its least number of bills and coins.
2. Describe each type of coin.
3. Translate each of the following into number of nickels:
   90 cents        75 cents        $1.15        60 cents

## ACTIVITY 3 (15 points)

Application Level - Choose two.
1. Estimate what 10 items you might buy for the change in the bag. (Each item costs approximately this amount.)
2. Determine the amount of money you would have if you did the following with the change in the bag at this station:
   deduct $\frac{1}{2}$
   add $\frac{1}{4}$
   double the amount
   multiply total by 5
   divide total by 7

## ACTIVITY 4 (20 points)

Analysis Level - Choose two.

1. Compare and contrast the coins in the bag to discover similarities and differences.
2. Differentiate between a Lincoln head penny and another kind of penny.
3. Discover the alloys in a quarter, a dime, and a penny.

## ACTIVITY 5 (25 points)

Synthesis Level - Choose two.

1. Invent a new coin. Explain your reason for creating this new coin. Propose its composition or make-up. Create its size, shape, denomination, and the pictures for the front and back of the coin. Will it have a motto? What is it?
2. Write an original story about "a day in the life of a quarter."
3. Design a personal "piggy bank" just for you or a brother or sister. Use the materials at the station.

## ACTIVITY 6 (25 points)

Evaluation Level - Choose two.

1. Defend the practice of parents rewarding their children with money for grades on report cards. Give five reasons.

2. Consider how your life would be different if there were NO paper money, just coins. Share at least five ideas.

3. Select the one quotation you like best. Justify your choice with at least three reasons.

   *The greatest waste of money is to keep it.* — J. Gleason

   *Money is round. It rolls away.* — S. Aleichem

   > *That money talks*
   > *I'll not deny,*
   > *I heard it once:*
   > *It said ''Goodbye.'* — R. Armour

   *When money talks, no one pays attention to the grammar.* — Anonymous

   *They say you can't take it with you, but have you ever tried to travel very far without it?* — Anonymous

## Changing Numbers

PURPOSE
To change Roman numerals into Arabic numerals; to change Arabic numerals into Roman numerals

SPECIAL MATERIALS NEEDED
None

DIRECTIONS  (100 points)
Use the following information to assist you in changing the numerals in the following activities.

| ROMAN NUMERALS | I | V | X | L | C | D | M |
|---|---|---|---|---|---|---|---|
| ARABIC COUNTERPARTS | 1 | 5 | 10 | 50 | 100 | 500 | 1000 |

Reminder: Add if smaller Roman numeral follows a larger Roman numeral. Subtract if a larger Roman numeral follows a smaller Roman numeral.

## ACTIVITY 1 (30 points)

Change these Roman numerals to Arabic numerals.
Example:  XXVIII = 28

1. LXI
2. CDVII
3. DCXVI
4. XCIV
5. MLIX
6. CML
7. MCMXCVI
8. XXXIV
9. LXVI
10. DLIX

11. - 15. Write five more of your own. Include answers.

## ACTIVITY 2  (30 points)

Change these Arabic numerals to Roman numerals.

Example:  117 = CXVII

1. 13
2. 1963
3. 59
4. 2001
5. 63
6. 112
7. 84
8. 1986
9. 75
10. 144

11. - 15. Write five more of your own. Include answers.

## ACTIVITY 3 (40 points)

Write the following in Roman numerals.

your birth year
your age
next year
number of desks (or chairs) in your classroom
year Declaration of Independence was signed
last four digits in your phone number
answer to:

3,462 - 2,956

179 + 43

87 X 8

4,980 - 5

## BONUS (20 points)

Produce five problems using Arabic numerals with Roman numeral answers.

Produce five problems using Roman numerals with Arabic numeral answers.

# Money Exchange

## PURPOSE
To investigate several examples of foreign currency; to change U.S. dollars into foreign currency

## SPECIAL MATERIALS NEEDED
Calculator (teacher option); access to reference materials

## DIRECTIONS  (100 points)
Complete all six activities below. Be sure to refer to the chart provided.

### FOREIGN EXCHANGE RATES
(based on U.S. $1.00)

| | |
|---|---|
| Austria (schilling) | 8.94 |
| Belgium (franc) | 26.12 |
| Britain (pound) | .60 |
| Germany (mark, DM) | 1.34 |
| Greece (drachma) | 205.08 |
| India (rupee) | 28.94 |
| Italy (lira) | 1,570.00 |
| Japan (yen) | 81.32 |
| Mexico (peso) | 5.44 |
| Sweden (krona) | 6.67 |

## ACTIVITY 1 (40 points)

Calculate $250.00 in each of the currencies listed above. Calculate $775.00 in each of the currencies.

## ACTIVITY 2  (10 points)

If you are traveling home from Germany and you have DM 400 left from your trip to exchange, how much is this in U.S. dollars?

## ACTIVITY 3 (10 points)

You will be flying to Japan to visit for two weeks. You have 3000 U.S. dollars. How many yen will you get when you exchange?

## ACTIVITY 4 (5 points)

For your trip to Greece from your hometown, you have purchased $950.00 in travelers' checks. How much drachma is this?

## ACTIVITY 5 (10 points)

You have 432 British pounds. How much will you have when you exchange this for U.S. dollars?

## ACTIVITY 6 (25 points)

Create five exchange problems focusing on the foreign exchange currencies not used in the previous problems. Show your solutions.

## BONUS (25 points)

Research to find at least five pieces of information about five of the foreign currencies listed on the chart. Organize your information in some manner to share it with your teacher.

# CHANGE - ANSWER KEY

## Changes in Language, Activity 2

| | | | | |
|---|---|---|---|---|
| bodies | ladies | calves | leaves | children |
| mice | cities | potatoes | dice | speeches |
| echoes | teeth | feet | vetoes | glasses |
| waltzes | geese | wolves | knives | women |

## Changes in Language, Activity 4

| | | | | | | |
|---|---|---|---|---|---|---|
| Past: | sang | wrote | ran | rang | brought | drove |
| Past Participle: | sung | written | run | rung | brought | driven |

| | | | | |
|---|---|---|---|---|
| Past: | told | watched | cried | saw |
| Past Participle: | told | watched | cried | seen |

## Changes in Language, Activity 5

| | | | |
|---|---|---|---|
| they've | don't | I'll | she's |
| you've | o'clock | he'd | |
| won't | we're | shouldn't | |

## Changes in Science, Activity 4

| | | | |
|---|---|---|---|
| 1. | joey | 10. | bunny |
| 2. | cygnet | 11. | pup |
| 3. | cub | 12. | lamb |
| 4. | puppy | 13. | calf |
| 5. | fawn | 14. | gosling |
| 6. | cub | 15. | squab |
| 7. | chick | | |
| 8. | calf | | |
| 9. | kid | | |

## Changing Numbers, Activity 1

| | | | | |
|---|---|---|---|---|
| 1. 61 | 2. 407 | 3. 616 | 4. 94 | 5. 1,059 |
| 6. 950 | 7. 1996 | 8. 34 | 9. 66 | 10. 559 |

## Changing Numbers, Activity 2

| | | | | |
|---|---|---|---|---|
| 1. XIII | 2. MCMLXIII | 3. LIX | 4. MMI | 5. LXIII |
| 6. CXII | 7. LXXXIV | 8. MCMLXXXVI | 9. LXXV | 10. CXLIV |

**Money Exchange, Activity 1**

$250.00                                    $775.00

| | schillings | 6,928.50 |
| 2,235 | schillings | 6,928.50 |
| 6,530 | francs | 20,243 |
| 150 | pounds | 465 |
| 335 | marks | 1,038.50 |
| 51,270 | drachma | 158,937 |
| 7,235 | rupees | 224,285 |
| 392,500 | lira | 1,216,750 |
| 20,330 | yen | 63,023 |
| 1,360 | pesos | 4,216 |
| 1,667.50 | krona | 5,169.25 |

**Money Exchange, Activity 2**
$298.50

**Money Exchange, Activity 3**
243,960 yen

**Money Exchange, Activity 4**
194,826 drachma

**Money Exchange, Activity 5**
$720.00

**Money Exchange, Activity 6**
(5 pieces of information about five foreign currencies)

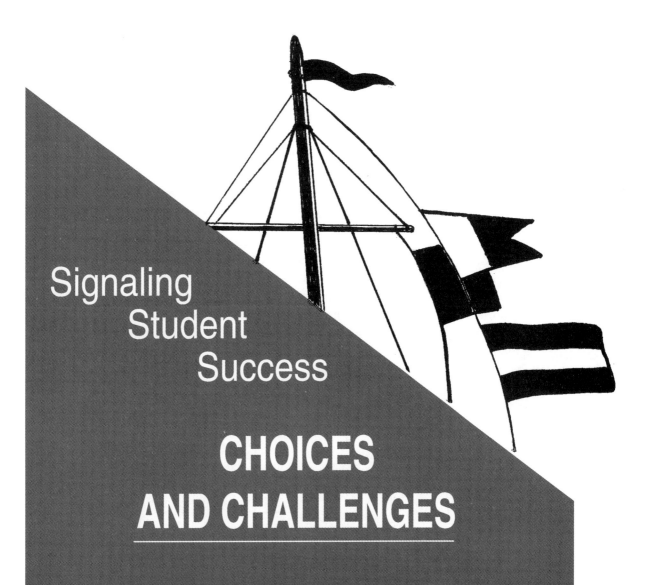

Signaling
Student
Success

# CHOICES
# AND CHALLENGES

- Making Economic Choices
- Challenges to Shape Your World
- The Challenge of Ethics
- Brainteasers That Challenge
- Challenge the System
- The Challenge of Inventing a Country
- Challenges From Our History
- Choices and Challenges of World Leaders
- Issues Challenging Americans Today
- The Challenge of Cultural Diversity
- Foreign Currency Challenges
- Challenging Your Memory
- Challenging Your Creative Self

National Middle School Association

**An Introduction to CHOICES AND CHALLENGES**

Today's world is full of changes in this Information Age. We have a multiple option society and a global economy that gives you many different choices for products, work, recreation, education, and life styles. It is important, then, for you to learn how to make both wise decisions and choices.

**Choices and Challenges** will introduce you to a wide variety of choices and challenges that focus on themes from your math, science, social studies, language arts, and exploratory subjects. Looking at ordinary things in unordinary ways can be an interesting means of reviewing old information and learning new information at the same time.

## THE GUIDING QUESTIONS

1. Why is it important to make good choices when engaged in problem solving and/or decision making?

2. How does one make wise choices?

3. What are some of the challenges that others have faced in the past and/or will face in the future?

4. How can I learn to accept challenge in this changing world?

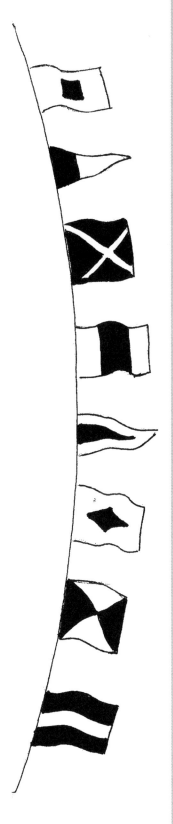

# At a glance — topics and tasks

- Examine the consumer buying and spending habits of many teenagers
- Show how geometry is an integrative force in the world of today
- Explore some of the ethical issues facing the biological sciences of today's modern world
- Construct a variety of puzzles and brainteasers that challenge the mind
- Study the various systems of the human body
- Invent a country based on one's study and knowledge base of countries around the world
- Examine the unique challenges faced by special groups of early Americans during the making of American history
- Survey a number of world leaders in the modern world to identify some of the challenges they face and the choices they make
- Identify and analyze a variety of issues and topics that are challenging the safety and security of the American people
- Use children's literature as the basis for recognizing the choices and challenges of cultural diversity in our pluralistic society
- Identify different foreign currencies and their conversion values compared with the U.S. dollar
- Examine ways one can challenge the memory to retain information as part of the learning process
- Challenge one's creative self

# Choices and Challenges Rubric

Name _____ Class _____

You may select from the following stations. Activities must be done completely, accurately, and neatly to earn full point values. The grading scale is as follows:

| **A**<br>**1840 pts.**<br>**Date Completed** | **B**<br>**1740 pts.**<br>**Activity** | **C**<br>**1640 pts.**<br>**Possible Points** | **D**<br>**1500 pts.**<br>**Points Earned** |
|---|---|---|---|
| _____ | Making Economic Choices | 60 - 140 | _____ |
| _____ | Challenges to Shape Your World | 160 | _____ |
| _____ | The Challenge of Ethics | 120 | _____ |
| _____ | Brainteasers That Challenge | 40 - 140 | _____ |
| _____ | Challenge the System | 60 - 140 | _____ |
| _____ | The Challenge of Inventing a Country | 120 | _____ |
| _____ | Challenges from our History | 160 | _____ |
| _____ | Choices and Challenges of World Leaders | 120 | _____ |
| _____ | Issues Challenging Americans Today | 160 | _____ |
| _____ | The Challenge of Cultural Diversity | 120 | _____ |
| _____ | Foreign Currency Challenges | 120 | _____ |
| _____ | Challenging Your Memory | 120 | _____ |
| _____ | Challenging Your Creative Self | 60 - 200 | _____ |

**TOTAL POINTS** _____

**GRADE** _____

## Making Economic Choices

PURPOSE
To examine the consumer buying and spending habits of many teenagers

SPECIAL MATERIALS NEEDED
None

DIRECTIONS  (60 points)
Complete any three of the following activities outlined below.

## ACTIVITY 1  (20 points)

VERBAL/LINGUISTIC
Research and write out the definitions of each of the following economic terms: consumer, goods, services, value, wages, cash flow, assets, budget, earnings, and bargain

## ACTIVITY 2  (20 points)

LOGICAL/MATHEMATICAL
Assume you had been asked by a parent group at school to serve as an advisor on a committee to examine the buying, spending, and earning habits of students in your age group. Outline a mock plan that would be considered ideal for today's typical teenager. Describe how students could earn money, save money, borrow money, acquire assets, and maintain a reasonable cash flow.

## ACTIVITY 3  (20 points)

VISUAL/SPATIAL
Use the information from the previous activities and create a budget for this typical teenager.

## ACTIVITY 4 (20 points)

BODY/KINESTHETIC
Create a display of actual products, replicas, or drawings/illustrations of the items most commonly purchased by today's typical teenager. Label each item as a good value or poor value and include the price.

## ACTIVITY 5 (20 points)

MUSICAL
Create a rap that talks about the buying and spending habits of kids today.

## ACTIVITY 6 (20 points)

INTERPERSONAL
Organize a panel of students to share their personal experiences with earning money, saving money, spending money, and loaning money. Compile a directory of creative ways that kids can earn money today if they are resourceful and motivated to do so.

## ACTIVITY 7 (20 points)

INTRAPERSONAL
Describe your own personal buying and spending habits. What do they reveal about your values, habits, and priorities?

## Challenges to Shape Your World

PURPOSE
To show how geometry is an integrative force in the world of today

SPECIAL MATERIALS NEEDED
None

DIRECTIONS  (160 points)
Complete each of these geometry activities in the order given.

## ACTIVITY 1 (20 points)

FLUENCY: Write down as many geometric terms, formulas, shapes, and symbols as you can think of in a period of five minutes.

## ACTIVITY 2  (20 points)

FLEXIBILITY: Look over your list from the Fluency Activity and write down any major concepts you may have overlooked in each of the four categories of geometric terms, formulas, shapes, and symbols.

## ACTIVITY 3 (20 points)

ORIGINALITY: Choose one formula, one shape, one geometric term, and one symbol from your list in the Fluency Activity above. Create an original geometry problem for each of these four concepts that other students in your class might be able to solve. Include an answer key.

## ACTIVITY 4 (20 points)

ELABORATION: Complete each of the following statements involving geometric concepts:

1.  A geometric formula I have learned to apply is . . . because . . .

2.  A geometric term I know how to define is . . .

3.  My favorite geometric shape is . . . because . . .

4.  A geometric symbol I think makes a lot of sense is . . . because . . .

## ACTIVITY 5 (20 points)

RISK TAKING: Give a brief personal example to illustrate any two of these figurative statements that make good use of geometric concepts:

1. Sometimes I am considered "to be a square" by my peers when I . . .

2. I would not appreciate being caught in a "love triangle" with someone I knew because . . .

3. People accuse me of "running around in circles" when I . . .

## ACTIVITY 6 (20 points)

COMPLEXITY: Explain or demonstrate the importance of geometry in the field of art or architecture.

## ACTIVITY 7 (20 points)

CURIOSITY: Make a list of five to ten careers that you feel require a solid understanding of and appreciation for the subject of "geometry."

## ACTIVITY 8 (20 points)

IMAGINATION: Visualize yourself in one of the following situations and respond accordingly:

1. Are you more like a circle or a square and why?

2. Are you more like an obtuse angle or an acute angle and why?

3. Are you more like the symbol for a set of parallel lines or a set of perpendicular lines and why?

4. Are you more like the formula for finding the area of a polygon or the perimeter of a polygon and why?

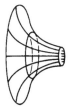

## The Challenge of Ethics

PURPOSE
To explore some of the ethical issues facing the biological sciences of today's modern world

SPECIAL MATERIALS NEEDED
Access to media center

DIRECTIONS  (120 points)
Complete each of the following activities in the order given.

## ACTIVITY 1  (20 points)

KNOWLEDGE
Locate information on at least one of the following "hot topics" facing scientists and the public in today's society:

1.   Organ donor and transplant programs
2.   Test-tube babies and surrogate parents
3.   Genetic engineering and determining the sex/intelligence of one's unborn child
4.   Mercy killings of terminally ill patients
5.   Mandatory abortions for incest and rape

## ACTIVITY 2  (20 points)

COMPREHENSION
Briefly summarize the main argument(s) for one of the "hot topics."

## ACTIVITY 3  (20 points)

APPLICATION
Construct a flow chart showing alternative choices and challenges in any one of the "hot topics."

## ACTIVITY 4 (20 points)

ANALYSIS

Draw conclusions as to why this decade has been referred to as the "Age of Life Science" rather than the "Age of Physical Science" or the "Age of Earth Science."

## ACTIVITY 5 (20 points)

SYNTHESIS

Choose one of the topics from the Knowledge Activity and write a passionate editorial about your feelings and opinions on the topic.

## ACTIVITY 6 (20 points)

EVALUATION

Argue for or against the quality of health care in this country today. Provide data and documentation for your position.

# Brainteasers That Challenge

PURPOSE
To construct a variety of puzzles and brainteasers that challenge the mind

SPECIAL MATERIALS NEEDED
Display of books that contain puzzles, brainteasers, and mindbenders

DIRECTIONS  (40 points)
Browse through the puzzle and brainteaser books on display. Select several of them to do. Then, accept the challenge of constructing two original puzzles or brainteasers from the options listed below. Your puzzles or brainteasers must reflect the science theme or topic of "rocks, minerals, fossils, and precious gems."

EXAMPLE:

## ACTIVITY 1  (20 points)

VERBAL/LINGUISTIC
Generate a list of relevant terms and their scientific definitions. Use these to construct a word finder puzzle or a crossword puzzle.

## ACTIVITY 2  (20 points)

LOGICAL/MATHEMATICAL
Examine a number of logic puzzles to determine how they are organized. Create a logic puzzle of your own that depends upon putting factual information together according to a given sequence or pattern in order to solve.

## ACTIVITY 3 (20 points)

VISUAL/SPATIAL
Mazes can be both fun to work and interesting to design. Try drawing a maze that has several alternative paths to a desired end result and that includes challenges to meet along the way.

## ACTIVITY 4 (20 points)

BODY/KINESTHETIC
Design a living puzzle or brainteaser that requires others to "act out" their responses in mime or charade fashion.

## ACTIVITY 5 (20 points)

INTERPERSONAL
Model a new game after the popular "Pictionary" or "Trivial Pursuit" formats to play with your friends.

## ACTIVITY 6 (20 points)

INTRAPERSONAL
Determine the type of puzzle or brainteaser that has the most appeal to you and create one of your own.

## Challenge the System

PURPOSE
To study the various systems of the human body

SPECIAL MATERIALS NEEDED
Display of reference books and multi-media on the human body

DIRECTIONS  (60 points)
It is always a challenge for one to understand how his/her body works and how to keep it in good working condition. Complete any three of the activities below to help you accept the challenge of being "fit as a fiddle" when it comes to bodily functions.

### ACTIVITY 1 (20 points)

VERBAL/LINGUISTIC
Write a brief paragraph for each system of the body that explains how it works.

### ACTIVITY 2 (20 points)

LOGICAL/MATHEMATICAL
Construct a chart that compares and contrasts the major body systems.

### ACTIVITY 3 (20 points)

VISUAL/SPATIAL
Draw a series of diagrams showing how each system of the body functions.

### ACTIVITY 4 (20 points)

BODY/KINESTHETIC
Work with a group of friends and construct a series of paper bag puppets for a major organ from each system of the body (such as a heart puppet, a kidney puppet, a stomach puppet, etc.). Use these puppets to write and put on a simple skit explaining the role of each of these organs in the functioning of the body.

## ACTIVITY 5 (20 points)

MUSICAL
Select musical pieces or compositions that seem to reflect each of the body systems. Arrange these into a musical collage.

## ACTIVITY 6 (20 points)

INTERPERSONAL
Work with a small group of friends to prepare a booklet of facts for each system of the human body. Design a cover, title page, dedication page, quiz page, and bibliography page for your booklet.

## ACTIVITY 7 (20 points)

INTRAPERSONAL
Write a learning log entry for each system of the human body that records both interesting facts you discovered from your study of the human body as well as questions or reactions you have to information uncovered in your study.

# The Challenge of Inventing a Country

PURPOSE
To invent a country based on one's study and knowledge base of countries around the world

SPECIAL MATERIALS NEEDED
Globe or world map

DIRECTIONS (120 points)
Think about all of the countries you have read about and studied during the past several years of school. Be able to identify the elements common to every country such as geographic location, political system, natural resources, and food/shelter.

Complete each of the activities outlined below to invent a new country of your own.

## ACTIVITY 1 (20 points)

VERBAL/LINGUISTIC
Describe the people who live in your country. Discuss where they live, what they eat, how they dress, what they do during the day, and how they earn a living and obtain an education.

## ACTIVITY 2 (20 points)

LOGICAL/MATHEMATICAL
Write a good paragraph describing their form of government. Is it a republic, a democracy, a monarchy, or a totalitarian government. Present this information in an outline or chart form with explanation.

## ACTIVITY 3 (20 points)

VISUAL/SPATIAL
Draw a map of your country and label its location, size in square miles, distinguishing land forms such as seaports, harbors, rivers, mountain ranges and its natural resources such as minerals, plants, animals, energy sources, etc.

## ACTIVITY 4 (20 points)

BODY/KINESTHETIC
Prepare a set of drawings showing the transportation and communication systems for your country.

## ACTIVITY 5 (20 points)

INTERPERSONAL
Conduct a town meeting with representatives from your country to discuss any ecology or pollution problems your country is experiencing at the present time. Record notes or minutes from your town meeting.

## ACTIVITY 6 (20 points)

INTRAPERSONAL
Design a set of postcards showing your favorite people, places, things, or events associated with your country.

# Challenges From Our History

PURPOSE
To examine the unique challenges faced by special groups of early Americans during the making of America from the 1700s through the 1800s

SPECIAL MATERIALS NEEDED
Social studies textbooks and reference books on American history

DIRECTIONS  (160 points)
Choose one of the following groups of early Americans to use in completing each of the activities outlined below.

1. Native Americans (American Indians)   3.  Pioneers
2. British Colonists                                      4.  African American Slaves

## ACTIVITY 1 (20 points)

FLUENCY
Write down as many challenges as you can think of that were faced by the group of early Americans you have selected to study for this exercise.

## ACTIVITY 2 (20 points)

FLEXIBILITY
Classify each of these challenges in some meaningful way.

## ACTIVITY 3 (20 points)

ORIGINALITY
Determine what special and unique character or personality traits were best exhibited by this group and which helped them to meet the challenges in their lives.

## ACTIVITY 4 (20 points)

ELABORATION
Elaborate on this idea as it relates to your group: *People can be taught to rise to a challenge.*

## ACTIVITY 5 (20 points)

RISK TAKING
Decide what thing you would fear the most about being a member of this group if you could go back in time and live among them.

## ACTIVITY 6 (20 points)

COMPLEXITY
Infer why there is so much evidence of some groups exploiting, terrorizing, or intimidating other groups in the course of making American history. Be specific in your explanations and examples.

## ACTIVITY 7 (20 points)

CURIOSITY
If your group were able to visit you and your community today, write down what you think they would be most curious to see and do.

## ACTIVITY 8 (20 points)

IMAGINATION
Imagine you could communicate with members of this group today by letting them know the legacy they have left for members of your generation. Record the message you would give them.

## Choices and Challenges of World Leaders

PURPOSE
To survey a number of world leaders in the modern era in order to identify some of the challenges they face and the choices they make

SPECIAL MATERIALS NEEDED
Access to media center reference books

DIRECTIONS  (120 points)
Complete each of the following activities in the order given.

## ACTIVITY 1 (20 points)

KNOWLEDGE
Research to find out both the leadership role as well as the country represented by each of the leaders listed below who are currently in positions of power or have been in positions of power during the last ten years.

| | |
|---|---|
| Corazon Aquino | Ibn Talal Hussein |
| Yasir Arafat | Daniel Ortega |
| Beatrix | Pope John Paul II |
| Menachem Begin | Mother Teresa |
| Willy Brandt | Margaret Thatcher |
| Fidel Castro | Bishop Desmond Tutu |
| Queen Elizabeth II | Lech Walesa |
| Mikhail Gorbachev | |

## ACTIVITY 2 (20 points)

COMPREHENSION
In your own words, summarize a major challenge or choice that each of these individuals has made as part of their professional leadership responsibilities.

## ACTIVITY 3 (20 points)

APPLICATION
Assuming you could interview one of these leaders through a satellite communications network, write down a list of five to ten questions you would want to ask him/her.

## ACTIVITY 4 (20 points)

ANALYSIS
Draw conclusions as to what common characteristics these leaders share with one another. Be able to support your ideas.

## ACTIVITY 5 (20 points)

SYNTHESIS
Select one of the leaders you most admire and create a student award in his/her name or honor. Create a design for the award and decide who would most likely receive it in your class or school.

## ACTIVITY 6 (20 points)

EVALUATION
Rank order any ten of these leaders according to the complexity of the challenges and choices they have made or are expected to make in the future with 1 being your first choice and 10 being your last choice. Be able to defend your first and last choices.

# Issues Challenging Americans Today

**PURPOSE**
To identify and analyze a variety of issues and topics that are challenging the safety and security of the American people

**SPECIAL MATERIALS NEEDED**
None

**DIRECTIONS** (160 points)
Complete each of the activities described below.

## ACTIVITY 1 (20 points)

FLUENCY: List as many specific problems as you can that are challenging the safety and security of the American people in our society today.

## ACTIVITY 2 (20 points)

FLEXIBILITY: Classify these problems into one or more of the following categories: Economic Problems, Social Problems, Health Problems, Political Problems, Psychological Problems, or Legal Problems

## ACTIVITY 3 (20 points)

ORIGINALITY: Select any one of the problems from the Fluency Activity and think of a very unusual, novel, or unique solution to the problem.

## ACTIVITY 4 (20 points)

ELABORATION: Write a detailed paragraph discussing this problem from several different perspectives.

## ACTIVITY 5 (20 points)

RISK TAKING: Determine how you or members of your family/race/community are or might be contributing to the magnitude of this problem.

## ACTIVITY 6 (20 points)

COMPLEXITY: Explain why this problem is not a simple one to solve.

## ACTIVITY 7 (20 points)

CURIOSITY: If you could talk to someone in authority about this problem, decide who that would be and what things you would be curious to ask him/her about the problem.

## ACTIVITY 8 (20 points)

IMAGINATION: Pretend you have been able to solve the problem. Visualize and describe how the society would be different.

# The Challenge of Cultural Diversity

PURPOSE
To use children's literature as the basis for recognizing the choices and challenges growing out of the cultural diversity in our pluralistic society

SPECIAL MATERIALS NEEDED
Display of children's picture books dealing with minority characters

DIRECTIONS (120 points)
Browse through the collection of children's picture books on display at the Learning Station. Choose one of these books to complete the tasks outlined below. Do your work on a separate piece of paper.

## ACTIVITY 1 (20 points)

KNOWLEDGE: Choose one minority character from the book you read and record the character's ethnic, racial, or religious background.

## ACTIVITY 2 (20 points)

COMPREHENSION: In your own words, summarize the challenges or struggles this character had to overcome because of his/her minority status. Write another paragraph describing the personality traits of that character that helped him/her overcome those difficulties.

## ACTIVITY 3 (20 points)

APPLICATION: Conduct a small group discussion with two friends on this topic: "What advice would you give to a new student who had just accepted the challenge of moving here from a foreign country for one year?" Record your ideas.

## ACTIVITY 4 (20 points)

ANALYSIS: Challenge your own ego and determine what you think people in other countries think of America, our people, and the American way of life.

## ACTIVITY 5 (20 points)

SYNTHESIS: Design a book mark that gives a brief synopsis of the book you have chosen for this activity.

## ACTIVITY 6 (20 points)

EVALUATION: Decide what country, other than your own, you most admire. Write the reasons for your choice.

## Foreign Currency Challenges

PURPOSE
To identify different foreign currencies and their conversion
values when compared with the U.S. dollar

SPECIAL MATERIALS NEEDED
None

DIRECTIONS (120 points)
Complete each of the activities listed below. Do your work
on separate pieces of paper.

## ACTIVITY 1 (20 points)

KNOWLEDGE
Record the name of the currency system for each of the following countries:
(See Activity 6)

| | | |
|---|---|---|
| Argentina | Belgium | Britain |
| China | Denmark | France |
| Germany | India | Ireland |
| Israel | Italy | Japan |
| Mexico | Saudi Arabia | Thailand |

## ACTIVITY 2 (20 points)

COMPREHENSION
In your own words, explain what makes the value of the American dollar go up
and down against the value of foreign currencies. Explain how these fluctuations
can challenge a country's tourist industry.

## ACTIVITY 3 (20 points)

APPLICATION
Plan a challenging trip to one of the countries listed in Activity 1. Budget your
dollars for a typical day in that country if a room cost $85.00, meals cost $36.00,
transportation cost $22.00, and fees for tourist attractions cost $44.00 in American money. Convert these figures into the foreign currency rates according to the
chart in this section. For example, using this chart, to change a U.S. dollar to
British pounds, you divide $1 by 1.5 to get .66 pounds. To change a British pound
to U.S. dollars, you multiply 1 pound times 1.5 to get $1.50 in U.S. dollars.

## ACTIVITY 4 (20 points)

ANALYSIS
Based on the foreign currency rates in this chart, choose the five countries that would offer an American traveler the best value. Challenge your thinking and draw conclusions as to why you think the currency rates in these five countries are so low.

## ACTIVITY 5 (20 points)

SYNTHESIS
Pretend you have been selected by the U.S. Treasury Department to create a challenging design for a new monetary system for the country. Submit three designs and have classmates choose the best one.

## ACTIVITY 6 (20 points)

EVALUATION
Determine which method of payment would be best to choose from if you were going on an extended trip to a foreign country   (1) foreign currency only that you had purchased in the States at a lower exchange rate than exists on the money market and sufficient "pocket money"; (2) credit cards only except for sufficient "pocket money"; or (3) traveler's checks only except for sufficient "pocket money." Defend your choice.

### MONEY IN OTHER COUNTRIES

| Countries | Name | Foreign | Currency in dollars (changes daily) |
|---|---|---|---|
| Argentina | Peso | 1.01 | |
| Belgium | Franc | .02 | |
| Britain | Pound | 1.5 | |
| China | Yuan | .17 | |
| Denmark | Krone | .15 | |
| France | Franc | .17 | |
| Germany | Mark | .58 | |
| India | Rupee | .03 | |
| Ireland | Punt | 1.43 | |
| Israel | Shekel | .34 | |
| Italy | Lira | .0005 | |
| Japan | Yen | .008 | |
| Mexico | Peso | .32 | |
| The Netherlands | Guilder | .52 | |
| Saudi Arabia | Riyal | .26 | |
| Thailand | Bhat | .03 | |

Using this chart, to change a U.S. dollar to British pounds, you divide  $\$1 \div 1.5 = £.66$ British. To change a British pound to U.S. dollars, you multiply £1 x 1.5 = $1.50 U.S.

# Challenging Your Memory

PURPOSE
To examine ways one can challenge the memory to retain information as part of the learning process

SPECIAL MATERIALS NEEDED
Reference materials on short and long term memory

DIRECTIONS (120 points)
It is always a challenge to remember facts and retain information in the teaching and learning process. Complete these activities to help you discover some tools and techniques for improving your short and long term memory skills.

## ACTIVITY 1 (20 points)

KNOWLEDGE
List situations where it is important for you and others to have a good memory.

## ACTIVITY 2 (20 points)

COMPREHENSION
In your own words, explain the memory function of the brain.

## ACTIVITY 3 (20 points)

APPLICATION
Practice using one or more of the memory aids suggested here. Write a short position paper describing which memory aids worked best for you and why.

1. Jog your memory with visual prompts such as a note or string around your finger.

2. Make lists to order and organize your memory.

3. Keep a drawing pad and pencil at hand and sketch or doodle information as it is presented.

4. Outline the essence of what you want to remember.

5. Use sticky notes and paste them in important places.

6. Force yourself to teach something to someone that you want to learn and remember.

7. Chunk little pieces of information together by using mnemonic devices. For example, you can remember the Great Lakes by the word HOMES (Huron, Ontario, Michigan, Erie, and Superior)

8. Say aloud what you see to help remember it.

9. Use index cards to record important information and always carry them with you to class in a pocket or purse.

10. Associate new information with pieces of old information you know on the topic.

---

## ACTIVITY 4 (20 points)

ANALYSIS

Analyze a typical day in your life at school. Record all of the things that you do which are done strictly from memory. Classify the things on your list in some organized way. What conclusions can you draw about memory from this exercise?

---

## ACTIVITY 5 (20 points)

SYNTHESIS

Create a short poem, story, or essay describing a wonderful memory that you have from your past.

---

## ACTIVITY 6 (20 points)

EVALUATION

Write down five to ten things you have been asked to memorize for classes at school. Rank order these items from 1 to 10 in terms of their value or importance to you.

---

## Challenging Your Creative Self

PURPOSE
To challenge one's creative self

SPECIAL MATERIALS NEEDED
None

DIRECTIONS  (60 points)
One of the greatest challenges facing today's society is finding ways to encourage and nurture the creative talents inherent in all people. Complete any three of the creative activities suggested below.

### ACTIVITY 1  (20 points)

**You are a Name Dropper:**  The mayor wants you to name four new recreation areas for the city. What exciting names will you give her?

### ACTIVITY 2  (20 points)

**You are an Improver:**  Write down three things which would greatly improve the appearance and appeal of your classroom setting or your school grounds.

### ACTIVITY 3  (20 points)

**You are a Designer:**  Create a new line of greeting cards for kids to send to one another.

### ACTIVITY 4  (20 points)

**You are a Problem Solver:**  You have just been discussing how much you dislike the name "Bertha" with a group of friends. Suddenly a new student approaches the group and introduces herself as "Bertha." How can you save the day?

## ACTIVITY 5 (20 points)

**You are a Word Specialist:** Write down ten words that make you want to laugh.

## ACTIVITY 6 (20 points)

**You are a Writer:** Write down ten titles for a creative poem or story. Choose one title and write it.

## ACTIVITY 7 (20 points)

**You are an Idea Person:** Think up 20 uses for a broken watch.

## ACTIVITY 8 (20 points)

**You are a Teacher:** Write out the directions for learning how to skateboard, roller blade, or play a game of pogs.

## ACTIVITY 9 (20 points)

**You are an Explorer:** You have just discovered a new species of plants. Draw it and describe it.

## ACTIVITY 10 (20 points)

**You are an Advisor:** Write out the advice you would give to a group of senior citizens who wanted to better understand the needs and characteristics of teenagers.

Signaling
Student
Success

# COOPERATION AND CONFLICT

- **Classroom Cooperation: Who's Who?**

- **Global Cooperation: the U.N.**

- **Global Conflict in the News**

- **Resolving Conflict**

- **Cooperation and Conflict in Nature**

- **Cooperative Problem Solving**

- **Synonyms and Antonyms**

- **Conflict in Singapore: You Be the Judge**

- **Cooperation, Teamwork, and Sports**

- **Ben and Jerry — A Cooperative Corporate Tale**

National Middle School Association

**An Introduction to COOPERATION**

*Cooperation* is defined as working with others to reach a common goal or desired end. Cooperation exits in many forms, among both people and animals. In today's team-oriented workplace, cooperation is a must! Students who are able to work with diverse ideas and people will be the leaders of tomorrow.

The opposite of cooperation is *conflict*. Conflict is a clash of opposing ideas, interests, or beliefs that often end in some type of disagreement. The ultimate conflict for man is war. Conflict, like cooperation, exists in nature and science as well as in our human world.

There are many ways to restore conflict once it has occurred. Cooperation is often a positive result of conflict. Historically, cooperation and conflict have both played significant roles. By understanding these two concepts, you will be better prepared to meet the challenges of tomorrow.

## THE GUIDING QUESTIONS

1. What is cooperation?

2. How will cooperation and collaboration affect my life? Why are they important skills for me to master and use?

3. What is conflict, and what causes it?

4. How is conflict resolved?

5. How are cooperation and conflict related?

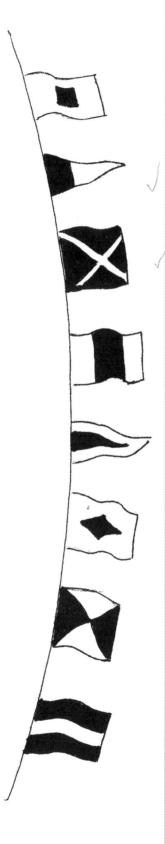

# At a glance — topics and tasks

- Become aware of diversity within your classroom and how cooperation is an important part of accepting one another
- Gain an understanding of global cooperation and why it is important in today's world
- Become globally and internationally more aware of current worldwide conflicts
- Learn about different ways to resolve conflict
- Learn about how cooperation and conflict exist in nature among animals
- Work together cooperatively to solve problems
- Practice using synonyms and antonyms in expressive writing
- Think about differences in sentencing procedures around the world and how these procedures can become a source of international conflict
- Evaluate the importance of both cooperation and competition in sports
- Introduce cooperation and compromise as tools of corporate success

## Cooperation and Conflict Rubric

Name _____ Class _____

You may select from the following stations. An activity must be done completely, accurately, and neatly to earn full point value. The grading scale is as follows:

| A | B | C | D |
|---|---|---|---|
| 830+ pts. | 780-829 pts. | 730-779 pts. | 680-729 pts. |

| Date Completed | Activity | Possible Points | Points Earned |
|---|---|---|---|
| _____ | Classroom Cooperation: Who's Who? | 100 | _____ |
| _____ | Global Cooperation: the U.N. | 100-150 | _____ |
| _____ | Global Conflict in the News | 50 | _____ |
| _____ | Resolving Conflict | 120-140 | _____ |
| _____ | Cooperation and Conflict in Nature | 60 | _____ |
| _____ | Cooperative Problem Solving | 80 | _____ |
| _____ | Synonyms and Antonyms | 110 | _____ |
| _____ | Conflict in Singapore: You Be the Judge | 60 | _____ |
| _____ | Cooperation, Teamwork, and Sports | 60-70 | _____ |
| _____ | Ben and Jerry: A Cooperative Corporate Tale | 90 | _____ |

**TOTAL POINTS** _____
**GRADE** _____

## Classroom Cooperation: Who's Who?

PURPOSE
To become aware of diversity within your classroom and how cooperation is an important part of accepting one another

SPECIAL MATERIALS NEEDED
Class survey; graph paper; words to "Colors of the Wind" from *Pocahontas*; *People* by Peter Spier; multi-cultural stories and books; Right/Left Brain Inventory; Modality Inventory; Multiple Intelligences Inventory

DIRECTIONS  (100 points)
Complete all of the activities at this station. This station is worth 100 points.

## ACTIVITY 1 (50 points)

This survey should be reproduced so that student information may be tallied. Instruments (Learning Styles Inventory/Right Brain/Left Brain Inventory, Gardner's 7 Intelligences) should be administered to the class before conducting the survey.

CLASS PROFILE SURVEY
Compile the data from the survey about your class members:

| Characteristics | Number of Students | |
|---|---|---|
| **Sex** | Boys _____ | Girls _____ |
| **Race** | African-American ____<br>White _____<br>Native American ____ | Asian _____<br>Hispanic _____<br>Other (Specify) _____ |
| **Religion** | Christian _____<br>Jewish _____ | Moslem _____<br>Other (Specify) _____ |
| **Language Spoken** | English _____<br>Spanish _____<br>Japanese _____ | Vietnamese _____<br>Other (Specify) _____ |
| **Learning Style** | Visual _____<br>Auditory _____ | Kinesthetic _____<br>Right Brain _____<br>Left Brain _____ |
| **Intelligence** (according to Gardner) | Linguistic _____<br>Logical-Mathematical _____<br>Bodily Kinesthetic ____ | Spatial _____<br>Musical _____<br>Intrapersonal ____<br>Interpersonal ____ |

Once the numbers of students have been tallied, create a bar graph to show the results. Display the graphs. This should provide all students with a good visual picture of their classroom population.

## ACTIVITY 2 (10 points)

Select one of these to complete.

A. The theme song from the Disney movie *Pocahontas* is entitled "Colors of the Wind." The song represents global acceptance and cooperation. Read the words and write your own interpretation of what the song means.

B. There have been other songs about acceptance, diversity and cooperation. Play, sing or share one with the class and discuss its meaning.

C. Write your own song sharing your thoughts about cooperation and acceptance of others.

## ACTIVITY 3 (10 points)

Select one of these to complete.

A. There are many children's literature books that deal with multicultural issues. Select one to read. Write a poem that summarizes the story or underlying theme of the story.

B. Create your own "Big Book" story around a multicultural theme. Read it to a class of elementary students. (Your teacher can help you schedule this.)

## ACTIVITY 4 (30 points)

In a cooperative group read the book *People* by Peter Spier. Discuss these questions in your group:

1. What is the special idea that Peter Spier conveys in this book?

2. How does he highlight or celebrate the differences in people?

3. How is this book a "smiling lesson of ecology"?

4. What if we were clones of one another? How would things be different?

5. What do you think makes you most unique or different from your friends? other family members?kids on television your age?

6. What key words best describe the illustrations in this book?

7. What things would you do to change the world?

# RIGHT/LEFT BRAIN INVENTORY

**Left-Brain Learner**

_____    responds well to verbal information and explanations

_____    prefers to talk or write

_____    is interested in reward

_____    tends to be reflective, analytical

_____    likes ordered information: logical, sequential, systematic

_____    relies on language in thinking and remembering

_____    likes multiple choice items on tests

_____    solves problems by logical analysis and systematic solutions

_____    is conscious of time, likes schedules

_____    can logically explain answers to math (or other) problems

**Right-Brain Learner**

_____    likes open-ended information

_____    responds well to demonstrations or symbolic instructions

_____    relies on images in thinking and remembering

_____    has difficulty with simultaneous number and word concepts

_____    likes to draw or manipulate objects

_____    has little sense of time; dislikes schedules

_____    prefers essay questions

_____    solves problems with intuition, playing hunches

_____    looks at the whole, rather than details

_____    often knows an answer but may not be able to explain why

# MODALITY INVENTORY

**Visual Student**

_____ thinks in pictures, visualizes details

_____ is distracted by clutter or movement

_____ can plan in advance; writes thoughts down

_____ stares or doodles or finds something to look at when inactive

_____ is often unaware of sounds

_____ remembers by writing things down

_____ likes order in appearance, notebook, locker, desk

_____ may repress emotion, cry easily, or show emotion through facial expression

_____ tends to be a good speller

_____ learns by reading or watching demonstrations

**Auditory Student**

_____ enjoys listening, but cannot wait to talk

_____ is easily distracted by sounds

_____ reads aloud or subvocalizes

_____ talks problems out

_____ remembers stories and directions after hearing them

_____ hums, talks to self or others

_____ enjoys music more than visual arts

_____ expresses displeasure by "blowing off steam" but calms down quickly

_____ remembers by auditory repetition and saying it

_____ may perform rote memory task well if "sung" to a tune

**Kinesthetic Student**

_____ drums fingers, taps toes, or asks to leave room frequently

_____ gestures when speaking

_____ is not attentive to visual or auditory presentations

_____ tends to be impulsive

_____ selects options with the greatest physical activity

_____ reflects emotion through body: stamps, pounds, jumps, hits, hugs

_____ pushes hard on pencil, breaks point easily

_____ learns by trying things out: touches and manipulates

_____ tends to have disheveled appearance because of activity

_____ likes sports and games with movement

84

# MULTIPLE INTELLIGENCES INVENTORY

Did you know there are seven different types of intelligence and that each of us possesses all seven, although one or more of them may be stronger than others? Dr. Howard Gardner, a researcher and professor at the Harvard Graduate School of Education, has developed the Theory of Multiple Intelligences to help us better understand ourselves and the way we acquire information. Try to rank order the seven intelligences below as they best describe the way you learn, with "1" being your strongest intelligence area and "7" being your weakest area. Try to think of examples and instances in the classroom when you were successful on a test, assignment, activity, or task because it was compatible with the way you like to learn.

**Linguistic Intelligence**

_____ Do you find it easy to memorize information, write poems or stories, give oral talks, read books, play word games like Scrabble and Password, use big words in your conversations or assignments, and do you remember what you hear?

**Logical-Mathematic Intelligence**

_____ Do you find it easy to compute numbers in your head and on paper, to solve brainteasers, to do logic puzzles, to conduct science experiments, to figure out number and sequence patterns, and to watch videos or television shows on science and nature themes?

**Spatial Intelligence**

_____ Do you find it easy to draw, paint, or doodle, work through puzzles and mazes, build with blocks or various types of building sets, follow maps and flow charts, use a camera to record what you see around you, and do you prefer reading material that has lots of illustrations?

**Bodily-Kinesthetic Intelligence**

_____ Do you like to engage in lots of sports and physical activities, move around rather than sit still, spend free time outdoors, work with your hands on such things as model-building or sewing, participate in dance, ballet, gymnastics, plays, puppet shows or other performances, and mess around with finger painting, clay, and papier-mâché?

**Musical Intelligence**

_____ Do you like to play a musical instrument or sing in the choir, listen to favorite records or tapes, make up your own songs or rap, recognize off-key recordings or noises, remember television jungles and lyrics of many different songs, and work while listening to or humming simple melodies and tunes?

**Interpersonal Intelligence**

_____ Do you find it easy to make friends, meet strangers, resolve conflicts among peers, lead groups or clubs, engage in gossip, participate in team sports, plan social activities, and teach or counsel others?

**Intrapersonal Intelligence**

_____ Do you find it easy to function independently, do your own work and thinking, spend time alone, engage in solo hobbies and activities, attend personal growth seminars, set goals, analyze your own strengths and weaknesses, and keep private diaries or journals?

# Global Cooperation: The U.N.

PURPOSE
To gain an understanding of global cooperation and why it is important in today's world

SPECIAL MATERIALS NEEDED
Reference materials; art paper; markers

DIRECTIONS (100 points)
Complete all of the activities at this station.

## ACTIVITY 1 (60 points)

Complete the following six exercises. You should read the information and then relate or apply it to help you complete your work. You may need additional reference materials. The bonus questions are optional.

U.N. stands for United Nations. The Charter of the U.N. was drawn up after the Second World War by the countries who had defeated Germany. It officially began on October 24, 1995. The 111 articles of the Charter were written to establish world peace. Another mission of the U.N. is to help underdeveloped countries become more self-supporting.
The U.N. offers support ranging from the lending of money to technical help with farming machinery or industrial equipment. The headquarters of the U.N. is in New York City. There are 184 member nations in the U.N. today.

LANGUAGE ARTS

1. Make a list of other important acronyms or initials that stand for important organizations. Classify your list in some way and explain your rationale for the grouping.

SOCIAL STUDIES

2. Choose one of the 51 countries that belonged to the U.N. in 1945 when the Charter was drawn up and develop a mini-report on its culture. Consider such countries as the Soviet Union, Nationalist China, France, India, Egypt, South Africa, Turkey, Greece, Canada, and the United Kingdom.

MATH

3. Investigate the monetary system for a major U.N. country and compare its values to that of U.S. currency.

SCIENCE

4.   Draw up a set of recommendations for the U.N. to consider in setting up their priority projects for the next fiscal year. Identify ten different countries that could benefit from monetary or technological assistance and write down exactly what you think each one would need and why.

ART

5.   Design a new flag to represent the U.N.

INDUSTRIAL ARTS and HOME ECONOMICS

6.   Plan a U.N. Fair complete with foods, games, events, displays, costumes, and artifacts representative of as many of the Charter nations as possible.

## BONUS (20 points)

Choose one.
1.   On a World Map, find and locate as many U.N. member nations as you can find. Label them and color your map.
2.   The United Nations historically has intervened in world affairs to help countries in warlike conditions. Research and write a brief report to tell about an incident where U.N. troops improved or stopped fighting between countries.

## ACTIVITY 2 (20 points)

### GLOBAL COOPERATION – LANGUAGES AROUND THE WORLD

There are more than 225 languages spoken in the world today. For each of those languages, there are hundreds of dialects and different versions spoken. Global communication can sometimes be a problem in global cooperation. In the chart below, fill in the blanks for the language given with the appropriate foreign words or missing country.

| LANGUAGE | HELLO! / GOOD DAY! | GOODBYE! |
|---|---|---|
| French | | |
| German | Guten Tag! | |
| Hebrew | | שלום pronounced Shalom! |
| Italian | | Addio! |
| Japanese | | |
| Portuguese | Alô! | |
| Russian | Здравствуйте! pronounced ZDRAHST-vooy-tyeh | |
| Swahili | Neno la kusalimu rafiki au mtani! | |
| Swedish | | Adjö! |
| Thai | Sa wat dee ka! | |
| Hawaiian | Aloha! | |

## BONUS (10 points)

Can you add other languages to the chart? Or can you share other words or expression from one of the languages listed in the chart?

## ACTIVITY 3 (20 points)

Ask your teacher or media specialist to provide you with a list of Pen Pals from around the world. Write a letter to a student you select sharing information about your family, school, hobbies, sports, etc. You'll be doing your part toward global cooperation by communicating with a student from a different country. Check to see what technology possibilities exist to communicate through the computer (on line) with another student somewhere else in the world.

## BONUS (20 points)

Select a world cause or organization that you'd like to help with a monetary contribution. Put a large jar in your cafeteria in which to collect pennies or small change from all students. Make a poster explaining what it's for and display it with the jar. Send money collected with a letter of support to the organization or country you selected to help.

88

# Global Conflict in the News

PURPOSE
To become globally and internationally more aware of current worldwide conflicts

SPECIAL MATERIALS NEEDED
News grids

DIRECTIONS  (50 points)
You must complete Activity 1; then select one other to complete from the remaining three.

## ACTIVITY 1  (30 points)

Watch the CNN news update (30 minute summary). Select five to ten different stories that they report and use the information to complete the News Grid.
Try to be brief and only use one or two words to convey information.

### NEWS EVENTS

| Who's Involved (people) | Where (Country or State) | What's the conflict? | Why is there conflict? | When? (timeline) | Solution (Yours or theirs?) |
|---|---|---|---|---|---|
|  |  |  |  |  |  |
|  |  |  |  |  |  |
|  |  |  |  |  |  |
|  |  |  |  |  |  |
|  |  |  |  |  |  |
|  |  |  |  |  |  |
|  |  |  |  |  |  |
|  |  |  |  |  |  |

## ACTIVITY 2  (20 points)

Keep a journal or diary about one event you see on the news. Trace it from the beginning of the conflict until the final resolution or solution. Be sure to include the fiveW's in reporting your information.

## ACTIVITY 3 (20 points)

Write your congressman sharing your thoughts about a particular international conflict.

Know your facts and combine them with your concerned opinion. Find out how you can help or make a difference! Use a business letter format. If you receive a response, share it with the class.

## ACTIVITY 4 (20 points)

Make a poster or draw a picture which describes the global conflict in the news that most interests you. Display your work.

## Resolving Conflict

PURPOSE
To learn about different ways to resolve conflict

SPECIAL MATERIALS NEEDED
Dictionaries

DIRECTIONS  (120 points)
Complete all of the activities at this station.

## ACTIVITY 1 (30 points)

Write a brief description of a conflict that has occurred in your life personally, either at school or at home.

- How did you resolve or solve the conflict?
- Was there a different or better way to solve it after the conflict was over and you've had time to reflect on it?

## ACTIVITY 2 (20 points)

In a cooperative group, select one of the student conflicts from Activity 1 and role play it for the class.

- Did the class agree with your way of resolving the conflict?
- If not, how would they have done it differently?

## ACTIVITY 3 (70 points)

The following list represents ways to settle or handle conflict. Define each one and give an example of how you've used this method in situations in your life.

| | | | |
|---|---|---|---|
| argue | mediate | reconceptualize | seek consensus |
| persuade | arbitrate | negotiate | humor |
| vote | delay | give-in | avoid |
| compromise | | | |

Rank order the three strategies that you feel are most important in resolving conflict and tell why.

## BONUS (20 points)

Take each students' ranking, combine them, and create a total class ranking of the best ways to resolve conflict.

91

## Cooperation and Conflict in Nature

PURPOSE
To learn how cooperation and conflict exists in nature among animals

SPECIAL MATERIALS NEEDED
Drawing paper; markers; resource materials

DIRECTIONS (60 points)
Complete three of the following activities.

### ACTIVITY 1 (20 points)

Symbiosis is described as the relationship of two or more different organisms living together in a close association especially when it is of mutual benefit. Some examples:

      A. Plovers (small birds)/Crocodiles
      B. Remoras/Sharks
      C. Cow Birds/Cows

Research and find other animals which have a symbiotic relationship. List them and write a brief description of how they benefit or cooperate with each other. Illustrate the examples you find on a chart to display in the classroom.

### ACTIVITY 2 (20 points)

Parasites live on the bodies of other living things. These are usually harmful relationships which deplete the host organism in some way. Research and find ten examples of parasites and what harm they cause their host. Write a brief descriptive paragraph about each of the parasites you discovered.

## ACTIVITY 3 (20 points)

The single names of most animals change when referring to that animal as a group. An example would be a wolf and a pack. In the chart below, fill in the group name for the single animal listed.

| Animal | Group | Animal | Group |
|--------|-------|--------|-------|
| Bear | Sleuth | Goose | |
| Cat | | Horse | |
| Cattle | Herd | Lion | |
| Chicken | | Monkey | |
| Dog | | Rabbit | |
| Elephant | | Sheep | |
| Fox | | Swan | |
| Goat | | Pig (Swine) | |
| | | Whale | |

Can you add others to the chart? Share them with the class.

While in the group, animals often work together and cooperate to make their lives easier or simply to survive. Choose three of the animals found in the chart and write specific examples on how they work together or cooperate in their group. Is conflict ever a part of the group? Explain.

## ACTIVITY 4 (20 points)

The food chain is one example of conflict among animals found in nature. The predator/prey relationship usually involves conflict. Draw a food chain showing examples of conflict found within one of these food chain situations.

## Cooperative Problem Solving

PURPOSE
To work together cooperatively to solve problems

SPECIAL MATERIALS NEEDED
Puzzle pieces; math homework

DIRECTIONS  (80 points)
Complete the activities at this station.

## ACTIVITY 1 (50 points)

This activity should be done in cooperative groups of three or six. Each group should be given an envelope of puzzle pieces. Each person should be given six pieces if in a group of three, or three pieces if in a group of six. There are six puzzles to complete. There is only one way to put all six puzzles together correctly. The student's goal is to make six perfect squares.

Rules:  You may not speak putting the puzzle pieces together. No
signaling or gesturing is allowed. Each student should lay the pieces he/she
has in the appropriate place.

Time the groups to see who completes it first. Then discuss these questions:
1.  What did you notice about the way your group members solved the puzzle?
2.  Were some members of the group more cooperative than others?
3.  What would have made this task easier?

Can you find other cooperative puzzles for your group to solve?

## ACTIVITY 2  (30 points)

Think/Pair/Share is another cooperative strategy. Using your math homework, complete the assignment by yourself – *Think*! Get a partner from your class and share your answers. Check them with each other. Discuss differences and correct them if there are any – *Pair!* With your partner, find another pair and repeat the process – *Share!*

What did you notice about this activity?

Does reviewing and restating something three times lock in learning?
Why or why not?

# PUZZLE SETS

Note to teacher: Puzzle pieces should be cut from poster board. You may choose to color code them.

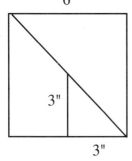

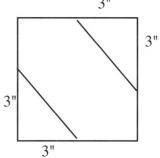

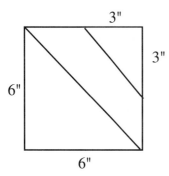

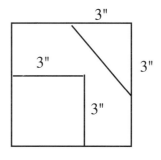

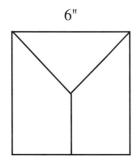

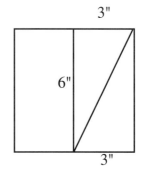

## Synonyms and Antonyms

PURPOSE
To practice using synonyms and antonyms in expressive writing

SPECIAL MATERIALS NEEDED
Thesaurus; drawing paper; markers

DIRECTIONS  (110 points)
Complete all of the activities at this station.

### ACTIVITY 1  (20 points)

In a cooperative group (or by yourself) brainstorm at least ten synonyms for cooperation and ten synonyms for conflict. List them. You may want to use a thesaurus.

### ACTIVITY 2  (20 points)

Using the synonyms from Activity One, create a comparative chart showing antonyms for all the words you listed.

### ACTIVITY 3 (20 points)

Write a story or poem using all the synonyms and antonyms from Activities 1 and 2. Illustrate your story or poem.

### ACTIVITY 4 (20 points)

Using all of the knowledge you've gained through this activity, write out good definitions for both of these terms.

Cooperation is: _____

_____

Conflict is:     _____

_____

### ACTIVITY 5  (30 points)

What would the world be like if there was no cooperation? What would the world be like if there were no conflict? Share your thoughts in a two-minute speech that you present to the class.

96

---

## Conflict in Singapore — You Be the Judge

PURPOSE
To think about differences in sentencing procedures around the world and how these procedures can become a source of international conflict

SPECIAL MATERIALS NEEDED
Background information; reference materials

DIRECTIONS  (60 points)
Read the following background information and complete three of the five activities listed.
You may choose which you want to complete.

### BACKGROUND INFORMATION

Michael Fay, an 18-year-old American living in Singapore, was arrested for vandalism in April of 1994. He was charged with spray painting cars and throwing eggs at property. He was found guilty and was sentenced to four months in jail, a $1,400.00 fine and six lashes on his bare buttocks with a rattan cane whip. In Singapore this kind of punishment is normal and accepted. Yet in the United States it is considered cruel, unusual, even torturous to some; and so an international outcry resulted.

---

### ACTIVITY 1 (20 points)

Answer the following questions:
1. What was your reaction to this incident? Did Michael get what he deserved?
2. How does the saying, "When in Rome, do as the Romans do!" apply here?
3. Should any individual be subjected to this kind of punishment? Is it O.K. for other countries to do this but not O.K. for America?
4. Why do you think this incident became an international conflict? Should our government have done more? done less?
5. Did you agree with how it was resolved? Why or why not?

---

### ACTIVITY 2 (20 points)

Make a chart comparing sentencing practices in the United states to those in Singapore and eight other foreign countries you choose. Do stiffer punishments reduce serious crimes? Which country do you think handles crimes and criminals best?

## ACTIVITY 3 (20 points)

Pretend you are an American judge. What would your sentence for Michael Fay have been? Should we in the United States have more severe punishments for certain crimes? Why or why not?

## ACTIVITY 4 (20 points)

Pretend you are going to interview Michael Fay for a teen magazine. Write five questions you would want to ask him and five possible responses he might give.

## ACTIVITY 5 (20 POINTS)

Research and find other incidents (kidnaping, terrorist acts, inhumane treatment of prisoners, etc.) that have caused international conflict. How were they resolved? Did you agree with the way the situations were handled? Why or why not?

**Cooperation, Teamwork, and Sports**

PURPOSE
To evaluate the importance of both cooperation
and competition in sports

SPECIAL MATERIALS NEEDED
Blank Venn diagrams

DIRECTIONS  (60 points)
You must complete Activity One. Choose one of
the remaining three to complete.

## ACTIVITY 1 (40 points)

Create a Venn Diagram using the concepts of cooperation and competition.

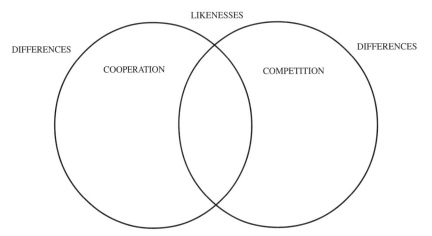

List characteristics of each concept in their separate, respective circles. Are there common characteristics to both? If so, place those in the overlap where the two circles meet. Share your diagram with others. Compare them and discuss the likenesses and differences between cooperation and competition.

## BONUS (10 points)

Could you add a third circle? Label it conflict. Does competition ever contribute to conflict?

## ACTIVITY 2 (20 points)

In a cooperative group, select three of your favorite sports. Role play the game first using cooperation and then with no cooperation. Was there a difference? What would team sports be like if there were no cooperation, only competition?

## ACTIVITY 3 (20 points)

Invent a new game. Tell how both cooperation and competition are important in your game. Get your P.E. teacher to let you play the game in class. Was it successful? You may want to write it up and present it to other schools.

## ACTIVITY 4 (20 points)

Write a one page reaction paper using this theme: "Cooperation is good, competition is bad." Do you agree with this statement? Why or why not?

## Ben and Jerry — A Cooperative Corporate Tale

PURPOSE
To introduce cooperation and compromise as tools of corporate success

SPECIAL MATERIALS NEEDED
Copies of *Ben and Jerry's – Ice Cream For Everyone* by Keith Greenberg (Woodbridge,CT: Blackbirch Press, 1994) or other reference books; drawing paper; markers

DIRECTIONS  (90 points)
Complete Activities 1 and 4. Select one other to complete.

Ben Cohen and Jerry Greenfield form a very successful team in today's corporate world. Their friendship began in a seventh grade classroom on Long Island, New York.

They began their dream together with a plan of opening a mail order bagel shop but realized early on that this would not gain them the success they wanted. So they turned to ice cream. From their first store in an abandoned gas station the company has grown to become the second largest ice cream corporation in the world. Their story is one of cooperation and compromise.

## ACTIVITY 1  (40 points)

Ben and Jerry list many qualities that helped make their company a success. Among them are:

    work can be fun (work ethic)
    humor
    giving back to the community (community service)
    equal opportunities for women and minorities
    caring/employee pride
    compromise and cooperation
    teamwork/ownership

Research and find out how those qualities helped to make them successful. Would these be important qualities for all businesses? Why or why not?

## ACTIVITY 2 (20 points)

How does the Ben and Jerry Story fulfill the "American dream?" It is said you can accomplish anything in America, if you want it bad enough and work hard. Create a timeline showing the success story of Ben and Jerry.

## ACTIVITY 3 (20 points)

Can getting "too big" for a company become a problem? Ben and Jerry hung a sign outside their business that read "We're Closed Because We're Trying to Figure Out What's Going On." What did they mean by this? How did they regroup and go on to make their company sell over a million dollars of ice cream in a year?

## ACTIVITY 4 (30 points)

Research and find five other companies that use teamwork and cooperation as the cornerstones of their success, for example, Ford Motor Company. Briefly describe how each company utilizes the principles of cooperation and teamwork.

## ACTIVITY 5 (20 points)

Create a bumper sticker to convey the message of teamwork and cooperation and their importance in today's corporate world.

**Example:** You can't "go it" alone in corporate America.

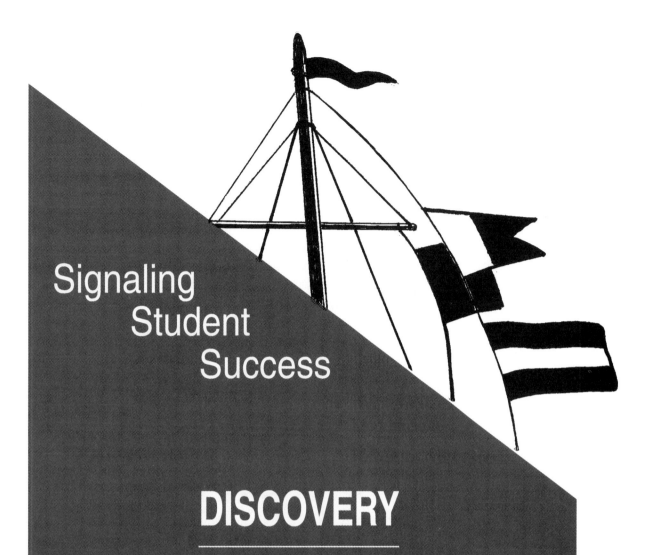

# Signaling Student Success

# DISCOVERY

- Discovering Surprises of Language

- Discovering Patterns of Poetry

- Discovering Speech Making Tricks

- Discovering the Impact of Juvenile Crime

- Discovering the Secrets of Archaeology

- Discovering Secrets of the Wild West

- Discovering the Secrets of the Pyramids

- Discovering Lines of Symmetry

- Discovering the Meanings in Mathematics

- Discovering the Secrets of Plants

- Discovering the Mysteries of the Sea

- Discovering Creative Brainstorming

National Middle School Association

**An Introduction to DISCOVERY**

**The world is an exciting place because every day there is something new to explore, to examine, to discover, and to wonder about. People in former years discovered the secrets of the past while people of today are discovering the secrets of the future.**

Every subject area – whether math, science, social studies, language arts, music, art, physical education, home economics, or industrial arts – is doubling its knowledge every two to five years because we discover new ideas and insights primarily through our access to technology and telecommunications.

The activities in this learning station will help you to uncover some of yesterday's mysteries and discover some of today's delights. Just remember our definition of *discover* as you do these activities: "…discovery consists of looking at the same thing as everyone else and thinking something different" (Albert Szent-Gyorgi).

## THE GUIDING QUESTIONS

1.  What are some of the important discoveries of the past?

2.  How can we use past information to understand the present?

3.  What key discoveries can I make in my studies of math, science, social studies, and language arts to help me be successful in the future?

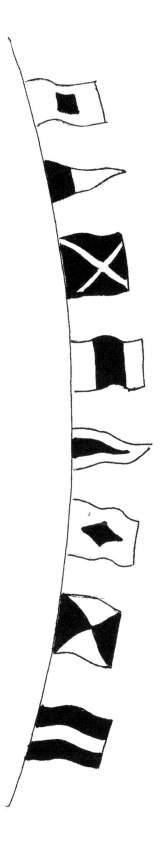

# At a glance — topics and tasks

- **Analyze words and their origins to discover patterns in the development of language**
- **Introduce students to varied patterns for creating original poems**
- **Provide practice in preparing and giving simple speeches with varied themes or purposes**
- **Examine the statistics of juvenile crime and its impact on schools and communities**
- **Define archaeology and discover some of the tools and methods used by archaeologists**
- **Examine the life-style of the American cowboy during the western movement in American history**
- **Explore the pyramids of ancient Egypt and discover information about them**
- **Experiment with the concept of symmetry**
- **Look at mathematics as a language complete with its symbols, definitions, applications, and interpretations**
- **Identify the characteristics of plants and flowers that distinguish them from other living things**
- **Study the flora, animals, birds, and creatures of the ocean**
- **Encourage creative thinking skills, especially brainstorming, in small group sessions**

# Discovery Rubric

Name _____ Class _____

You may select from the following stations. The activity must be done completely, accurately, and neatly to earn full point value. The grading scale is as follows:

| A<br>1940 pts. | B<br>1820 pts. | C<br>1700 pts. | D<br>1600 pts. |
|---|---|---|---|
| Date Completed | Activity | Possible Points | Points Earned |
| _____ | Discovering Surprises of Language | 160-180 | _____ |
| _____ | Discovering Patterns of Poetry | 160-180 | _____ |
| _____ | Discovering Speech Making Tricks | 100-120 | _____ |
| _____ | Discovering the Impact of Juvenile Crime | 120-140 | _____ |
| _____ | Discovering the Secrets of Archaeology | 120-140 | _____ |
| _____ | Discovering Secrets of the Wild West | 140-160 | _____ |
| _____ | Discovering the Secrets of the Pyramids | 140-160 | _____ |
| _____ | Discovering Lines of Symmetry | 120-140 | _____ |
| _____ | Discovering the Meanings in Mathematics | 140-160 | _____ |
| _____ | Discovering the Secrets of Plants | 140-160 | _____ |
| _____ | Discovering the Mysteries of the Sea | 160-180 | _____ |
| _____ | Discovering Creative Brainstorming | 60-220 | _____ |
| | | **TOTAL POINTS** | _____ |
| | | **GRADE** | _____ |

## Discovering Surprises of Language

PURPOSE
To analyze words and their origins in order to discover patterns in the development of language

SPECIAL MATERIALS NEEDED
None

DIRECTIONS  (160 points)
Complete each of the following activities as described.

### ACTIVITY 1 (20 points)

An *initialism* is a series of letters that stand for names or words. It is a kind of code used to shorten words and names.

> **Examples**:  — BLT is a bacon, lettuce, and tomato sandwich.
> — IQ means intelligence quotient.
> — COD means collect on delivery.

Can you think of five more initialisms?

### ACTIVITY 2 (20 points)

A *euphemism* is a word or phrase used to make another word sound better. Often they are used to hide the real meanings of words with negative connotations.

> **Examples:**  — We say someone "passed away" instead of saying someone died.
> — We call a garbage man a sanitation engineer.
> — We refer to a spy as an intelligence agent.

Can you think of five more euphemisms?

### ACTIVITY 3 (20 points)

A *stink pink* is a pair of words that rhyme, have the same number of syllables, and that fit a given definition.

> **Examples:**  — A stupid fruit is a "dumb plum."
> — A monster movie is a "creature feature."
> — An usual couple is a "rare pair."

Can you think of five more stink pinks?

## ACTIVITY 4 (20 points)

A *pun* is a "play on words" that creates humor by using word sounds and meanings.

**Examples:**
— A good name for a referee might be Otto Bounds.
— A good name for a plumber might be Rusty Pipes.
— A good name for a wealthy socialite might be Vera Rich.

Can you think of five more puns?

## ACTIVITY 5 (20 points)

A *Tom Swifty* is a sentence that says things in a special way so that they relate to another word or idea in the sentence.

**Examples:**
— Move to the back of the boat," Tom said sternly.
— "Did you study for the exam?" Tom asked testily.
— "My pencil needs sharpening," Tom said pointedly.

Can you think of five more Tom Swifties?

## ACTIVITY 6 (20 points)

A *wordle* is a group of words or letters written so that they stand for a familiar phrase.

**Example:**

| | |
|---|---|
| Time Time | "double-time" |
| C | |
| I | |
| H | "hiccup" |
| The ears wet | "wet behind the ears" |

Can you think of five more wordles?

## ACTIVITY 7 (20 points)

A *picture word* is a word that is written in such a way that it reflects the actual meaning of the word.

**Examples:**

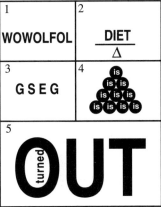

*See below for answers.*

Can you think of five more picture words?

## ACTIVITY 8 (20 points)

A *cliché* is a worn-out expression that has been used so often and so universally that it has become completely predictable.

**Examples:**
— Her stomach is a "bottomless pit."
— He is a "chip off the old block."
— They tried to budget and "make both ends meet."

Can you think of five more cliches?

## BONUS (20 points)

Collect three favorite proverbs and rewrite them using sophisticated language and fancy synonyms and phrases for the original word choices.

**ANSWERS FOR ACTIVITY SEVEN:**
1. Reverse image.   2. Balanced diet.
3. Scrambled eggs.   4. Tennis balls.   5. Turned inside out.

# Discovering Patterns of Poetry

PURPOSE
To introduce students to varied patterns for creating original poems

SPECIAL MATERIALS NEEDED
None

DIRECTIONS (160 points)
Select an interesting living or nonliving object that has special interest or appeal to you. This can be anything from a butterfly or a cloud to a frisbee or a rose. Use the eight different poetry patterns below to write eight different poems or perspectives about your given object. Title your collection of poems: "Eight Ways to Look at a ..."

# ACTIVITY

### POETRY PATTERN 1 (20 points)

**Cinquain**

       Line 1: a noun
       Line 2: two adjectives describing line 1
       Line 3: three verbs related to line 1
       Line 4: a four word phrase about line 1
       Line 5: a synonym for line 1 (noun)

### POETRY PATTERN 2 (20 points)

**Triplet**

       A triplet:  has three lines
                   can be rhymed or unrhymed
                   has lines that can be of same length or vary in length
                   may use any of these rhyming patterns: aaa, aab, aba, abb, or abc

### POETRY PATTERN 3 (20 points)

**Tanka**

       A tanka is usually unrhymed, has five lines, and a total of 31 syllables. Its pattern is:

             Line 1: 5 syllables
             Line 2: 7 syllables
             Line 3: 5 syllables
             Line 4: 7 syllables
             Line 5: 7 syllables

POETRY PATTERN 4  (20 points)

**Dial-A-Poem**

This poem has seven lines, can be rhymed or unrhymed, and uses words and phrases totaling a certain number of syllables. To use this pattern, you . . .

> Write your phone number vertically.
> Each number indicates the number for syllables for that line.
> Any number of syllables may be assigned to zero.
> Use words or phrases, not sentences.

POETRY PATTERN 5  (20 points)

**Action Acrostic**

The letters of this type of poem are written vertically. These letters indicate the first letter of each line of the poem. Acrostics may be made with complete sentences, words, or phrases.

POETRY PATTERN 6  (20 points)

**5 "W" Poetry**

The pattern for 5 "W" poetry is:

> Line 1: Tells who.
> Line 2: Adds did what (an action for "who").
> Line 3: Tells where the action took place.
> Line 4: Tells when the action happened.
> Line 5: Explains why the action happened.

POETRY PATTERN 7  (20 points)

**Definition Poem**

A definition poem is made of a selection of phrases that defines an idea or concept. The first line of the poem either asks a question such as "What's a butterfly?" or makes a statement such as "A butterfly is an insect that . . ." The next 8 lines define the idea or concept using a verb or verb form to begin each line. The last line says "That's a . . ."

POETRY PATTERN 8  (20 points)

**Concrete Poem**

A concrete poem is written in the shape of the topic of the poem. It does not have to rhyme. Use descriptive words or thoughts about the object of the poem and arrange these visually to form the shape of your object. For example, a concrete poem about butterflies would contain a variety of words, phrases, or sentences describing a butterfly arranged in a butterfly pattern or outline.

## BONUS (20 points)

Choose a poetry theme such as nature, love, cats, food, feelings, or people. Collect 5-10 poems on that theme and copy them for a poetry booklet. Illustrate these poems with drawings, computer graphics, or cut-out magazine illustrations. Add a cover and Table of Contents to your booklet.

## Discovering Speech Making Tricks

PURPOSE
To provide practice in preparing and giving simple speeches with varied themes or purposes

SPECIAL MATERIALS NEEDED
None

DIRECTIONS  (100 points)
It is important that every student learn how to prepare and deliver a short but interesting speech. A general outline to follow in writing and giving a speech follows: (1) Choose a topic; (2) Research and collect ideas on the topic; (3) Organize the facts in a logical sequence; (4) Plan the beginning and closing; and (5) Write the whole speech in more detail. In delivering your speech, it is important to: (1) Practice your speech before a mirror and/or small audience; (2) Maintain eye contact with your audience; (3) Project your voice; (4) Speak slowly and deliberately; (5) Look at your audience and only glance at your notes.

You will be planning and delivering a series of short talks or speeches. These will be performed before a small group of peers and not for the entire class. Read through the speech guidelines which follow and "take one speech at a time." The teacher will assign you to a small cooperative learning group of six students for this purpose.

## ACTIVITY

### SPEECH NUMBER 1  (20 points)

Browse through some joke books in the library and find one of several lines that has appeal to you. Copy down the joke, practice telling it, and be prepared to share it with your group.

### SPEECH NUMBER 2  (20 points)

Browse through some children's poetry books in the library and find a short one that you like. Copy down the poem, memorize it, and be prepared to share it with your group.

### SPEECH NUMBER 3  (20 points)

The teacher will put six to eight topics in a "hat" and you will draw one out at random and give a 60 to 90 second impromptu speech on the topic for members of your group. Some typical speech topics are like the ones suggested below. Use these for practice.
    1.   Describe the best or worst meal you have ever eaten.
    2.   Give a description of the nicest person you know.

3. Tell about your favorite holiday.
4. Summarize your television viewing habits.
5. Describe a perfect birthday for you.
6. Discuss a pet peeve that you have.

### SPEECH NUMBER 4  (20 points)

Plan, write, and deliver a short book review. Your review should include the following parts:

1. Tell what the story is about.
2. Describe the main character and discuss his/her appeal.
3. Think of one high point in the story and describe it.
4. State your opinion of the story and give reasons for feeling as you do.

### SPEECH NUMBER 5  (20 points)

Plan, write, and deliver any one of the types of speech suggested here. The topic of your speech is up to you although some suggestions have been given for you to think about. Your speech is to be approximately three minutes long and should include an effective opening and closing statement. Consider using humor, quotations, startling statements, unusual facts or examples, testimonials, personal experiences/anecdotes, or a rhetorical question for this purpose.

Option 1:   A Speech to Demonstrate. Give a speech that shows someone how to do something such as prepare a recipe, build a card house, play a game, or organize a stamp collection.

Option 2:   A Speech to Inform. Give a speech that tells someone about a person, place, or thing such as information about shells, information about a state you visited, or information about a local politician.

Option 3:   A Speech to Persuade. Give a speech that attempts to persuade the audience into believing something such as: video games are destroying kids' minds; homework is (or is not) beneficial; or professional sports is ruining this country.

## BONUS  (20 points)

Create a rubric for others to use in assessing the quality of your speech to demonstrate, inform, or persuade.

## Discovering the Impact of Juvenile Crime

PURPOSE
To examine the statistics of juvenile crime and their impact on schools and communities

SPECIAL MATERIALS NEEDED
Copies of crime statistics below

*CRIME STATISTICS*

- Since 1965, the juvenile arrest rate for violent crime has tripled.The fastest growing segment of the criminal population is our nation's children.

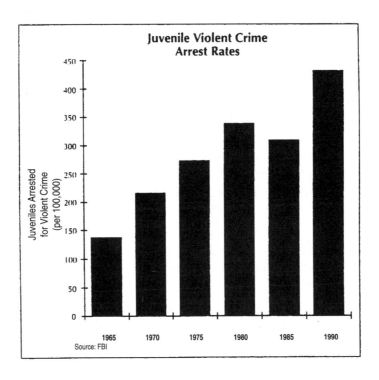

| Juvenile Violent Crime Arrest Rates | |
|---|---|
| Year | Arrest Rates (per 100,000) |
| 1960 | NA |
| 1965 | 137.0 |
| 1970 | 215.9 |
| 1975 | 272.4 |
| 1980 | 338.1 |
| 1985 | 308.6 |
| 1990 | 430.6 |
| Source: FBI | |

- Between 1982 and 1991, the arrest rate for juveniles for murder increased 93 percent, the arrest rate for aggravated assault increased 72 percent, for forcible rape 24 percent, and for motor vehicle theft 97 percent.

- Because the population group of 10- to 17-year-olds is going to increase significantly in the 1990s, the violent upsurge will probably accelerate.

- There has been a 1,740 percent rise in the number of children and teenagers treated for knife and gunshot wounds since 1986 at the Children's National Medical Center in Washington.

- About 3 million thefts and violent crimes occur on or near a school campus each year, representing nearly 16,000 incidents per day.

- Twenty percent of high school students now carry a firearm, knife, razor, club, or some other weapon on a regular basis.

- In 1991, children under age 10 committed more than 1,000 acts of aggravated assault and 81 cases of forcible rape. Juveniles 12 and under committed the following crimes:

| Offenses Committed by Juveniles Under 12: 1991 | | |
|---|---|---|
| Type of Offense | Under Age 10 | Ages 10–12 |
| Murder | 6 | 29 |
| Forcible Rape | 81 | 441 |
| Robbery | 238 | 1,924 |
| Motor Vehicle Theft | 253 | 2,423 |
| Aggravated Assault | 1,068 | 3,859 |
| Arson | 1,068 | 1,571 |
| Burglary | 3,395 | 11,959 |
| Larceny-Theft | 11,663 | 50,505 |
| Source: FBI | | |

- In 1991, the violent crime arrest rate for African-American youth was five times higher than that of white youth.

- Today, 70 percent of the juvenile offenders in long-term correctional facilities grew up without a father in the household.

- Only 5 percent of all young violent offenders are tried as adults. In many states a youthful offender under the age of 16 cannot be sentenced past the age of 25 no matter how serious the crime.

- When asked to name a cause for the increase in youth violence, law enforcement officials largely single out the nation's system of so-called juvenile justice. Set up some 30 years ago to protect immature kids who might get arrested for truancy, shoplifting, or joyriding, it is ill equipped to deal with the violent children of the 1990s who are robbing, raping, and murdering." — *The Wall Street Journal*

- Crime does not wash over all Americans equally. It especially terrorizes the weakest and most vulnerable among us. Three quarters of America's 64 million children live in metropolitan areas, a fifth live in low-income households, at least a tenth come home after school to a house containing no adult, and most are physically immature and incompletely formed in character. These are the people who suffer most when law and order decay. "Children need order. Aside from love and sustenance, there is nothing they need more than order." — Karl Zinsmeister, American Enterprise Institute

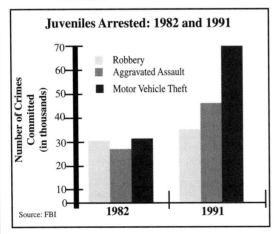

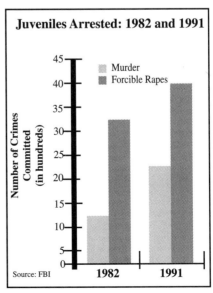

SOURCE: Bennet, W. J. (1994).

*The index of leading cultural indicators.*

New York: Simon & Schuster-Touchstone.

DIRECTIONS  (120 points)
Use the juvenile crime statistics provided to help you complete each of the tasks outlined below.

## ACTIVITY 1  (20 points)

KNOWLEDGE
Record three facts from any of the charts or statistics on the pages entitled "Juvenile Crime Facts and Statistics" that have special meaning or interest to you. Be prepared to discuss your choices.

## ACTIVITY 2  (20 points)

COMPREHENSION
In your own words, explain why you think so many kids today are attracted to gangs.

## ACTIVITY 3  (20 points)

APPLICATION
Determine why you think each of these facts or statistics has become a reality:
1. In 1991 the violent crime arrest rate for African American youth was five times higher than that of white youth.
2. Today, 70 percent of the juvenile offenders in long-term correctional facilities grew up without a father in the household.
3. Twenty percent of high school students now carry a firearm, knife, razor, club, or some other weapon on a regular basis.

## ACTIVITY 4  (20 points)

ANALYSIS
Research has demonstrated that watching violence on television can have four distinct effects: (1) An increase in meanness and violent behavior (called the "aggressor" effect); (2) an increase in fearfulness, mistrust, and self-protective behaviors (called the "victim" effect); (3) an increase in callousness, apathy, and desensitization (the "bystander" effect); and (4) an increase in the desire for more media violence and participation in violent events (the "appetite" effect).

Examine each of these issues and decide whether they make sense to you or not. Write your thoughts up in an opinion and reflection paper.

## ACTIVITY 5 (20 points)

SYNTHESIS

Plan a "Juvenile Crime Awareness" booth and/or fair for your class. Who will you invite? When and where will it be held? What resource people and materials will you feature? How will you promote it? Why will people want to attend?

## ACTIVITY 6 (20 points)

EVALUATION

Risk factors which increase the likelihood that child will become a victim or perpetrator of violence include the following:

1. Poverty
2. Prejudice against ethnic, religious, or social groups
3. Drug or alcohol involvement for the young person and family
4. Access to firearms
5. Family experience with violence
6. Previous experience as a victim or witness of personal, family, peer violence or hate crimes
7. Problems with impulse control
8. Inadequate social problem-solving skills
9. The absence of adults in a family
10. Fatalistic beliefs that violence is inevitable and that fighting is an appropriate way to resolve conflicts
11. A history of depression or suicidality
12. Dropping out of school

Rank order each of these risk factors from 1 to 12 with 1 being, in your opinion, the most significant for members of your school/community and 12 being the least significant for members of your school/community. Give reasons for your first and last choices.

Note: This information was taken from the Center for School Counseling Practitioners. Coping with Violence in the Schools: a Report of the 1993 Summer Conference of the Center for School Counseling Practitioners. Cambridge, MA: 1994.

## BONUS (20 points)

Design a billboard to inform kids about the dangers of juvenile crime.

## Discovering the Secrets of Archaeology

PURPOSE
To define archaeology and discover some of the tools and methods that are used by archaeologists

SPECIAL MATERIALS NEEDED
Resource materials and reference books about archaeology

DIRECTIONS  (120 points)
Complete each of the archaeology activities outlined below.

### ACTIVITY 1  (20 points)

KNOWLEDGE
Define the following terms as they relate to archaeology: archaeologist, artifacts, archaeological site, culture, digs, excavation, fossils, prehistory, primary sources, and secondary sources.

### ACTIVITY 2  (20 points)

COMPREHENSION
In your own words, explain the work of an archaeologist and why they have been called "detectives of the past." Give some specific examples of archaeological expeditions, finds, or digs as part of your explanation.

### ACTIVITY 3 (20 points)

APPLICATION
Archaeologists use artifacts to reconstruct the life of a given culture in a given time. Prepare an artifact box of at least 20 items that you feel best represent the "pop culture" of today's teenager in your school and community. Construct a chart that lists each artifact, gives its description, and tells its purpose/use/value to the pop culture.

### ACTIVITY 4 (20 points)

ANALYSIS
Hammurabi was a powerful leader in Babylonia in 1792 B.C. He is best known for the Code of Hammurabi. These were laws that covered religion, irrigation, trade, property, slavery, family matters, crime, etc. Locate these laws set forth by Hammurabi in an encyclopedia and draw conclusions as to whether they made sense and were fair or not. Share your analysis in written form.

120

## ACTIVITY 5 (20 points)

SYNTHESIS

Work with a small group of students and "invent a culture." Record information about your culture on 5 X 8 file cards using one card for each type of information required. You should have one card that tells:

1. The name and geographic location/features of your culture.
2. A physical description/drawings of the people in your culture.
3. The values, rules, and beliefs that guide the behavior of the people in your culture.
4. The major foods, fashions, and shelter accommodations of the people in our culture.
5. The marriage/family/funeral rites of the people in your culture.
6. The religious practices and rituals of the people in your culture.
7. The form of government, including its laws, that determine the political norms of the people in your culture.
8. The alphabet and number systems used throughout your culture.
9. The art, music, and dance types that are popular with people of your culture.
10. The games, hobbies, and leisure time activities that are popular with people of your culture.

## ACTIVITY 6 (20 points)

EVALUATION

It was common for ancient cultures to bury their dead with things they valued while alive and with things they thought they would need in the afterlife. List five items you would choose to have buried with you now and give reasons for these choices.

## BONUS (20 points)

The geometric square is the basic unit of measurement used by archaeologists on a dig. Complete each of these square activities:

1. Draw an array to illustrate a square number of your choice.
2. Construct the numbers from 1 to 100 on a sheet of paper with 10 numbers down and 10 numbers across. Circle all of the square numbers.
3. Write down some unique characteristics of a square.
4. Describe some practical applications of squares in our everyday life.

## Discovering Secrets of the Wild West

**PURPOSE**
To examine the life style of the American cowboy during the western movement in American history

**SPECIAL MATERIALS NEEDED**
Resource materials and reference books about cowboys and the western movement

**DIRECTIONS** (140 points)
Complete each of the seven activities described below. The Bonus is optional.

### ACTIVITY 1 (20 points)

VERBAL/LINGUISTIC
Develop a glossary of terms associated with the life and work of the American cowboy on a wagon train, on a cattle drive, or on a gold mining expedition.

### ACTIVITY 2 (20 points)

VISUAL/SPATIAL
Create a mural showing scenes and events depicting the life style of yesterday's American cowboy.

### ACTIVITY 3 (20 points)

LOGICAL/MATHEMATICAL
Read to locate information about the work of a cowboy on a wagon train, on a cattle drive, or on a gold mining expedition. Determine which of these work options was the most important, most dangerous, most productive, and most popular for the times.

### ACTIVITY 4 (20 points)

BODY/KINESTHETIC
Create a humorous WANTED POSTER for a favorite cowboy. Include as much factual information as you can about his life.

## ACTIVITY 5 (20 points)

MUSICAL
Learn a square dance and/or a line dance number and teach it to the rest of the class.

## ACTIVITY 6 (20 points)

INTERPERSONAL
Organize a "cowboy/cowgirl" day for your class. Plan costumes, foods, entertainment, and decorations around this theme.

## ACTIVITY 7 (20 points)

INTRAPERSONAL
Describe qualities that you do or do not possess which would have made you a popular/unpopular cowboy or cowgirl during the days of the Wild West.

## BONUS (20 points)

Prepare a medley of cowboy songs and music. Tape record your musical selections.

# Discovering the Secrets of the Pyramids

**PURPOSE**
To explore the pyramids of ancient Egypt and discover information about them

**SPECIAL MATERIALS NEEDED**
Reference books and resource materials about the pyramids of ancient Egypt with special emphasis on the Giza Pyramids

**DIRECTIONS** (140 points)
Complete each of the following activities as part of your study of ancient Egypt.

## ACTIVITY 1 (20 points)

VERBAL/LINGUISTIC
Pretend you are a travel agent who has prepared a special school-sponsored excursion for middle and high school students to the Giza Pyramids of Egypt. Prepare a descriptive flyer that includes the following information:

1. Diagram of the pyramids
2. Facts about the pyramids
3. Description of chambers within the pyramids
4. History of the pyramids

## ACTIVITY 2 (20 points)

VISUAL/SPATIAL
Prepare a simple picture essay that explains the mummification process associated with the Giza Pyramids.

## ACTIVITY 3 (20 points)

LOGICAL/MATHEMATICAL
Use the following facts about the Giza Pyramids to construct at least three different word problems in math for others to solve. Include an answer key with your problems.

1. The Giza Pyramids are 480 feet tall.
2. The average weight of one of a pyramid's stone blocks is 2 1/2 tons. Some blocks even weighed as much as 15 tons with varied weights somewhere in between.
3. The coffin of King Tut was made out of 2,500 pounds of gold.
4. It was not uncommon for 10,000 men to work on the pyramids for up to 20 years.
5. It takes up to 410 yards of linen to wrap a mummy.

## ACTIVITY 4 (20 points)

BODY/KINESTHETIC
Role play a scene where you are interviewing for a job as a worker to help with the construction of the pyramids.

## ACTIVITY 5 (20 points)

MUSICAL
Create a dance for one of the following hypothetical situations:
1. The Dance of the Mummies
2. The Dance to Honor the Sphinx
3. The Funeral Dance of King Tut

## ACTIVITY 6 (20 points)

INTERPERSONAL
The Giza Pyramids are one of the seven wonders of the ancient world. Work with a group of three other students and together decide on the seven wonders of the modern world. To help you with this task, consider the following questions:
1. What criteria will you use in making your decision?
2. Will you try to get one from each major part of the world such as one per continent or will you ignore geographic location and size of area?
3. What options are you going to consider and how will you narrow down your choices?

Develop a presentation to share your final decision and rationale with the rest of the class.

## ACTIVITY 7 (20 points)

INTRAPERSONAL
Write a short paragraph expressing your feelings about why you would or would not want to be part of this school-sponsored excursion to the Giza Pyramids.

## BONUS (20 points)

Design a modern pyramid for your community. Where would it be located? Who would use it? How would it be used? Why would people want it?

# Discovering Lines of Symmetry

**PURPOSE**
To experiment with the concept of symmetry

**SPECIAL MATERIALS NEEDED**
None

**DIRECTIONS** (120 points)
Symmetry is the exact matching of shapes or figures on opposite sides of dividing lines or around a simple point. The dividing line is called the axis of symmetry. A line of symmetry is a line which divides the figure into two parts which are reflections of each other. Complete each of the symmetrical activities outlined below.

## ACTIVITY 1 (20 points)

**KNOWLEDGE**
Draw three different geometric shapes and fill in the lines of symmetry for each one. A square, for example, has four lines of symmetry because there are four ways that the square can be folded so that one half of the figure falls exactly on the other.

## ACTIVITY 2 (20 points)

**COMPREHENSION**
In your own words, explain why symmetrical figures are not necessarily congruent. You may include a drawing or diagram to help you.

## ACTIVITY 3 (20 points)

**APPLICATION**
Search through several magazines looking for examples of symmetry in the real world. Share your findings in some way.

## ACTIVITY 4 (20 points)

**ANALYSIS**
Search to discover an example of symmetry in any two of the following areas: art, architecture, music, plants, insects, animals, or humans. Draw a diagram to illustrate each example.

## ACTIVITY 5 (20 points)

SYNTHESIS
Symmetry is a mathematical idea often used in art because a design must have a balance or harmony to be visually attractive. Construct an original symmetrical design using colored pencils, crayons, or markers.

## ACTIVITY 6 (20 points)

EVALUATION
Decide whether most people prefer symmetrical or asymmetrical patterns and figures in their lives. Devise an experiment to defend your position.

## BONUS (20 points)

Imagine that you are a judge in a design contest. Create a good and a bad example of two designs that are similar but where one is more pleasing than the other.

## Discovering the Meanings in Mathematics

**PURPOSE**
To look at mathematics as a language complete with its symbols, definitions, applications, and interpretations

**SPECIAL MATERIALS NEEDED**
None

**DIRECTIONS** (140 points)
Complete each of the activities as directed.

---

## ACTIVITY 1 (20 points)

**VERBAL/LINGUISTIC**
In a one page essay, describe in what ways mathematics is really a language.

---

## ACTIVITY 2 (20 points)

**VISUAL/SPATIAL**
Construct a chart of the following math symbols that has three columns: Picture of symbol in first column; definition of symbol in second column; and math sentence showing application of symbol in third column.

$$+ \quad - \quad \chi \quad = \quad \neq \quad > \quad < \quad \varnothing \quad \{\}$$
$$\geq \quad \leq \quad : \quad \infty \quad \angle \quad \llcorner \quad \perp \quad \| \quad \sqrt{}$$

---

## ACTIVITY 3 (20 points)

**LOGICAL/MATHEMATICAL**
Develop a logical explanation for one of the following statements:
1. Calculators should be used extensively in the classroom.
2. Algebra is becoming an obsolete area of mathematics in today's world.
3. Formulas should be provided to students during testing situations.
4. Girls have been discriminated against in math classes.
5. Computers and software will eliminate the need for teaching many math concepts in the classroom.

## ACTIVITY 4 (20 points)

BODY/KINESTHETIC
Create a list of math symbols, phrases, problems, and concepts and use this list to organize a game of "math charades" where individuals act out the math ideas generated.

## ACTIVITY 5 (20 points)

MUSICAL
Create a rap to teach/learn a major set of related math concepts such as the decimal system, basic math functions, measurement, geometry, money, graphs, statistics, or probability concepts.

## ACTIVITY 6 (20 points)

INTERPERSONAL
Organize a panel of business people to share with the class how math is used in their jobs or work roles.

## ACTIVITY 7 (20 points)

INTRAPERSONAL
Create a personal mini-poster that shows a wide range of math skills, problems, and computations that you know how to do at this point in time.

## BONUS (20 points)

Develop a lesson plan for using the out-of-doors to teach a math concept. Use it with a group of your classmates.

## Discovering the Secrets of Plants

PURPOSE
To identify the characteristics of plants and flowers that distinguish them from other living things

SPECIAL MATERIALS NEEDED
Resource materials and reference books about plants and flowers

DIRECTIONS  (140 points)
Complete each of these activities in your study of plants and flowers.

### ACTIVITY 1  (20 points)

In your own words, explain what "makes a plant a plant."

### ACTIVITY 2  (20 points)

Draw a simple diagram of a plant and label, define, and describe the job of each of the following parts: stems, roots, and leaves.

### ACTIVITY 3  (20 points)

Write an informative paragraph explaining the processes of "photosynthesis" and "respiration."

### ACTIVITY 4  (20 points)

Examine a packet of seeds. Note what type of information, instructions, and pictures are shown on the seed package. Use this knowledge to "invent a seed" and create a packet to describe and sell your new seeds that will eventually become a new plant form.

## ACTIVITY 5 (20 points)

Make a hypothesis about how soaking time will affect the time it takes seeds to sprout. Design an experiment to test your hypothesis. Describe the steps for conducting your experiment and plan a data table for recording your observations. Make a chart or graph that shows the results of your investigation.

## ACTIVITY 6 (20 points)

Compose a picture essay to describe ways that human activity threatens different plant species and what the destruction of such plant life will have, in turn, on human beings.

## ACTIVITY 7 (20 points)

Work with a small group of students to create a set of "trading cards" to highlight common plants and flowers. Put a simple drawing of the plant or flower on one side and interesting facts about it on the other side.

## BONUS (20 points)

The sassafras tree has been called "the everything tree" because of its many uses. Find out how the pioneers used it. Design your own everything tree. It should provide for all your needs. What will you fertilize it with and under what special climatic conditions will it survive?

## Discovering the Mysteries of the Sea

PURPOSE
To study the flora, animals, birds, and creatures of the ocean

SPECIAL MATERIALS NEEDED
Resources and reference books on the ocean and the science of oceanography

DIRECTIONS  (160 points)
Complete each of the activities outlined below.

### ACTIVITY 1 (20 points)

FLUENCY
List as many ocean-related words as you can think of in two minutes.

### ACTIVITY 2  (20 points)

FLEXIBILITY
Classify your list of words into the following categories: Ocean terms, ocean creatures, ocean flora, ocean birds, ocean animals, and ocean names. Use reference books to fill in any gaps on your list.

### ACTIVITY 3  (20 points)

ORIGINALITY
Choose five of the ocean words from your list and create a set of five original word problems in math for others to solve. Provide an answer key with your problems.

### ACTIVITY 4 (20 points)

ELABORATION
Divide the words from your Fluency/Flexibility activity among a small group of students. Give each student at least 10 words to research. Each word should be written on one side of a separate file card and students should record the definitions, descriptions, examples, and explanations for each word on the other side, making flash cards for the group. Diagrams or drawings might also be added where appropriate to do so.

## ACTIVITY 5 (20 points)

RISK TAKING
Choose one of the following sea creatures that you most resemble. Write a paragraph describing that resemblance. Consider: *sardine, sea urchin, sea slug, jellyfish, crab, barnacle, mussel, clam, eel,* or *barracuda.*

## ACTIVITY 6 (20 points)

COMPLEXITY
Many of our beaches and oceans are becoming polluted because people are indifferent, careless, ignorant, lazy, and selfish. Write a short position paper explaining why you think this is so and what we can do about it.

## ACTIVITY 7 (20 points)

CURIOSITY
Suppose you could interview a mermaid to discover the many secrets of the ocean. Make a list of questions you would want to ask her.

## ACTIVITY 8 (20 points)

IMAGINATION
Use your imagination and write an ocean fable responding to one of the following topics:

How the Eel Got Its Electricity
How the Sea Urchin Got Its Spines
How the Octopus Got Its Tentacles
How the Angler Fish Got Its Light
How the Angelfish Got Its Name
How the Starfish Got Its Fingers
How the Sponge Got Its Holes
How the Blood Star Got Its Color

## BONUS (20 points)

Design and sketch out an underwater home or city.

# Discovering Creative Brainstorming

PURPOSE
To encourage creative thinking skills, especially brainstorming, in small group sessions

SPECIAL MATERIALS NEEDED
None

DIRECTIONS  (60 points)
Work with a partner and complete any three (as well as Activity 10) of the following creative thinking or brainstorming tasks outlined below.

## ACTIVITY 1 (20 points)

Imagine that your teacher returns to class after a conference with a parent and finds the room an absolute mess and the students out of control. Think of and present 10 explanations for the situation.

## ACTIVITY 2 (20 points)

Imagine that you go outside your house one morning and discover an angry bull in your backyard. Think of 10 things you could do to relieve his temper.

## ACTIVITY 3 (20 points)

Imagine that you have been accused of pulling the fire alarm in your local community library. What are 10 reasons why you couldn't have done it?

## ACTIVITY 4 (20 points)

Imagine that you have been hired to sell a haunted house in the neighborhood. Think of 10 reasons why somebody would want to buy it.

## ACTIVITY 5 (20 points)

Imagine that you have been asked by the retail owners of a large department store during the holiday season to convince suspicious kids that Santa Claus does really exist. Think of 10 arguments you could use with these non-believing children.

## ACTIVITY 6 (20 points)

Imagine that you have been chosen to name a new theme park for Orlando to compete with Disney World. Think of 10 unusual names/themes you could suggest for this purpose.

## ACTIVITY 7 (20 points)

Imagine that you have had to show up at school with two missing front teeth. Think of 10 inventive ways to explain your predicament.

## ACTIVITY 8 (20 points)

Imagine that you have been told to remove the snow off your driveway and sidewalks. Think of 10 innovative ways to do this without using a shovel.

## ACTIVITY 9 (20 points)

Imagine that you have forgotten to do your homework for the second night in a row. Think of 10 irrefutable excuses to give your teacher the next morning.

## ACTIVITY 10 (20 points)

Imagine that you and a friend will be spending one solid month in a cabin in the wilderness with a relative during the summer. There is no electricity or running water and it is miles away from the nearest town. The location is beautiful with both lakes and mountains nearby. Think of 10 wonderful ways you can spend your time there without benefit of television, radio, video games, or CDs.

## BONUS (20 points)

Study a U.S. map and determine a wilderness location that you think would be wonderful for your month-long vacation in the summer. Describe it.

Signaling
Student
Success

# FREEDOM AND INDEPENDENCE

- An Independent Nation

- Awesome Amendments

- Freedom of Expression

- Personal Freedom: "I Believe…"

- Symbols of Freedom

- Stand Up and Be Counted

- Fighting for Social and Political Freedom

- ABCs of Freedom

- The Underground Railroad

- Immigrants

- Born Free

- Creative Freedom

National Middle School Association

**An Introduction to FREE-
DOM and INDEPENDENCE**

**Freedom is defined as being free and not imprisoned, enslaved, or controlled by the will of another. *Independence* is defined as being self-sufficient, self-supporting, self-reliant, self-governing, and free from the influence or control of others.**

Historically, the colonies fought for their freedom and independence from the rule of Great Britain. The slaves wanted freedom from the plantation owners of the South.

The Bill of Rights grants five basic freedoms to all American citizens: religion, speech, press, assembly, and petition. These are the cornerstones of American democracy, government, and independence.

Additionally, some groups have been oppressed for religious, political, racial, or gender reasons by other groups. The Nazis and the Jewish people have battled over basic freedoms. The Native Americans have struggled for freedom within their own country. Women have fought for equal rights. And the list goes on.

Each of you has probably wanted more freedom and independence from your parents or guardians as you have grown up.

In short, freedom and independence are ideals or concepts that Americans value greatly. For many, it is something to fight for, even die for.

## THE GUIDING QUESTIONS:

1. **What is freedom?**

2. **What is independence?**

3. **What freedoms are most important to me?**

4. **Why are freedom and independence the basis for our democratic government and way of life?**

# At a glance — topics and tasks

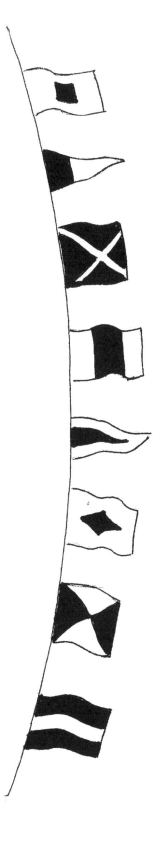

- Define freedom and independence
- Interpret and understand the Declaration of Independence
- Create a timeline of events that led to our country's independence and ultimate freedom
- Understand the Bill of Rights and other amendments to our Constitution
- Express individual feelings and beliefs about freedom in writing
- Share personal beliefs and ideas
- Understand existing symbols of freedom and independence and design new ones
- Understand how votes are counted and the "majority vote" is determined
- Understand the importance of freedom and what people have gone through in order to keep or regain their freedom
- Learn more about holidays and freedom fighters who made significant efforts to obtain freedom or independence
- Simulate the feelings of escaping slavery
- Appreciate the millions of people who came to a new land in search of opportunity and freedom
- Think about animals in captivity who have lost their freedom
- Create a new recipe, song, or game using one's right or freedom to be creative

138

## Freedom and Independence Rubric

Name _____ Class _____

You may choose to complete activities from all of the stations to earn points or you may choose to complete more work from only some of the stations to earn points. Your activities should be done completely, accurately, and neatly to earn full credit. The grading scale is as follows:

| A 850 + pts. | B 750-849 pts. | C 650-749 pts. | D 550-649 pts. |
|---|---|---|---|

| Date Completed | Activity | Possible Points | Points Earned |
|---|---|---|---|
| _____ | An Independent Nation | 190-215 | _____ |
| _____ | Awesome Amendments | 75-100 | _____ |
| _____ | Freedom of Expression | 100-150 | _____ |
| _____ | Personal Freedom: " I Believe . . ." | 45 | _____ |
| _____ | Symbols of Freedom | 50-100 | _____ |
| _____ | Stand Up and Be Counted | 50 | _____ |
| _____ | Freedoms to Fight For: Social and Political Freedom | 60 | _____ |
| _____ | ABCs of Freedom | 100-110 | _____ |
| _____ | The Underground Railroad | 60 | _____ |
| _____ | Immigrants | 100-150 | _____ |
| _____ | Born Free | 40-70 | _____ |
| _____ | Creative Freedom | 30 | _____ |
| | | **TOTAL POINTS** | _____ |
| | | **GRADE** | _____ |

## An Independent Nation

**PURPOSE**
To interpret and understand the Declaration of Independence; to create a timeline of events that led to our country's independence and ultimate freedom

**SPECIAL MATERIALS NEEDED**
Copies of the Declaration of Independence; construction, chart, or butcher paper; markers

**DIRECTIONS** (190 points)
Complete the activities at this station. The Bonus section is optional.

---

## ACTIVITY 1 (110 points)

It is important that all Americans understand and be familiar with the statement of philosophy found in the Declaration. This forms the basis of our Constitution and democratic government. Read through the Declaration and answer the following questions about it:

1. What are the four self-evident truths found in the Declaration?
2. What are the three inalienable rights found in the Declaration?
3. What is meant by "it is their right - it is their duty - to throw off the government"? When should this occur?
4. What do the colonists state they have done to defend against the king's "oppressions"?
5. What five powers are claimed by the "free and independent states"?
6. Who is the ultimate power that is asked to give protection?
7. Why could the Declaration be considered a propaganda or campaign piece as well as a statement of philosophy?
8. Define the following terms found in the Declaration of Independence in your own words:
   a. inalienable
   b. usurpations
   c. magnanimity
   d. conjured
   e. consanguinity
   f. oppressions
9. What part of this document is the most important to you? Why?

## ACTIVITY 2 (80 points)

On the butcher or chart paper provided at this station, create a timeline of events that led to the independence of the colonies and ultimately the United States. Find an event, cause, or action for each of the following dates. There may be more than one listing for each year.

1763, 1764, 1765, 1766, 1767, 1769, 1770, 1772, 1773, 1774, 1775, 1776, 1777, 1778, 1781, 1783

## BONUS (25 points)

Create a Declaration of Independence for Teenagers. Include the issues that would be important in a statement of philosophy about growing up and gaining personal independence.

# Awesome Amendments

**PURPOSE**
To understand the Bill of Rights and other amendments to our Constitution

**SPECIAL MATERIALS NEEDED**
Amendment worksheet; copies of the amendments to the Constitution; markers; chart paper

**DIRECTIONS** (75 points)
Complete Activity One and one other activity.

## ACTIVITY 1 (50 points)

There are 26 amendments to the United States Constitution. They guarantee certain freedoms for all Americans. The first ten are known as the Bill of Rights. Identify which amendment number matches with each right or freedom listed below.

_____ 1. Gave women the right to vote

_____ 2. Protects the rights of people in criminal cases; the accused must be told the charges against him and be allowed to obtain a lawyer

_____ 3. Limits the President to serving two terms

_____ 4. Right to vote cannot be denied because of race

_____ 5. Protects the rights of people in criminal cases – right to a fair trial

_____ 6. Defines citizenship

_____ 7. Provides that U.S. senators must be elected by the people

_____ 8. Powers not given to the federal government belong to the states

_____ 9. Choices for President and Vice-President must be designated

_____ 10. Abolished slavery

_____ 11. States that soldiers can be housed in private homes only with the owner's permission

_____ 12. Gives citizens in Washington, D.C. the right to vote for President and Vice-President

_____ 13. Although all rights are not listed specifically in the Constitution, people still retain these rights

_____ 14. Presidential and Vice-Presidential terms begin on January 20 while congressional terms begin on January 3

_____ 15. Repealed the eighteenth amendment

_____ 16. Found in the Bill of Rights, it guarantees the right to trial by jury in civil cases

_____ 17. Gives state militias the right to bear arms

_____ 18. Gives Congress the right to impose individual federal income tax

_____ 19. Unreasonable searches and seizures are prohibited

_____ 20. Outlines the procedure for presidential succession in case of presidential disability

_____ 21. Protects freedom of religion, speech, press, and assembly

_____ 22. Prohibits the manufacture and sale of alcohol

_____ 23. Payment of tax is not required in order to vote

_____ 24. Lowered the voting age to 18

_____ 25. Prohibits courts from setting unreasonably high bail and forbids cruel and unusual punishment

_____ 26. Prohibits federal courts from hearing cases lodged against a state by a citizen of another state

## ACTIVITY 2 (25 points)

Construct a chart that illustrates the dates the amendments were added and that gives a brief explanation of each amendment.

## ACTIVITY 3 (25 points)

Write a new amendment that you would like to see added to the Constitution. Present your amendment to the class. When all new amendments have been written and presented, take a class vote. Issues that the class decides are of great importance could be directed to congressional representatives in the form of a letter.

# Freedom of Expression

PURPOSE
To express individual feelings and beliefs about freedom in writing

SPECIAL MATERIALS NEEDED
Samples of editorials from the newspaper; list of censored books

DIRECTIONS  (100 points)
Complete the activities at this station. The Bonus is optional.

## ACTIVITY 1 (50 points)

An editorial in a newspaper expresses one's feelings and beliefs about an issue. Freedom of speech and expression allows us to write our views in newspapers. Choose one of the following issues and write a one-page essay or editorial, taking a stand on what you believe about it.

| | |
|---|---|
| Death penalty | The homeless |
| Teen curfews | AIDS research |
| Legalized drugs | The military draft |
| Teen birth control | Gun control |
| School dress codes | Abortion |
| Prayer in public schools | Women's rights |
| Violence on TV/movies | Censorship of books |
| Illegal immigrants/laws | Salary caps in sports |
| Free agencies in sports | Driving/drinking age |

## ACTIVITY 2 (50 points)

Find a book that has been censored – banned – from a library for some reason. Some famous ones include . . .

*The Adventures of Huckleberry Finn,* Mark Twain
*Brave New World,* Aldous Huxley
*Catch-22,* Joseph Heller
*Chocolate War*, Robert Cormier
*Farewell to Arms*, Ernest Hemingway
*Lord of the Flies,* William Golding
*1984,* George Orwell
*The Outsiders,* S. E. Hinton
*The Pigman,* Paul Zindel
*The Slave Dancer,* Paula Fox
*Then Again, Maybe I Won't,* Judy Blume

Read it yourself. In one page, write your reaction to the book, answering the following guiding questions:

1. How did it make you feel?
2. Did it make you think about an issue in a different way?
3. Should this book have been censored? Why or why not?

**BONUS (25 points)**

Get your editorial from Activity One published in your school or local newspaper.

**BONUS (25 points)**

Read the following article on censorship from the newspaper. Summarize it and write 10 important facts you learned about censorship from reading the article.

"Florida Schools Rank High in Censorship," by Mary Shedden
*The Gainesville Sun,* Thursday, August 31, 1995

Two local controversies over middle school paperbacks helped keep Florida ranked among the top 10 in a national report on education censorship.

Both Westwood and Fort Clarke middle schools last year fielded challenges to material that parents considered inappropriate for their children. The incidents are among the 458 cited Wednesday by the People for the American Way, a nonpartisan civil-liberties organization based in Washington, D.C.

Both of the Gainesville principals who handled the complaints said the censorship label was inappropriate.

"We don't really ban books in this district," said Mike Joyner, the former Westwood principal and acting director of secondary education for the school district.

The 13th annual report said that while fewer attempts were made to ban books than in previous years, those complaining about offensive material were more successful during the 1994-95 school year. And broad-based attacks on school policy and programs have increased.

"The real story has been the increase in the complexity of the issue," said Deanna Duby, director of education policy for the group. "They aren't going after only books, they're going after curriculum like sex education and evolution."

Florida ranked 10th in the nation with 16 incidents, down from a year earlier when it ranked third with 22 cases. Three years ago, Florida led the nation with 34 complaints, said

Susan Glickman, Florida director for People for the American Way. While book-banning challenges permeate the report, other broad-based challenges included attempts to abolish Halloween celebrations, end counseling services for gay teen-agers and lobby efforts against education reform laws.

Other incidents cited in the report include:

• A California parent objected to Sesame Street being shown to kindergartners because Ernie and Bert lived together, suggesting homosexuality.

• Pennsylvania school board members objected to a book referring to homeless people. "My problem with the book is that I didn't think it was a fair depiction of the vast majority of the United States," an objector stated.

In Alachua County, the parent of a Westwood sixth-grader challenged three books in sixth-grade reading classes because of violence or sex that was lurid, if not explicit.

*Fall into Darkness* and *Final Friends, Book 3: The Graduation*, both by Christopher Pike and *Broken Hearts* by R. L. Stine all were reviewed by a school committee that included parents, teachers, and Joyner.

*Final Friends* was removed altogether from Westwood, and the other two were moved to an eighth-grade reading room because they were appropriate for "more mature" students.

At Fort Clarke, a teacher who also was the parent of a sixth-grader requested that Judy Blume's popular teen romance novel *Forever* be removed from an eighth-grade reading room because the book implies it is acceptable for teens to have sex and smoke marijuana.

A school review committee agreed *Forever* should be removed from the reading shelves, but former principal Chet Sanders – now at Mebane Middle School – said the decision would not have prevented a student from reading the book for a class assignment if the child and parent wanted to.

"This whole idea of us being ultra-conservative and censoring what the students could read is really inaccurate," Sanders said.

Jim Moffett, district director of instructional technology, said once a person files a complaint, appropriate material is determined by a review committee that represents the school "community."

"What may be right for Mebane Middle School may not be right for Howard Bishop Middle School or vice versa," Moffett said. Among the books challenged nationally, often because they contain profanity, violence, or sexual scenes, were such classics as Nobel Prize winner John Steinbeck's *Of Mice and Men* and Maya Angelou's *I Know Why the Caged Bird Sings*.

The most frequent complaints against a book was that its treatment of sexuality was offensive. Profanity was the next most frequent complaint.

People For the American Way said it documented 338 attempts to remove or restrict access to a book and said 50 percent, or 169, were successful. The year before, 375 attempts were documented and 46 percent, or 157, were successful.

But conservatives accused the group of exaggerating the number of incidents and of attacking parents' legitimate concerns.

"When a government restricts what its citizens can read, that's censorship," said Gary L. Bauer of the Family Research Council in Washington. "But when parents have input on what local officials do in the schools, that's democracy."

The report listed only instances when a parent or community member tried to keep a book not just from one child, but from all children, said group education director Duby.

"If a parent has a concern about what their child is learning, they have every right to go to the school board . . . and look for an alternative," Duby said.

"If they go to the next step, saying this disagrees with my politics or religion and they want to remove it from all children, then that is censorship. That tramples on the rights of other parents."

# Personal Freedom: "I Believe..."

PURPOSE
To share personal beliefs and ideas

SPECIAL MATERIALS NEEDED
Chart paper; markers

DIRECTIONS  (45 points)
Complete the activities at this station.

## ACTIVITY 1  (20 points)

Personal freedom allows you to think and feel the way you choose. Share some of your personal beliefs and ideas by completing the following starter statements:

1. I am . . .
2. I most admire . . .
3. When I am 30, I expect to . . .
4. I am proud of myself when . . .
5. My favorite qualities are . . .
6. One thing special about me is . . .
7. One thing I really believe is . . .
8. A good teacher is . . .
9. Something that is unfair is . . .
10. My favorite place to travel . . .
11. I am happiest when . . .
12. The most important thing to consider in choosing a career is . . .
13. The freedom I value most is . . .
14. When I make a mistake, I . . .
15. People my age need . . .
16. My family is . . .
17. All people should . . .
18. My wish for the world . . .
19. Conflict is . . .
20. The future depends on . . .

## ACTIVITY 2  (25 points)

Make a chart showing the freedoms you think you're old enough to experience and have, as opposed to the freedoms your parents or guardians think you're old enough to experience or have.

148

## Symbols of Freedom

PURPOSE
To understand existing symbols of freedom and independence and to design new ones

SPECIAL MATERIALS NEEDED
Drawing paper; scissors; markers; magazines; glue; copies of "The Star-Spangled Banner." For the Bonus activity, students will need gardening tools; seeds; and a small plot of ground.

DIRECTIONS (50 points)
Choose one of the activities at this center and display your work. The Bonus is optional.

### ACTIVITY 1 (50 points)

Create a banner, mosaic, or collage (from magazines), using any symbols of freedom: flag, eagle, lit candle, sunburst, star, Statue of Liberty, closed fist, etc. Can you add others?

### ACTIVITY 2 (50 points)

Design a flag that shows respect for the things you believe. Symbolize your beliefs through color, graphics or icons, and design. Draw your flag and write a brief explanation of its meaning.

### ACTIVITY 3 (50 points)

Read the words to "The Star-Spangled Banner," our national anthem. This poem was written in the War of 1812 by Francis Scott Key. Think about the meaning of the words. Rewrite the song in your own words, sharing your interpretation of its meaning.

## ACTIVITY 4 (50 points)

Design a statue or a monument in honor of a historical event that symbolizes freedom or independence for a group of people. Example: a monument for the military who fought in the Gulf War. Draw it or create a model of it. With a group of students, try to become the monument and share it with the class.

## BONUS (50 points)

*Victory Garden*

During World War II, patriotic Americans wanted to do something to help in the war effort. Shortages of food at home and overseas were common. In an attempt to help solve this problem, many Americans grew "Victory Gardens." People grew vegetables whereever they could find a space to help supplement food shortages.

The Victory Garden is a symbol of a citizen's support of their cause. Choose an issue that you and the national government support. Select a small plot of ground at school or at home. Investigate which vegetables grow best in your area for the particular time of year it is. Post a sign in your garden stating the issue or cause you are supporting. Also, display the national flag.

Water and weed your garden often. You may want to research basic gardening tips before you begin. When your vegetables have grown, dig them up, cook and/or eat them and have a Victory party or celebration. Capture your garden in photographs and make a photographic essay illustrating your work and effort. Share this at your party.

## Stand Up and Be Counted

PURPOSE
To understand how votes are counted and to compute percentages to determine the "majority vote"

SPECIAL MATERIALS NEEDED
None

DIRECTIONS  (50 points)
The right to vote is a treasured process in the United States. In a democratic society, the majority vote wins. A majority is achieved when more than one half of the votes are cast for a particular party or candidate.. In order to determine the majority, percentages are used. Use percentages and their equivalents to solve the following problems. You may want to review percentages in your math book.

## ACTIVITY

1.  In the last election for city council mayor, 50% of the registered voters in Hastings cast their ballots. There are 10,000 voters in Hastings. How many people voted?

2.  Mayor Jim LaMorte won the election in Hastings. He won 80% of the votes. How many people voted for him?

3.  Two-thirds of Hastings' registered voters are age 55 or older. How many voters does Hastings have who are 55 or older?

4.  The residents of Cedar Key voted to elect a temporary sheriff. 60,000 people voted. Those who voted made up 90% of the registered voters. How many registered voters are there in Cedar Key?

5.  How many registered voters in Cedar Key didn't vote?

6.  In Yankeetown, 850 people voted for School Superintendent. The number of registered voters is 1,575. What percentage of registered voters voted?

7.  How many people would need to vote in Yankeetown in order to have 80% of the registered voters actually to cast ballots?

8.  Michael Jones was elected the new Superintendent of Schools in Yankeetown. He had 736 votes cast for him. What percentage of voters voted for him? (Round off your answer.)

Using information from your community, create two math problems using percentages related to voting. Solve your problem – give it to a friend to work on!

9.

10.

## Fighting for Social and Political Freedom

PURPOSE
To understand the importance of freedom and what people have gone through in order to keep or regain their freedom

SPECIAL MATERIALS NEEDED
Copies of books from this bibliography or others that are similar in their theme; dodecahedron patterns; tagboard or card stock paper; markers; stapler; and Book Report forms

DIRECTIONS  (60 points)
Complete one activity at this station.

Many books have been written that focus on political or social freedom as the theme. Select one of the following books to read.

Avi. *Nothing but the Truth.* New York: Avon Books, 1991.

Carter, Forrest. *The Education of Little Tree.* Albuquerque: University of New Mexico Press, 1976.

Drucker, Malka, and Halperin, Michael. *Jacob's Rescue: A Holocaust Story.* New York: Yearling Book, 1993.

Fox, Paula. *The Slave Dancer.* New York: Dell Yearling, 1973.

Frank, Anne. *Anne Frank: The Diary of a Young Girl.* New York: Doubleday, 1967.

Lowry, Lois. *Number the Stars.* New York: Dell Yearling, 1989.

Matas, Carol. *Daniel's Story.* New York: Scholastic, 1993.

Pettit, Jayne. *A Place to Hide: True Stories of the Holocaust.* New York: Scholastic, 1993.

Uchida, Yoshiko. *Journey to Topaz.* Creative Arts Book Co., 1971.

Van der Rol, Rund, and Verhoeven, Rian. *Anne Frank: Beyond the Diary.* New York: Viking, 1993.

## ACTIVITY 1  (60 points)

Using the dodecahedron pattern, trace and cut out 12 panels or sides to your geometric figure. On each panel or side, illustrate and describe a character from the book you have read. Include the following information in your description: physical appearance, events of the plot, and the freedom issues relevant to the story.

Staple the sides of the figure — using the display model as a guide. Hang up your dodecahedron in the classroom.

## ACTIVITY 2 (60 points)

Complete the following Historical Book Report Form:

## Historical Book Report

Title: _____ Author: _____

**Knowledge:** What historical event or character is the focus or subject of this novel?

**Comprehension:** Describe the time and setting in which your novel takes place.

**Application:** Using the information from the book, write five newspaper headings that may have appeared in a newspaper during that period in history.

**Analysis:** Compare and contrast the historical events of this story with those that are happening around the world today.

**Synthesis:** Rewrite part of the story that would alter or change the course of history. Would it have made things better or worse?

**Evaluation:** Tell what human values or ideas are expressed in this story and how they relate to your life. Do you agree with them? Why or why not?

## ABCs of Freedom

PURPOSE
To learn more about holidays and/or freedom fighters (people who have made significant efforts to obtain freedom or independence in some way)

SPECIAL MATERIALS NEEDED
Samples of ABC books; magazines; scissors; glue. Resource books on holidays and historical freedom fighters will need to be provided or access to the media center for research time.

DIRECTIONS  (100 points)
Develop and write an ABC report. Select an entry for each letter of the alphabet. Your report should be either The ABCs of Holidays or The ABCs of Freedom Fighters. Select your entries from the lists provided. You may use any learning station materials or other resources from the media center. Illustrate each entry in some way (magazine pictures or drawings).

## ACTIVITY

### ABCS OF HOLIDAYS

Holidays are special occasions that people all over the world celebrate. However, there are many holidays that are not shared by everyone. The freedom to learn about these holidays and to choose which ones we celebrate is an individual's right.

As you develop your ABC report, be sure to include the following information about each entry:
1. Purpose of the holiday
2. Customs or traditions associated with the holiday

A       Admissions Day, Advent, All Saints' Day, Anzac Day, April Fool's Day, Arbor Day, Ash Wednesday, Ascension Day, Armistice Day, Australia Day, Abolition Day, Alaska Day, American Family Day

B       Bastille Day, Battle of New Orleans Day, Bird Day, Bennington Battle Day, Bunker Hill Day, Boxing Day, Bonfire Night, Buddha's Birthday

C       Canada Day, Candlemas Day, Ch'usok, Children's Day, Chinese New Year, Christmas, Cinco de Mayo, Columbus Day, Confederate Memorial Day, Cherokee Strip Day, Constitution Day

| | |
|---|---|
| D | Day of the Dead, Defenders' Day, Delaware Day, Discovery Day, Dolls' Festival, Divali |
| E | Easter, Epiphany, Election Day, Evacuation, Emancipation Day |
| F | Father's Day, Feast of Hungry Ghosts, Feast of St. Nicholas, Flag Day, Friendship Day, F. D. Roosevelt's Birthday, Fast Day |
| G | Good Friday, Ground Hog Day, Guy Fawkes Day, Guadalupe Day, Grand-parents' Day |
| H | Halloween, Hanukkah, Hogmanay, Huey P. Long Day |
| I | Independence Day, Indian Day |
| J | Jean Baptiste Day, Jefferson Davis's Birthday |
| K | King Kamehameha Day, Kwanzaa |
| L | Labor Day, Lent, Leif Ericson Day, Lincoln's Birthday, Lee-Jackson-King Day, Lyndon B. Johnson's Birthday |
| M | Mardi Gras, Martin Luther King's Birthday, May Day, Maundy Thursday, Mother's Day, Moomba Festival, Midsummer Day, Muhammad's Birth-day, Memorial Day, Maryland Day, Minnesota Day, Mecklenburg Independence Day |
| N | Navajo National Fair, National Day, New Year's Eve, New Year's Day, Nevada Day |
| O | Oklahoma Day, Oktoberfest, Olympic Games |
| P | Pancake Day, Passover, Patriot's Day, President's Day, Pioneer Day, Pascua Florida Day, Pentecost, Palm Sunday, Purim, Pulaski Day |
| Q | Quebec National Day, Quinceaños |
| R | Rosh Hashana, Ramadan, Robert E. Lee's Birthday, Remembrance Day, Republic Day, Rondy, Rizal Day |
| S | Shavuot, Separation Day, Senior Citizens Day, San Jacinto Day, Seward's Day, Susan B. Anthony Day, Sukkoth, Simhat Torah, St. Patrick's Day, Shrove Tuesday, St. Valentine's Day, St. Lucia Day, Simon Bolivar's Birthday, Shichi-Go-San |

| | |
|---|---|
| T | Thanksgiving, Texas Independence Day, Three Kings' Day, Town Meeting Day, Thomas Jefferson's Birthday, Truman Day, Tanabata Matsuri |
| U | United Nations Day |
| V | Veterans Day, Victory Day, Victoria Day |
| W | Washington's Birthday, Waitangi Day, Will Rogers Day, West Virginia Day |
| Y | Yom Kippur, Youth Day |

## BONUS (10 points)

Invent a new holiday of freedom for your community or country. Describe:
1. Date
2. Purpose
3. Customs and traditions

## ACTIVITY

## ABCS OF FREEDOM FIGHTERS

Freedom fighters are people who historically have worked very hard to insure freedom of some kind for all of us. In some cases they fought for it and in other cases they even died for it. Choose from the list below (or find your own) and write a brief biographical sketch about the contributions of any ten individuals.

| | |
|---|---|
| A | Abraham Lincoln, Alexander Hamilton |
| B | Benjamin Franklin, Betsy Ross, Booker T. Washington |
| C | Crispus Attucks, Christopher Gadsden, Cesar Chavez |
| D | Dred Scott, Denmark Vesey |
| E | Edmund Randolph, Esteban Dorantes, Eleanor Roosevelt, Elizabeth C. Stanton |
| F | Frederick Douglass, Franklin Roosevelt |
| G | George Washington |
| H | Horace Mann, Harriett Beecher Stowe, Harriett Tubman |
| I | Ida Wells |

| J | James Madison, John Hancock, John Adams, John F. Kennedy, John Quincy Adams, Joseph Galloway, John Brown, James Pierce Beckwith, Joseph Cinque, Jesse Jackson |
| K | |
| L | Lucretia Mott |
| M | Martin Luther King, Jr., "Minutemen," Mae Jemison, Mary McLeod Bethune, Malcolm X |
| N | |
| O | |
| P | Patrick Henry, Paul Revere, Peter Zenger, "Patriots" |
| Q | |
| R | Richard Henry Lee, Robert E. Lee, Robert Kennedy, Rosa Parks |
| S | "Sons of Liberty," Samuel Adams, Sojourner Truth, Sequoya, Susan B. Anthony |
| T | Thomas Jefferson, Thomas Paine |
| U | |
| V | |
| W | William Davies, William DuBois, Whitney Young, Jr. |
| X | |
| Y | |
| Z | |

---

**Two software programs related to this learning station are:**

**Freedom** by MECC for Apple computers. Grade Level is 4-8.

**The American People: Fabric of a Nation,** by *National Geographic* on laserdisc. Grade Level is 4-8.

# The Underground Railroad

PURPOSE
To simulate the feelings of escaping slavery and becoming free

SPECIAL MATERIALS NEEDED
Readings and information about the Underground Railroad

DIRECTIONS  (60 points)
Read background information about the Underground Railroad for slaves in the United States during the Civil War. Harriet Tubman is well known for her efforts to help slaves escape from the shackles of the South for freedom in the North. It was not an actual railroad but rather a route of houses, shelters, and people who were sympathetic to the slaves and who would help them move from one location to the next. With a small group of students, develop a skit, role play, or simulation that depicts or tells the story of the Underground Railroad. Some of you will need to be the slaves who were seeking freedom; others of you will be the "conductors" or those who helped the slaves in their travels. Still others of you will need to be the slave owners or law enforcers. When your skit or simulation is developed, present it to the class. Share your thoughts about this important piece of history through your presentation.

158

## Immigrants

PURPOSE
To appreciate the millions of people who came to a new land in search of opportunity and freedom

SPECIAL MATERIALS NEEDED
Chart paper; markers; drawing paper

DIRECTIONS  (100 points)
Complete the activities at this station.

The Statue of Liberty has always been a symbol of the millions of immigrants who have come to America in search of a better life. Our country is truly a "melting pot" for different nationalities of people.

### ACTIVITY 1 (50 points)

From the book *Immigrants* by Martin Sandler, or any other book on the topic, look at the pictures depicting the faces, conditions, homes, workplaces, etc. of the immigrants. Create a visual timeline by drawing pictures that might show an immigrant leaving his or her country, making the journey, and living in America after his/her arrival.

### ACTIVITY 2 (50 points)

Create a pie graph or bar graph showing immigration into the United States, by country, during the years 1820-1925.

### BONUS (50 points)

Using the Almanac, create a graph showing immigration into the United States, by country, during the years of your life. Use your birthdate to represent the time period, e.g., 1981-1996.

## Born Free

### PURPOSE
To think about animals in captivity who have lost their freedom

### SPECIAL MATERIALS NEEDED
Animal videos; VCR recorder and projector

### DIRECTIONS (40 points)
Complete the following activity. The bonus is optional.

## ACTIVITY

Freedom is also experienced by animals who live in their natural habitats or surroundings. Several popular films tell the story of animals who have had their freedom removed or restricted by humans in some way. View one of these videos: *Free Willy, Born Free, Andre*, or another similar film. Write a short summary of the movie and a reaction paragraph, stating your beliefs about animals in captivity.

## BONUS (30 points)

*A Trip to the Zoo*

Visit a zoo in your community or think about a zoo you have visited before. What are the good things about zoos for the animals, for people? What are the negatives about zoos for animals and for people? Construct a chart showing your ideas.

## Creative Freedom

**PURPOSE**
To create a new recipe, song, or game using one's right or freedom to be creative

**SPECIAL MATERIALS NEEDED**
None

**DIRECTIONS** (30 points)
Creativity is defined as the freedom to make something original or to be expressive. Complete one of the following activities to show how creative you can be.

## ACTIVITY 1 (30 points)

*Create a Recipe*
Choose any ingredients you wish and create a new dish. You can make a dessert, main dish, a vegetable casserole, a salad, an appetizer, or a bread. Make it different from something you've tried before. You should bring samples of your new "food" to share with the class together with the recipe. Record comments from your family and friends about your new creation after they try it.

## ACTIVITY 2 (30 points)

*Create a Song*
Choose a song or tune that you are familiar with and rewrite the words to express some of your ideas about freedom. Patriotic songs and/or spirituals may work well. Once your new song is created, you should sing or play it to the class. You may involve a few others in order to have "a chorus."

## ACTIVITY 3

*Create a Game*
You have been hired by the Olympic committee to create a new game. Given these guidelines, what would your game be like?
1. Use a soccer ball
2. Play on a football field or outdoor court
3. Include six person teams

Describe your game briefly and draw a picture of what your game would look like. Be sure to include how points would be scored.

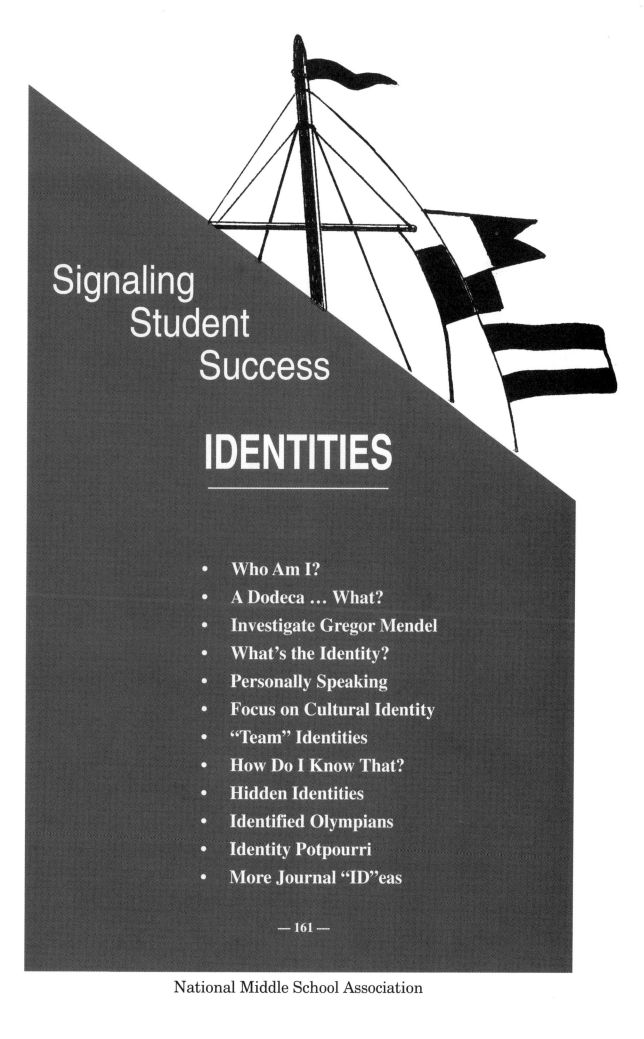

# Signaling Student Success

## IDENTITIES

- Who Am I?
- A Dodeca ... What?
- Investigate Gregor Mendel
- What's the Identity?
- Personally Speaking
- Focus on Cultural Identity
- "Team" Identities
- How Do I Know That?
- Hidden Identities
- Identified Olympians
- Identity Potpourri
- More Journal "ID"eas

National Middle School Association

**An Introduction to IDENTITIES**

**Who are you? What makes you distinguishable from others? Why are you considered an individual? What are your favorite foods, music, books, hobbies . . . ? What other kinds of *identities* might you explore? How do you make identifications?**

The formal definition of *identity* is the condition or fact of being a specific person or thing; individuality. As you work through the learning stations, you will focus on your own identity and personal relationships as well as the identity and relationships of figures from history, fictional characters, famous Olympians, current teams, and even chemical elements, to name just a few. Please be honest and thorough with your responses and research.

You will be required to keep a daily journal in which you reflect on your activities (complete or not) and your reactions to them. The journal suggestions will be included at each station. Your teacher will determine what the actual journal will look like and whether or not it will be included in your final grade. There is even a special journal learning station especially for those of you who enjoy writing about yourselves.

## THE GUIDING QUESTIONS

1. How does my identity influence my world, and how does my world influence my identity?

2. What are some ways to discover and/or protect identities?

3. In what ways does being part of a group affect my identity?

163

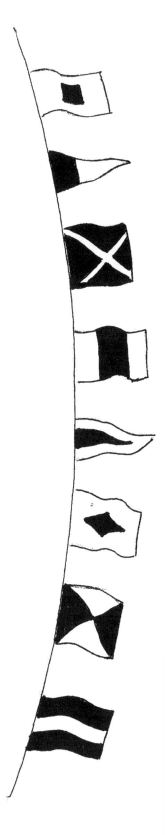

# At a glance — topics and tasks

- Introduce key identity vocabulary
- Discover individual identities through fingerprinting.
- Complete two profiles
- Share information
- Consider how you learn best
- Construct a dodecahedron which will feature something about you on each face
- Investigate a famous scientist and relate his/her findings to the theme of identities
- Identify chemical elements of the Periodic Table
- Explore personal and family history
- Consider differences and similarities in cultures through reading children's literature
- Discover the identities of athletic and school teams
- Identify character traits
- Investigate masks and their uses
- Examine famous Olympians and their Olympic games
- Explore several types of identities
- Respond in writing in a daily journal

164

## Opening (full class) Activities

PURPOSES
To introduce key module vocabulary and to discover individual identities through fingerprinting

SPECIAL MATERIALS NEEDED
Dictionary; white construction paper; three or four black ink stamp pads; colored pencils and markers

DIRECTIONS
Complete both activities and discuss your results. Note that these full class activities are not learning stations. Your teacher may assign points if needed.

## ACTIVITY 1

As new units of study are begun, there are always key vocabulary terms which must be introduced because they are the basis of the content or focus. Define these words that are important to our study of identities and give some kind of example or way to use each one.

| | |
|---|---|
| accomplishment | goal |
| autobiography | origin |
| biography | personal |
| challenge (n.) | preference |
| culture | relationship |
| encourage | success |
| experience (n.) | trait |
| characteristics | unique |
| (physical) | personality |

## ACTIVITY 2

Fingerprints are the impressions made by the ridges on the bulbs, or end joints, of the fingers and thumbs. Fingerprint patterns are formed by these ridges. Fingerprinting is a method of personal identification.

Fingerprints fall into three main groups: the arch, the loop, and the whorl. The arch pattern shows ridges which arch across the bulb of the finger (think of a rainbow). The loop pattern shows one or more curved ridges that form a loop on the bulb of the finger. The whorl pattern is a spiral or circular formation on the finger. Which kind of fingerprint do you have?

a. Trace your right or left hand onto a piece of white construction paper.

b. Use the ink pad to "fingerprint" each finger and thumb onto your traced hand.

c. Put your name above or below your hand in large letters with a marker.

d. Decorate this if you wish and add your fingerprint poster to the bulletin board or wall collage in your classroom.

e. Class discussion should center on your fingerprints and the conclusions you can draw from what you see. Which kind of fingerprint do you have?

f. Discover how many of each kind (arch, loop, whorl) are represented in your class or on your team.

---

## BONUS

What is DNA? Why is it used today? Compare and contrast DNA to ink pad fingerprinting. Are you aware of any court trial in which DNA has played an important part? Did the DNA evidence play a role in the outcome? If so, what case is it? What else do you know about DNA?

---

SUGGESTED JOURNAL STARTER STATEMENTS

I did/did not enjoy the fingerprint activity because . . .

_____ is a new word I learned today. It means . . .

My fingerprints most closely match . . . The difference is . . .

Our classroom collage is . . .

**Include any other kinds of appropriate responses you wish to make.**

Also, feel free to illustrate your journal entry.

# Identities Rubric

Name _____  Class _____

Here is a list of the learning stations from which you may choose to work to earn your points. The two which are starred (*) are required. All activities must be done completely, accurately, and neatly to earn full point value. The grading scale is as follows:

| A | B | C | D |
|---|---|---|---|
| 880-940 pts. | 799-879 pts. | 705-798 pts. | 611-704 pts. |

| Date Completed | Activity | Possible Points | Points Earned |
|---|---|---|---|
| _____ | *Who Am I? | 65-85 | _____ |
| _____ | A Dodeca . . . What? | 100 | _____ |
| _____ | Investigate Gregor Mendel | 90-100 | _____ |
| _____ | What's The Identity? | 30-40 | _____ |
| _____ | Personally Speaking | 100-200 | _____ |
| _____ | *Focus On Cultural Diversity | 75 | _____ |
| _____ | "Team" Identities | 40-80 | _____ |
| _____ | How Do I Know That? | 100-120 | _____ |
| _____ | Hidden Identities | 100 | _____ |
| _____ | Identified Olympians | 55 | _____ |
| _____ | Identity Potpourri | 65-170 | _____ |
| _____ | More Journal "ID"eas | 100 | _____ |

**TOTAL POINTS** _____

**GRADE** _____

## Who Am I?

PURPOSE
To complete two profiles; to share information; to consider how you learn best

SPECIAL MATERIALS NEEDED
personal profile sheet
informal inventory activity sheet
construction paper
colored pencils and markers

DIRECTIONS  (65 points)
There are four identity activities suggested for this learning station. There are two bonus activities. Be sure to read all introductory information carefully.

## ACTIVITY 1  (10 points)

Use the colored pencils or markers and construction paper at this station to create your own personal name tag – one that you would be comfortable wearing during class time. This is a sample:

## ACTIVITY 2  (20 points)

**PERSONAL PROFILE**

Directions: Read and complete this personal profile as completely as possible.

| First Name | Middle Name | Last Name |
|---|---|---|

Nickname _____ Age _____ Birthdate _____

Month  Day  Year

Parent/Guardian Names

_____

Name(s) of brother(s)

_____

Name(s) of sister(s)

_____

Names and kinds of pets

_____

_____

Current grade _____ School Name _____

Favorite subject(s) _____

Other "favorites":

      hobby _____

      book(s) _____

      music _____

      TV show _____

      actor/actress _____

      food(s) _____

      other? _____

Extracurricular activities _____

**(PERSONAL PROFILE  continued)**

What 8-10 words best describe your personality and physical characteristics?

_____        _____

_____        _____

_____        _____

_____        _____

Place a check mark ($\sqrt{}$ ) next to the two descriptors above that you are proudest of. Place a minus sign ( - ) next to the one trait that you would most like to change or improve.

Finish these sentence starters honestly and completely. Be sure to tell why.

I always enjoy _____

  because _____

I truly dislike _____

  because _____

I sometimes do _____

  because _____

I will never say _____

  because _____

I appreciate _____

  because _____

## ACTIVITY 3  (20 points)

### MY LEARNING PROFILE

**Directions:** Because you spend so much time in school, you probably know how you learn best in classroom settings. Please read carefully the following lists and circle the items which are most like you in learning situations. Then complete the activities which follow.

| A | B |
|---|---|
| am organized in my approach | talk aloud to myself |
| like to read | am easily distracted |
| am usually a good speller | like to be read to |
| memorize by seeing pictures | enjoy music |
| have good handwriting | whisper to myself when I read |
| remember faces | remember names |
| use graphic organizers | am friendly and outgoing |
| often doodle | enjoy listening activities |
| notice details | often hum or sing |

| C | D |
|---|---|
| am moving most of the time | prefer essay tests |
| use my hands while talking | have musical ability |
| will try new things | picture things in my mind |
| enjoy physical activities | am creative and spontaneous |
| am a poor speller | follow written or demonstrated |
| like to solve problems by physically |    directions |
|    working through them | enjoy using language |
| tap my pencil or foot while | prefer objective (T/F, matching, |
|    studying |    multiple-choice) tests |
|    or reading | talk to think and learn |
| like to role play | am logical and structured |
| write lists | follow spoken directions |
| take notes to learn | |

Now count the number of items circled in the above lists.
How many describe you? _____

**(MY LEARNING PROFILE continued)**

Explain your reasons for the items circled in section D. Do you see a pattern?

_____

_____

Complete this bar graph with your responses.

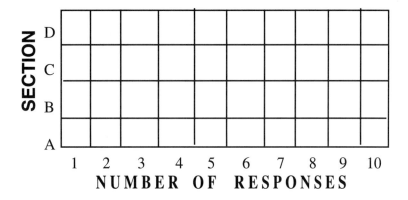

Draw conclusions about how you learn best from the graph above. Explain.

_____

_____

Design a personal logo (picture, drawing) which reflects the way(s) you learn best. Use the markers and construction paper provided at the center.

Support one of the following statements with at least two examples.

1.  Studying is best done alone with soft background music.
2.  Studying is best done aloud with a partner.
3.  Studying is best done alone in a quiet setting.
4.  Studying is best done at school in a cooperative group.

My choice is # _____ Why? _____

_____

172

## ACTIVITY 4 (15 points)

Answer the following questions about your name. You may need to ask a parent or guardian for help with this.

1. What does your given first name mean?

2. Who gave you this name?

3. Are you named for someone? If so, who?

4. Is there something unique or special about your name? If so, what is it?

5. Can you tell a story about your name? (Yes or no will do for now.)

6. Do you have a nickname? If so, what is it? Why do you have this nickname?

7. Does your name fit you? Why or why not?

8. If you could change your first name or your nickname, would you? Why?

9. What is the origin of your last name?

10. Share your name story with someone else at this station.

## BONUS (10 points)

**(choose one)**

Create an acrostic/name poem for your first name (middle name, too, if your first name is four or fewer letters). All of the words used should describe you.

Name poem sample:
    *K*   ind and friendly
    *A*   thletic and skilled
    *T*   welve, going on 18
    *H*   appy-go-lucky
    *Y*   oung but growing up

*OR*

Write a television or radio announcement about your next birthday. Include:

> full name
> date of birthday
> age at birthday
> type of celebration, where, when, who's invited, and what will be served
> kinds of gifts accepted
> other

---

### SUGGESTED JOURNAL STARTER STATEMENTS FOR THIS STATION

One of the things I've always been afraid of is . . . because . . .

The kind of test I like best is . . . because . . .

I can (or cannot) study with the stereo on because . . .

As I completed the Personal Profile, I realized . . .

After I completed the Learning Profile activities, I . . .

Wearing any kind of name tag . . .

**Include any other kinds of appropriate responses you wish to make.**

Also, feel free to illustrate any of your journal entries.

## A Dodeca What?

PURPOSE
To construct a dodecahedron which will feature something about you on each face

SPECIAL MATERIALS NEEDED
Dodecahedron pattern; construction paper; scissors; colored pencils or markers; magazines and/or actual photographs

DIRECTIONS (100 points)
Read through the following information and begin. Note that this is the only activity at this station.

Grading Criteria:     6 points each "face" = 72
                              1 illustration
                              1 sentence
                  10 points correct spelling
                  12 points complete sentences
                     6 points overall appearance, neatness

## ACTIVITY 3 (20 points)

The dodecahedron is a twelve-sided geometric shape which is a perfect vehicle to focus on *you* – who you are, who and what are important to you, and many of your personal favorites.

At this learning station you will construct a personal dodecahedron. On each "face" will be a complete sentence and an illustration about you. Here are the topic requirements for the 12 faces:

| | |
|---|---|
| 2 - family | 1 - you at the present time |
| 1 - hobby | 2 - interest/sport |
| 1 - favorite food | 1 - favorite actor/actress/musician |
| 1 - you as an infant | 1 - home state or town |
| 1 - favorite color | 1 - your choice |

Use the pattern provided to cut the circles from construction paper at the station. Make the folds so that you can write, draw, and/or paste on each "face." When all 12 faces are ready, staple your circles together to form the three-dimensional "ball." Your teacher may want to display this in the classroom or media center. (You may use photographs or representative pictures as well as your own drawings for all illustrations. Be colorful and creative.)

**SUGGESTED JOURNAL STARTER STATEMENTS FOR THIS STATION**

While working on my dodecahedron, I was surprised that . . .

It was difficult to find (or draw) a picture of . . . because . . .

The picture of me as a baby . . .

I miss . . . because . . .

This activity . . .

I do (or do not) want my dodecahedron to be displayed because . . .


**Include any other kinds of appropriate responses you wish to make.**


Also, feel free to illustrate any of your journal entries.

**DODECAHEDRON PATTERN**

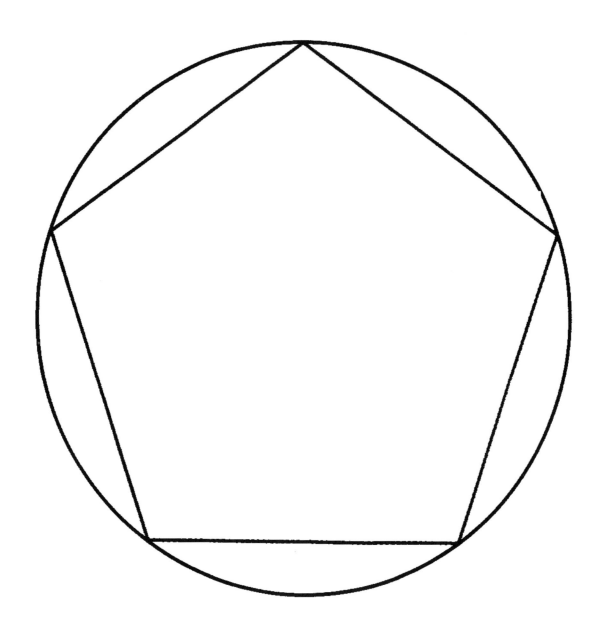

## Investigate Gregor Mendel

PURPOSE
To investigate a famous scientist and relate his findings to the theme of identities

SPECIAL MATERIALS NEEDED
Science textbook(s); encyclopedias; other reference sources and/or the CD-ROM; mirror; white paper; colored pencils or crayons

DIRECTIONS  (90 points)
Complete these activities in order.

---

## ACTIVITY 1 (50 points)

Gregor Mendel was an Austrian botanist and monk. Use the materials and resources available to research and find out more about him. You are to include who he was, what he discovered, and why it is important to include him in our Identities learning stations. Gather your information from at least two different sources. Your final product should be at least three well-developed paragraphs written in ink or on the computer.

---

## ACTIVITY 2 (25 points)

Define these terms which relate to our topic. Use your own paper and any resources you may need.

| | |
|---|---|
| trait | inheritance |
| chromosome | gene |
| dominant (genes) | sickle-cell anemia |
| color blindness | DNA |
| heredity | recessive (genes) |
| pedigree | molecule |
| albino | random |

Next, illustrate and label at least five of the above terms.

---

## ACTIVITY 3 (15 points)

Brainstorm a list of 8-10 questions you would like to ask Gregor Mendel.

Identify at least four of your features:
eye color
hair color and whether straight or curly
shape of nose
shape of mouth
other

(If you live with or know one or both of your natural parents/grandparents, answer the next questions.)

Who else in your family has each of your features?
Have you noticed the resemblance before this?
These are inherited traits. What other physical traits have you inherited?
Which of your traits do you like the best? the least? Why?

OR

Draw and color a self-portrait. Use the mirror for details.

**SUGGESTED JOURNAL STARTER STATEMENTS FOR THIS STATION**

I learned . . . about Gregor Mendel.

The most interesting part of Mendel's discoveries is . . . because . . .

Being color blind . . .

I was surprised about . . .

I would like to know more about . . .

The physical trait of mine I like most is . . . because . . .

**Include any other kinds of appropriate responses you wish to make.**

Also, feel free to illustrate any of your journal entries.

# What's the Identity?

PURPOSE
To identify chemical elements of the Periodic Table based on their physical descriptions

SPECIAL MATERIALS NEEDED
Resource materials which include information on the Periodic Table

DIRECTIONS  (30 points)
Identify at least ten of the following Periodic Table chemical elements by name, symbol, and atomic number.

Example:      bluish white
              usually found in combination
              used as protective coating for iron

Answer:       zinc - Zn - 30

## ACTIVITY 2 (25 points)

A. named after recently discovered plant
   hard, heavy, silvery, radioactive
   important in atomic energy

B. heavy, yellow, inert, metallic
   precious metal
   used in manufacture of coins and jewelry

C. nonmetallic
   basic element in coal, charcoal, soot
   found in all organic compounds

D. rare, gaseous
   inert to all reagents except fluorine
   means "hidden," was difficult to isolate

E. silvery, malleable, ductile, metallic
   highly resistant to corrosion
   used as chemical catalyst

F. pale-yellow, nonmetallic, found in crystalline form
   burns with blue flame and stifling odor
   used in making gunpowder and insecticides

180

G. silvery, lightweight, and metallic
   resists corrosion
   found abundantly, but only in combination

H. white, metallic, ductile, and malleable
   best metal conductor of heat and electricity
   precious metal, capable of high polish

I. radioactive
   discovered in 1952
   now produced by irradiating plutonium with neutrons

J. colorless, odorless, tasteless, gaseous
   forms one-third of volume of the atmosphere
   most common element in earth's crust

K. radioactive and gaseous
   formed with alpha rays
   first product in atomic disintegration of radium

L. light, silver-white
   used in making several alloys
   burns with hot, white light

M. inert, heavy, colorless, noble, gaseous
   found in small quantities in earth's atmosphere
   used to discharge tubes and gas lasers

O. corrosive, poisonous, pale greenish-yellow
   most reactive nonmetallic element known
   forms fluorides with almost all known elements

## BONUS (10 points)

Use the format from Activity 1 to write your physical description as if you were a chemical element on the Periodic Table. Give your element a name, symbol, and atomic number.

## SUGGESTED JOURNAL STARTER STATEMENTS FOR THIS STATION

To me, the most interesting element is . . . because . . .

I'd like to know more about . . . because . . .

This activity . . .

I *do/do* not understand the arrangement of the Periodic Table. It . . .


**Include any other kinds of appropriate responses you wish to make.**


Also, feel free to illustrate any of your journal entries.

## Personally Speaking

### PURPOSE
To explore one's personal and family history

### SPECIAL MATERIALS NEEDED
Adding machine tape (or something wide); ruler; construction paper or poster board; colored pencils or markers

### DIRECTIONS
At this station there are two activities which relate directly to you and your family. You will need to read the requirements carefully and you may have to ask your parents/guardians for assistance. You may select one or both activities.

## ACTIVITY 1 (100 points)

### PERSONAL TIMELINE
Using the adding machine tape and a ruler provided at this station, you are to draw your own personal timeline. Begin with the date of your birth and include "milestones" and important happenings through your next birthday. Try to include at least two or three things per year if at all possible. Some things to consider:

> when you began to talk
> when you took your first step
> major illnesses
> family moves
> birth of brothers/sisters
> important visits/visitors
> vacations
> parent job change
> when you began school, name of school, location
> when you learned to count, to read
> death of a friend or relative
> many others - your choice

You may want to make a list on notebook paper to begin. This can be taken home today to discuss with a parent/guardian. Tomorrow you can complete the timeline.

Scale: 1 year =3 or 4 inches. Be sure to label years and dates. Use colored pencils if you wish and illustrate where appropriate. When finished, post in your classroom as directed by your teacher.

## ACTIVITY 2 (100 points)

FAMILY TREE

Family trees are charts showing relationships of family members dating back to the earliest known ancestor. Usually full names are included, along with year of birth (and death). Sometimes the relationship (son, daughter, mother, father, wife, etc.) is also given.

Some form of a branching tree is suggested for this activity. The trunk of the tree will begin with your name and birthdate. Each fork of the branch represents other family members as far into the past as possible. One side of the tree will focus on the mother's side of the family; the other side of the tree will focus on the father's side.

Your assignment is to construct your own family tree as completely as you can. It will be necessary to involve your parents in this activity. If you are unable to do so, borrow or adopt the family of a famous person you would like to know more about, an interesting neighbor, a guardian, or a teacher.

Grading criteria:
> Information is complete (names, dates)
> Information is clear (maternal/paternal sides)
> Information is readable
> Names are capitalized properly
> Spelling is correct
> Appearance is very neat, colorful, and visually pleasing

---

**SUGGESTED JOURNAL STARTER STATEMENTS FOR THIS STATION**

My favorite relative is . . . because . . .

I never knew . . .

My family tree . . .

Relationships are . . . because . . .

I miss . . . because . . .

This family tree activity . . .

I was surprised . . . because . . .

**Include any other kinds of appropriate responses you wish to make.**

Also, feel free to illustrate any of your journal entries

## Focus on Cultural Identity

PURPOSE
To consider differences and similarities in cultures through the reading of children's literature

SPECIAL MATERIALS NEEDED
Suggested titles for use at this station:

*Amazing Grace*, Mary Hoffman, Dial Books for Young Readers
*All the Color of the Earth*, Sheila Hamanaka, Morrow Jr. Books
*But Names Will Never Hurt Me*, Bernard Waber, Houghton Mifflin
*Charlie the Caterpillar*, Dom DeLuise, Simon & Schuster
*Cinder-Elly*, Frances Minters, Viking, U.S.A.
*An Enchanted Hair Tale*, Alex DeVeaux, Harper Trophy
*The Faithful Elephants: A True Story of Animals, People and War*,
    Yukio Tsuchiya, Houghton Mifflin
*The Fall of Freddie the Leaf: A Story of Life for All Ages*,
    Leo Buscaglia, Charles B. Slack, Inc.
*Fly Away Home*, Eve Bunting, Clarion Books
*Hey Al*, Arthur Yorink, Sunburst Books
*The House That Crack Built*, Clark Taylor, Chronicle Books
*The Lotus Seed*, Sherry Garland, Harcourt Brace Jovanovich
*My Father Always Embarrasses Me*, Mew Shalev, Wellington Pub.
*My Working Mom*, Peter Glassman, Morrow Jr. Books
*Nana Upstairs, Nana Downstairs*, Tomie de Paola, Putnam
*Nathaniel Talking*, Eloise Greenfield, Black Butterfly Children's Books
*Oliver Burton is a Sissy*, Tomie de Paola, Harcourt
*The Paper Bag Princess*, Colin Thompson, Knopf
*The Paper Crane*, Molly Bang, Mulberry Paperback Books
*People*, Peter Spier, Doubleday
*Seeing Eye Willie*, Dale Gottlieb, Knopf
*Sleeping Ugly*, Jane Yolen, Coward McCann
*Sootface: An Ojibwa Cinderella Story*, Robert D. SanSouci,
    Doubleday Books
*That's What a Friend Is*, P. K. Hallinan, Children's Press
*The Wall*, Eve Bunting, Clarion Books
*Weird Parents*, Audrey Wood, Dial Books for Young Readers
*Where Did Your Family Come From?* Melvin & Gilda Berger, Ideals
*Why Mosquitoes Buzz in People's Ears: A West African Folk Tale*, Verna
    Aardema, Dial Books for Young Readers

DIRECTIONS (75 points)
Read the following information:

It is recommended that a study of cultures reflect those universal elements present in all cultures. Some of these elements might include the following:

| | |
|---|---|
| language | families |
| dress | neighborhoods |
| foods | climate |
| monetary systems | plant and animal population |
| games | rituals, customs |
| art, songs, dances | geographical boundaries |

Culture is defined as the sum total of the beliefs, accomplishments, and behavior patterns of a group of people, acquired by members of the group through social learning and transmitted from one generation to another.

Diversity means a wide range of cultures and subcultures that represent differences in values, beliefs, symbols, rituals, languages, etc. Some types of diversity are age, gender, religion, race, nationality, color, ability and disability, to name a few.

Basic human needs such as food, shelter, clothing, water, love, and esteem are universal (no matter who or where we are). As we learn about and try to understand cultures different from our own, we must keep in mind those links that we all share as human beings.

One way we can explore other cultures is through the use of children's literature.

## ACTIVITY 1

Now select any three of the children's literature books representing three different cultures, available at this station. Sit back, relax, read each story, and enjoy the illustrations. Then, for each story, complete the following activities.

1. Write the title, author, and illustrator of the book.
2. Explain what the title means in a 4-6 sentence paragraph. Be specific.
3. Illustrate a "key" event in the story and then explain what is happening in a sentence or two.
4. Identify four or more cultural elements listed above.
5. Imagine yourself as the title character. What would you do differently, and why? OR Create a new title for the book and defend your creation.
6. Rank this story on a scale from 1-5. One is poor, 5 is excellent. Give three reasons for your ranking.
7. After reading the three stories and completing the activities above, compare and contrast your three selections.

186

## SUGGESTED JOURNAL STARTER STATEMENTS FOR THIS STATION

The story I enjoyed the most is . . . because . . .

I would love to be (character) . . . because . . .

I never knew . . .

Why do people always . . .

Different cultures are interesting to me because . . .

The best illustrations were in . . . I liked them because . . .

I might write a children's story entitled . . . It would tell . . .

**Include any other kinds of appropriate responses you wish to make.**

Also, feel free to illustrate any of your journal entries

## "Team" Identities

PURPOSE
To discover the identities of athletic and school teams

SPECIAL MATERIALS NEEDED
Recent world almanac; daily and Sunday newspapers; and school newsletters or team handbooks

DIRECTIONS  (40 points)
Use the books, newspapers, and materials provided at this station to discover as many team names as you possibly can to fit the categories for the following activities.

## ACTIVITY 1 (25 points)

Many middle schools use a team configuration by or across grade levels. After you have written your school name at the top of your paper, add your mascot, school colors, and slogan. Then discover and list the team names and grade levels for your school. If other identity information is available (colors, logo, slogan, etc.), be sure to include that, too. What does your team or school identity mean to you?

## ACTIVITY 2  (15 points)

What are the identity/identities of your school sports teams? your local high school(s) athletic teams? What are the identities of other organized teams in your local community? What part does team identity play in sport rivalry?

## BONUS  (40 points)

Identify as many state, national, international, and professional teams as you can. Be sure to include explanatory information. (For example, Cleveland Indians – National League.) You may include drawings and/or pictures if you wish. Why do team fans dress in decorated tee shirts, hats, etc. when they attend a sporting event? Besides the tee shirts and hats, what other sports memorabilia do fans collect to show team identity?

**SUGGESTED JOURNAL STARTER STATEMENTS FOR THIS STATION**

My favorite athletic team is . . . because . . .

My school team is the . . . Our name came from . . .

The athletic team I enjoy being on is . . . We . . .

React to this: A team HAS to work together because . . .

Team colors are/are not important because . . .

Our team/school slogan is . . . To me, it means . . .

When teachers team . . .

**Include any other kinds of appropriate responses you wish to make.**

Also, feel free to illustrate any of your journal entries.

## How Do I Know That?

PURPOSE
To identify character traits

SPECIAL MATERIALS NEEDED
Several short stories which focus on character traits and relate directly to curriculum requirements selected by the teacher. (Examples: "The Tell-Tale Heart," "The Necklace," "Raymond's Run," "Charles"). For Activity Two, an envelope of 50-100 pictures of unknown faces (cut from magazines). For Activity Three, a grammar/composition textbook.

DIRECTIONS  (120 points)
Select two of the suggested short stories. Read carefully and then consider the traits of each main character (one from each story). Continue with the next activities.

## ACTIVITY 1 (25 points)

After reading the stories, head your paper correctly and write the titles of the two stories you chose to read. Make two columns on your paper. Each main character's name is the heading. Below each name list the character traits (descriptive words about personality and attitude) which each possesses. Try to list five in each column. Next, answer these questions in complete sentences.

1. Are the characters similar in any way? Explain.
2. How do the characters differ?
3. Which character did you like best? Why?

## ACTIVITY 2  (25 points)

Select one picture from the envelope of pictures provided at this station. Write at least a one-paragraph character sketch, giving this person a name, a hometown, a complete physical description, several identifying personality traits, an occupation, and anything else you might want to include. Attach the picture to your writing.

## ACTIVITY 3 (25 points)

Write a letter of at least three complete paragraphs or make a videotape for an imaginary or real pen pal in another state or country. Introduce yourself and share identifying features and qualities you possess. Include your interests, hobbies, favorites, family and school information, and other facts you care to share. Be sure to ask questions of your pen pal. (Use correct friendly letter format.)

## ACTIVITY 4 (25 points)

As you read through the following list, decide on the identity of people you know (both adults and peers) who might be likely to do these things either presently or in the future. Complete at least ten; include full name and your reason for identifying this person.

Example:     Write a novel – Mrs. Sue Atkinson – English teacher who
             writes beautifully

Here is the list. Who is the most likely to . . .

> act in a movie or TV series
> become a scientist or researcher
> invent something new
> write a novel
> invest in real estate
> walk on Mars
> become President of the United States
> cook for a crowd of 50 or more
> communicate mainly by computer
> become an elementary teacher
> control a nuclear submarine
> create a new fad
> entertain a large radio audience
> become a country or rock star
> drive a race car
> conduct an orchestra

## BONUS (20 points)

Identify two poems, two short stories, one nonfiction selection, and one biography or autobiography you would recommend to students about the topic of IDENTITIES. Give reasons for each of your titles.

---

**SUGGESTED JOURNAL STARTER STATEMENTS FOR THIS STATION**

My best character trait is . . . because . . .

My worst character trait is . . . because . . .

My closest friend's best/worst character trait is . . . because . . .

Another short story that has great characters is . . . because . . .

I enjoy stories about . . . because . . .

My pen pal . . .

When I grow up, I am most likely to be/become . . . because . . .

A living "character" I know well is . . . because . . .

**Include any other kinds of appropriate responses you wish to make.**

Also, feel free to illustrate any of your journal entries.

192

## Hidden Identities

PURPOSE
To investigate masks and their uses

SPECIAL MATERIALS NEEDED
Access to reference materials; construction paper; markers; glue; glitter; feathers; ribbons; sample masks (if available)

DIRECTIONS  (100 points)
Complete the following activities in order.

---

## ACTIVITY 1  (5 points)

KNOWLEDGE
List at least ten different kinds of masks.

---

## ACTIVITY 2  (10 points)

COMPREHENSION
Suggest three or four reasons for someone to use/wear a mask.

---

## ACTIVITY 3  (15 points)

APPLICATION
Discover the origin of masks as we know them today. Write a well-developed paragraph.

---

## ACTIVITY 4  (20 points)

ANALYSIS
Compare and contrast two of the following masks:
    Indian medicine man
    Japanese Kabuki dancer
    Phantom of the Opera
    dramatic comedy/tragedy.

## ACTIVITY 5 (25 points)

SYNTHESIS
Design a mask that reflects one of your interests or hobbies. Use the construction paper and markers at the station.

## ACTIVITY 6 (25 points)

EVALUATION
Recommend a different kind of mask for at least four of the following persons, and state your reasons for each.

| | |
|---|---|
| your principal | your sister or brother |
| your mother or father | your best friend |
| your math teacher | a neighbor |
| a grandparent | a media specialist |

### SUGGESTED JOURNAL STARTER STATEMENTS FOR THIS STATION

The best activity above was . . . because . . .

My favorite kind of mask is . . . because . . .

Halloween is . . .

I didn't know . . . about masks.

I will/will not wear the mask I created because . . .

**Include any other kinds of appropriate responses you wish to make.**

Also, feel free to illustrate any of your journal entries

## Identified Olympians

PURPOSE
To examine famous Olympians and the Olympic games

SPECIAL MATERIALS NEEDED
Access to the media center and references

DIRECTIONS  (55 points)
Complete the activities in any order you wish.

### ACTIVITY 1 (20 points)

1.  Identify the event(s), year(s), and country for at least ten of these
    famous Olympians.

    | | |
    |---|---|
    | Eric Heiden | Bruce Jenner |
    | Jesse Owens | Katarina Witt |
    | Kristi Yamaguchi | Jackie Joyner-Kersee |
    | Nadia Comaneci | Carl Lewis |
    | Bonnie Blair | Mary Lou Retton |
    | Franz Klammer | Steffi Graf |

2.  With which of these gold medal winners do you most identify? Why?

### ACTIVITY 2 (10 points)

Answer the following questions in complete sentences.

1.  What event would be your first choice to participate in if you were selected
    to represent the United States in the summer or winter Olympics? Why?
2.  What event is your favorite event to watch in the Summer Olympics? the
    Winter Olympics? Why?
3.  How would you feel marching in the opening ceremonies carrying the flag
    of your country? Explain.
4.  Have you ever attended the Olympic games? If so, when, where, and what
    were your impressions? If not, which ones have you watched on TV?

## ACTIVITY 3 (25 points)

Investigate the Olympic games to discover:

origin                             Olympic rings

occurrence                 awards/medals

events/competitions       other pertinent information

List at least 10-12 facts from your investigation.

**SUGGESTED JOURNAL STARTER STATEMENTS FOR THIS STATION**

The Olympic rings . . .

My Olympic hero/heroine is . . . because . . .

I was surprised . . .

Women's/men's gymnastics . . .

The Olympic opening ceremonies . . .

In the past, the Olympics . . .

**Include any other kinds of appropriate responses you wish to make.**

Also, feel free to illustrate any of your journal entries.

## Identity Potpourri

**PURPOSE**
To explore several types of identities

**SPECIAL MATERIALS NEEDED**
Access to the media center; construction paper (including white); scissors; magazines; glue sticks; ruler

**DIRECTIONS** (65-170 points)
Select any three of the activities at this station.

## ACTIVITY 1 (50 points)

Identify a famous inventor with whom you would like to have a conversation. In several sentences, state this person's name and your reasons for selecting him/her. Then design at least 20 questions you would like to have answered by this person, and list at least 10 things about yourself you would like to share.

## ACTIVITY 2 (30 points)

Discover the IDENTITY of the following:

A. foster father of Edgar A. Poe
B. father of Pocohantas
C. sister of Anne and Emily Bronte
D. author of Hatchett
E. nickname for the helicopter
F. creator of peanut butter
G. discoverer of penicillin
H. President in 1954
I. vice-president in 1975
J. painter of the "Mona Lisa"

Now write five more of your own, complete with the answers.

## ACTIVITY 3 (25 points)

Create a "Student Search" activity sheet with at least 15-30 items. You will want others in your class to find "Someone who . . ." You should decide on the directions and the format for this activity. Sample identifying traits to search for:

        someone who . . .    has brown eyes
                                 enjoys dancing
                                 has naturally curly hair
                                 speaks a foreign language

*(Please try not to use these in your activity.)*

## ACTIVITY 4 (25 points)

Use the materials provided at this center to create a two-sided collage to hang in your classroom. Cut pictures which reflect your interests and favorites from magazines. Arrange in a random fashion and glue them on both sides of one piece of construction paper.

## ACTIVITY 5 (20 points)

Use the materials provided at this station to design a personal comic strip about a recent experience in your life. The strip should have six or eight cartoon drawings, including one with a title and your name.

## ACTIVITY 6 (20 points)

Use the materials provided at this center to design your own personal logo for the front and/or back of a tee shirt that you will wear on "Celebrate My Identity Day."

**SUGGESTED JOURNAL STARTER STATEMENTS FOR THIS STATION**

The inventor I chose to converse with is . . . because . . .

I enjoyed . . . because . . .

My best "someone who" statement is . . . because . . .

The collage I created . . .

I learned . . . about . . .

    **Include any other kinds of appropriate responses you wish to make.**

Also, feel free to illustrate any of your journal entries.

## More Journal "ID"eas

PURPOSE
To respond and react in writing in my own journal


SPECIAL MATERIALS NEEDED
Personal journal


DIRECTIONS  (100 points @ 20 points each)
Read through these journal starter statements. You must select at least five topics. At this station, your individual topics/responses should be in paragraph form, not just simple sentences.

## ACTIVITY 1 (50 points)

If I could be any kind of animal, I would be . . . because . . .

My feelings about animal rights are . . .

I'll never forget the time that my pet . . .

These are my favorite pet names . . . because . . .

The vacation I will never forget is . . . because . . .

My favorite color is . . . because . . .

My most embarrassing moment was . . .

Four questions I have about . . . are . . .

A friend is . . . My best friend is . . . He/she . . .

I am proudest of myself for . . .

I am unique because . . .

One goal I have set for myself is . . . because . . .

I am a volunteer at . . . because . . .

Kids my age should do some kind of volunteer work because . . .

My . . . always says . . . and it makes me . . . because . . .

One thing about my appearance I want to change is . . . because . . .

I have a collection of . . . because . . .

**Include any other kinds of appropriate responses you wish to make.**

Also, feel free to illustrate your journal entry.

IDENTITIES - ANSWER KEY

## WHAT'S THE IDENTITY?

A.    uranium - U - 92
B.    gold - Au - 79
C.    carbon - C - 6
D.    krypton - Kr - 36
E.    platinum - Pt - 78
F.    sulfur - S - 16
G.    aluminum - Al - 13
H.    silver - Ag - 47

I.    einsteinium - Es - 99
J.    oxygen - O - 8
K.    radon - Rn - 86
L.    magnesium - Mg - 12
M.    xenon - Xe - 54
N.    neon - Ne - 10
O.    fluorine - F - 9

## IDENTIFIED OLYMPIANS

(Name: event(s), year(s), country)

Eric Heiden          men's speed skating, 1980, U.S.A.
Jesse Owens          100 and 200 meter dash and running broad jump, 1936, U.S.A.
Kristi Yamaguchi     figure skating, women's singles, 1992, U.S.A.
Nadia Comaneci       gymnastics - all around, balance beam, 1976, Romania
                     floor exercises and balance beam, 1980, Romania
Bonnie Blair         women's speed skating, 1992, U.S.A.
Franz Klammer        downhill skiing, 1976, Austria
Bruce Jenner         track and field, decathlon, 1976, U.S.A.
Katarina Witt        figure skating, women's singles, 1984, E. Germany
Jackie Joyner-Kersee track and field, long jump, 1988, U.S.A.
Carl Lewis           100 and 200 meter dash, 1984, U.S.A.
                     long jump, 1988, 1992, 1996, U.S.A.
Mary Lou Retton      gymnastics, all around, 1984, U.S.A.
Steffi Graf          women's singles, tennis, 1988, W. Germany

## IDENTITY POTPOURRI
   A. John Allen
   B. Powhatan
   C. Charlotte Brontë
   D. Gary Paulsen
   E. chopper, eggbeater, whirlybird, or flying windmill
   F. George Washington Carver
   G. Alexander Fleming
   H. Dwight D. Eisenhower
   I. Gerald R. Ford
   J. Leonardo da Vinci

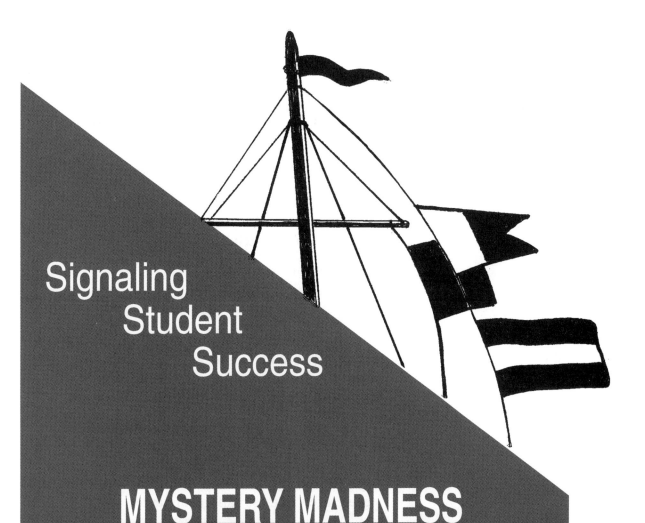

# Signaling
# Student
# Success

# MYSTERY MADNESS

- **Read A Mystery**
- **Mysterious Words**
- **Mysterious Characters – "Who Done It?"**
- **Private Eyes/Detectives**
- **Mysteries of Science and Nature**
- **Baffling, Mysterious Phenomena**
- **Mathematical Mysteries and Codes**
- **Real Life Mysteries**
- **Fears and Phobias**
- **Halloween – A Mystery Holiday**
- **Mystery Station Class Project**

National Middle School Association

**An Introduction to
MYSTERY MADNESS**

"Near the front door was a small chest of drawers with a mirror hanging above it. A tube of Chris's lipstick rested on the chest and there was writing in bright red.

You'll Never Get Away From Me.
A.

Then he looked at the front door and saw that the chain was off the latch."

SOURCE: Stuart Woods, *Dead Eyes* (New York: HarperCollins, 1994)

......

And so the stage is set for one of the most popular writing styles of fictional readers, the MYSTERY. Hundreds of spine-tingling, suspense-filled stories are written and read across the world daily.

Other kinds of mysteries fascinate or sizzle us. This kind of mystery pertains to phenomena, events, or animals that cannot be explained or easily understood. The Bermuda Triangle, Stonehenge, UFOs, Bigfoot, and the Loch Ness monster are a few of these baffling mysteries.

A mystery can also be a feeling or a quality associated with the unexplained, a secret, or the unknown. Mysteries make us think and try to find answers.

Mysteries of any kind will continue to intrigue and captivate people as they seek to unravel the clues and find the truth or solution to the problem or crime.

## THE GUIDING QUESTIONS

1. What is a mystery?

2. What different types of mysteries are there?

3. How do mysteries affect my life?

# At a glance — topics and tasks

- Read a fictional book classified as a mystery and discover the elements of a mystery

- Become familiar with words frequently used with mysteries or suspense; create an original mystery story

- Use descriptive words in writing a character sketch

- View a movie or TV show to learn more about the elements of a mystery and more about detectives and their jobs

- Investigate strange animals and things that seem to defy reality and aren't easily explained

- Explore mysterious and strange events that have occurred and have been documented without scientific explanation or that are just plain hard to believe

- Explore the mysteries of numbers and investigate the use of codes

- Investigate and explore mysteries and crimes as they have occurred in real life

- Learn about different kinds of fears and phobias

- Understand the historical significance of Halloween and how it evolved into today's celebration or holiday

# Mystery Madness Rubric

Name _____ Class _____

You may select from the following stations. The activity must be done completely, accurately, and neatly to earn full point value. The grading scale is as follows:

| A 660+ pts. | B 560-659 pts. | C 450-559 pts. | D 350-449 pts. |
|---|---|---|---|
| **Date Completed** | **Activity** | | 20-40 |

| Date Completed | Activity | Possible Points | Points Earned |
|---|---|---|---|
| _____ | Read a Mystery | | |
| _____ | Mysterious Words | 120-180 | _____ |
| _____ | Mysterious Characters – "Who Done It?" | 60-80 | _____ |
| _____ | Private Eyes/ Detectives | 60-80 | _____ |
| _____ | Mysteries of Science and Nature | 120-140 | _____ |
| _____ | Baffling, Mysterious Phenomena | 20-140 | _____ |
| _____ | Mathematical Mysteries and Codes | 20-40 | _____ |
| _____ | Real Life Mysteries | 40-60 | _____ |
| _____ | Fears and Phobias | 40-80 | _____ |
| _____ | Halloween – A Mystery Holiday | 80-100 | _____ |
| _____ | Mystery Station Class Project | 80-100 | _____ |

**TOTAL POINTS** _____

**GRADE** _____

## Read a Mystery

PURPOSES
To read a fictional book classified as a mystery and to understand the elements of a mystery

SPECIAL MATERIALS
Mystery books from the media center. A bibliography of mysteries may be helpful.

DIRECTIONS  (120 points)
Complete either the following Bloom activities or the Super Sleuth worksheet on the book you have read.

## ACTIVITY 1  (20 points)

KNOWLEDGE
Who was the detective, sleuth or crime solver in your mystery? Write a descriptive paragraph about this character.

## ACTIVITY 2  (20 points)

COMPREHENSION
List the conflicts in the story and tell how they were resolved or solved?

## ACTIVITY 3  (20 points)

APPLICATION
A person's fingerprints often help solve the mystery. Write a brief description about each kind of fingerprint. How can this information be helpful? Can you determine what your fingerprint pattern is?

## ACTIVITY 4 (20 points)

ANALYSIS
Make a timeline of events in your mystery and tell how each had an effect on the solution to the mystery (crime).

## ACTIVITY 5 (20 points)

SYNTHESIS
Write a different ending for the mystery you read.

## ACTIVITY 6 (20 points)

EVALUATION
List and explain the elements in the story which prove it to be a mystery: alibi; clues; crime; detective (detection); excitement; solution; suspense.

## Super Sleuths (120 points)

DIRECTIONS

1. Select a mystery novel to complete this assignment.

2. Use this sheet as a PATTERN for reporting on the book you read.

## TITLE

Author's first and last name

Description of the crime (include as many facts as you can)

Details about the detective (name, description, special skills)

Details about the suspect(s) (name, description, reasons)

Information about other main characters (name, description, the role they play)

Clues to the solution (in order)

Details about the final solution

Tell whether you were surprised at the ending and why or why not.

Tell whether you would have changed the ending in any way and why or why not.

## Mysterious Words

PURPOSES
To become familiar with words frequently used with mysteries or suspense; to create an original mystery story

SPECIAL MATERIALS
Dictionaries; thesaurus; drawing paper; crayons or markers

DIRECTIONS  (60 points)
Complete all three of the following activities. The "Bonus" is optional.

### ACTIVITY 1  (20 points)

Make a list of 50 words that are usually found in a mystery (see examples). Alphabetize your list and look up the words you don't understand and write out their meanings!

EXAMPLES:  baffling, detective, suspect, investigate, haunted, chilling

### ACTIVITY 2  (20 points)

Using the words in your word list, see if you can find a synonym for each word, creating a new word list.

### ACTIVITY 3  (20 points)

Using your word list, write a mystery of your own. Be sure to include the elements of a mystery. Share your mystery with a partner or the class.

### BONUS  (20 points)

Illustrate a scene from your mystery. Display your picture at this station.

## Mysterious Characters
## "Who Done It?"

**PURPOSE**
To use descriptive words in writing a character sketch

**SPECIAL MATERIALS**
Drawing paper; markers

**DIRECTIONS** (60 points)
Complete the writing activities for Mysterious Characters. Display your "Wanted" poster in the classroom.

---

### ACTIVITY 1 (20 points)

Write a good character description of someone in your class. Include physical features as well as other personal qualities or characteristics that would help identify the person. Write your character description in a "Who Am I"? format and post on your class bulletin board so that your fellow classmates can guess who it is.

---

### ACTIVITY 2 (20 points)

Using a villainous character from a mystery you've read, design a wanted poster that would display a drawing of the person as well as giving a written description of him/her, of the crime, of the award money, who to contact if seen, etc. Display your wanted poster in the classroom.

---

### ACTIVITY 3 (20 points)

In a small group of 4-6 members, create character descriptions by using the Round Table format. The group will decide what kind of villainous character they're depicting. The first person writes 2 sentences of description and passes the paper to the left. That person adds 2 more lines of description and the process continues until the whole group has written descriptive sentences about their character. The group then reads the total description and creates or draws their character from what they've written. Then name the character and display the poster.

## BONUS (20 points)

1. Visit the United States Post Office and find where the "Wanted" posters are displayed. Interview a postal employee about the poster.

   Do all post offices still provide this service?
   Does anyone ever get apprehended as a result?
   How has the Wanted poster changed over the years?
   Share your finding with the class.

2. Write the FBI (Federal Bureau of Investigation) or contact a branch office near you. Interview an employee or ask question in writing about the history of the "Wanted" poster and how it has changed through the years. Share your findings with the class.

## Private Eyes Detectives

PURPOSE
To view a movie or TV show for the purpose of learning more about the elements of a mystery; to learn more about detectives and their jobs

SPECIAL MATERIALS
Two Bloom Sheets (Detectives 1 and Detectives 2)

DIRECTIONS  (120 points)
Choose one of the two Bloom Sheets on Detectives and complete all of the activities.

## — DETECTIVES 1 —

DIRECTIONS
There are several mystery shows on television that have become weekly viewing rituals for many Americans. Some of them are seen as reruns because of their popularity. A few of them are: Perry Mason, Burke's Law, Murder She Wrote, Diagnosis Murder, Matlock, Colombo, and Hart to Hart. Choose one of these shows or another mystery of your own choosing to watch and complete a Bloom Sheet. You will need to do this activity at home.

### ACTIVITY 1 (20 points)

KNOWLEDGE
What is the name of the show you chose? List or describe the 5 W's of the mystery you selected to watch. (Who, What, Where, When and Why)

### ACTIVITY 2 (20 points)

COMPREHENSION
Describe both the main character (hero) of the program as well as the bad guy or villain in the program you watched.

### ACTIVITY 3 (20 points)

APPLICATION
Pretend you are the main character or detective in the story. Write an advertisement for the show to try to convince people to watch it. "Sell" your show to the class.

## ACTIVITY 4 (20 points)

ANALYSIS
Create a film clip of the mystery you watched breaking it down scene by scene or clue by clue. Illustrate the plot in this creative way. (You may want to ask your media specialist how to make a filmstrip and actually put your illustrations on it or use overhead transparencies to create your film clip segments.)

## ACTIVITY 5 (20 points)

SYNTHESIS
Rewrite the ending of the story so that the good guy doesn't win. Which version do you like best? Why?

## ACTIVITY 6 (20 points)

EVALUATION
Conduct a survey or poll with your classmates to find out which mysteries are viewed the most by them or their families on TV. Make a bar graph poster to show your findings. Share it with the class.

## BONUS (20 points)

Watch a mystery movie and complete the Bloom Sheet for it also.

— DETECTIVES 2 —

## ACTIVITY 1 (20 points)

KNOWLEDGE
List at least ten television, movie, or fictional detectives.

## ACTIVITY 2 (20 points)

COMPREHENSION
Define the following in your own words: detective, mystery, villain, witness, clue, description, sleuth, crisis, cliff-hanger.

## ACTIVITY 3 (20 points)

APPLICATION
Discover the detectives created by these mystery writers: Agatha Christie, John D. McDonald, Ellery Queen, Rex Stout, Donald J. Sobol, G. K. Chesterton, Erle Stanley Gardner, Sir Arthur Conan Doyle, Franklin W. Dixon, Carolyn Keene.

## ACTIVITY 4 (20 points)

ANALYSIS
Select a detective short story to read. Identify the following: the crime, the detective, the important clues, the suspects, the solution.

## ACTIVITY 5 (20 points)

SYNTHESIS
Write your own detective short story. Include all the elements: crime, detective, clues, suspects, and solution. Design a cover and pictures to use throughout.

## ACTIVITY 6 (20 points)

EVALUATION
Recommend your favorite detective for an award. Defend your choice. What kind of an award would it be; when would it be; and when would you give it and why?

## Mysteries of Science and Nature

PURPOSE
To investigate strange animals and things that seem to defy reality and aren't easily explained

SPECIAL MATERIALS
Access to the media center; resource materials for research; drawing paper; markers

DIRECTIONS  (20 points)
Choose at least one of the activities at this station to complete. You may do more than one if this topic is of interest to you.

## ACTIVITY 1  (20 points)

Select one of the topics below to research. Use your information to write a 1-2 page report or share your information in a creative format (poster report, diorama, video interview, etc.). Include illustrations or diagrams where appropriate. You will need to go to the media center to find information on the topic you chose.

| | |
|---|---|
| Stonehenge | Black Holes |
| Ancient Astronauts | Great Sphinx/Great Pyramid |
| Lines of Nazca | Acupuncture |
| Bigfoot | Admiral Piri Re'is' Map |
| Easter Island | The Human Mind |
| ESP | Ghosts/Apparitions |
| The Moon | Dead Sea Scrolls |
| Telepathy/Teleporting | The Milky Way |

## ACTIVITY 2  (20 points)

THE LOCH NESS MONSTER
Read the information provided below and complete the activities which follow.

Loch Ness is a lake in northern Scotland. Some people believe that a large creature, nicknamed "Nessie," lives in this lake. Hundreds of people have reported seeing the creature, but to date there is no hard evidence to prove its existence. Some descriptions include length up to 30 feet, flippers, one or two humps, and a long, thin neck. Perhaps Nessie is related to the dinosaur or the manatee or the seal.

The first reported sightings date from 565 A.D. During the 1930s a new road was built in the area, and sightings increased. Films have been made and photographs have been taken which show an object, but nothing is clear. Scientific investigations have explored the lake and sonar has been used. These reveal large bodies moving in the waters of Loch Ness. Experts do not agree on what is actually shown.

1. Calculate the number of years since the first sighting of the Loch Ness monster.

2. According to the physical description, what known animals share some of Nessie's physical description?

3. On the back of this sheet, generate an original drawing of the Loch Ness monster based on the description.

4. Propose at least one other means which could be used to try to prove Nessie's existence.

5. Decide whether or not a Loch Ness monster really exists. Defend your decision.

## BONUS (20 points)

Do more extensive research and reading on Nessie. Organize your facts and references.

## ACTIVITY 3 (20 points)

### CREATURES OF THE DEEP SEA

The animals and fish that live in the deepest part of the ocean have developed many adaptations in order to survive at that depth. Some are blind; others have electric lights on their bodies while still others have developed special appendages which allow them to feel and explore things through touching. Investigate these sea creatures and draw a mini mural showing what they look like. Identify them by name and write three facts you found about each sea creature.

216

## BONUS (20 points)

Read the poem, "The Fish With The Deep Sea Smile." Create your own poem about one of the animals you drew in your mural.

## ACTIVITY 4 (20 points)

MYSTERIOUS "WHYS"?
Write a brief answer to the following "WHY" questions. Use materials at the station or reference books in the media center to find your answers.

1. Why do some plants eat animals?
2. Why do leaf cutter ants cut leaves?
3. Why does an elephant have a trunk?
4. Why do some animals have no eyes?
5. Why does a snake's tongue flicker in and out?
6. Why do "Sticklebacks" (fish) change colors?
7. Who do grebes (bird) dance?
8. Why do marsupials have pouches?
9. Why does an antelope leap in the air?
10. Why do beavers build dams?
11. Why does a chameleon change color?
12. Why does a squid squirt ink?

## BONUS (20 points)

Want some more? Try these tougher ones!

1. Why does the Black Widow Spider eat her mate?
2. Why is it said that cows, worms, and snakes can predict earthquakes?
3. Why and where do farmers use toads to protect their grain?
4. Why does a roach explode when it comes in contact with boric acid?
5. Why do some farmers give cows magnets to swallow?
6. Why does a grasshopper spit "grink?"
7. Why will a queen bee only sting another queen bee?
8. Why does a horse sleep best standing up?

## Baffling, Mysterious Phenomena

PURPOSE
To explore mysterious and strange events that have occurred and have been documented without scientific explanation or that are just plain hard to believe

SPECIAL MATERIALS
Reference books or passes to the media center; poster board; markers; maps of North and South America

DIRECTIONS  (20 points)
Complete one of the activities at this station.

## ACTIVITY 1  (20 points)

BAFFLING

In pairs choose at least five (5) of the following "baffling" topics. Research to find why they are considered mysteries. Use your own paper and follow the format suggested. Choose at least one (1) of the five to illustrate on poster board with magic marker.

| | |
|---|---|
| Ambrose Bierce | Caroll A. Deering (ship) |
| Amelia Earhart | Flight 19 |
| Dorothy Arnold | Joshua Slocum |
| Judge Justice Crater | Donald Crowhurst |
| Benjamin Bathurst | Devil's Sea |
| Sherman Church | Crystal Skull |
| Mary Celeste (ghost ship) | Atlantis |
| Shroud of Turin | Lemuria |
| Philadelphia Experiment | Kaspar Hauser |

As you complete your research, be sure to include the following information. Add more if available.

TOPIC                                                    DATE(S)

WHAT IS MYSTERIOUS, OR BAFFLING?

KNOWN FACTS

POSSIBLE EXPLANATION(S)

## ACTIVITY 2 (20 points)

BERMUDA TRIANGLE
Use available reference materials to answer the questions and complete the activities provided on this page.

The Bermuda Triangle is a triangular section of the Atlantic Ocean stretching from Bermuda to southeastern Florida to Puerto Rico and back. It is an area where many ships and planes have mysteriously disappeared.

1. Draw the Bermuda Triangle on the map on the next page.
2. Find the approximate area of the Bermuda Triangle based on your drawing. (1 cm = 500 mi.)
3. How many recorded disappearances have there been?
4. Why is the Bermuda Triangle often referred to as the "Graveyard of the Atlantic?"
5. Discover at least three theories which account for the vanishing episodes in the Bermuda Triangle. Which of these do you accept, or do you have another theory? If so, explain.
6. Research to find the names of at least ten (10) planes or ships which have disappeared over the Bermuda Triangle. Arrange your findings in this manner:

*Ship or Plane*        *Circumstances*        *Year*

Star (*) those which originated in the United States.

7. Locate the following major cities by letter on your map. One has been done for you.

A. Mexico City            F. Bogota
B. Santiago               G. Buenos Aires
C. Caracas                H. Lima
D. Brasilia               I. Santo Domingo
E. San Salvador           J. Tegucigalpa

8. If you were to travel by air from each of these cities to Washington, D.C., from which cities would you most likely fly through the Bermuda Triangle?
9. Select three different colored pencils to color North America, Central America, and South America on your map.

## BONUS (20 points)

Mysterious disappearances have occurred in approximately ten (10) other areas of the world. Five are said to be in the northern hemisphere and five in the southern hemisphere. Where are they and what is mysterious about their locations?

# THE BERMUDA TRIANGLE

# Mathematical Mysteries and Codes

PURPOSE
To explore the mysteries of numbers and to investigate the use of codes

SPECIAL MATERIALS
Dictionaries; passes to the media center or resource books on codes; dice

DIRECTIONS  (40 points)
Complete the activities under number puzzles and mind stretchers. Choose two of
the activities under the codes section to complete.

## ACTIVITY 1 (20 points)

NUMBER PUZZLES
Complete the following number puzzles. Find a couple of your own to share with
friends. See if you can fool them.

   A.  Throw a pair of dice three times. Write down your numbers.
           1.  Multiply first throw by 2.
           2.  Add 5 to the answer.
           3.  Multiply the new number by 5.
           4.  Add the second throw to it.
           5.  Multiply the answer by 10.
           6.  Add the third throw.
           7.  Subtract 250.
           8.  The answer is always the three numbers thrown!

   B.  Think of any number. Remember it! You'll need it for the last step.
           1.  Multiply the number by 2.
           2.  Add 12 to the answer.
           3.  Add 5 to the answer.
           4.  Subtract 3 from the answer.
           5.  Divide number by 2.
           6.  Subtract the first number.
           7.  The answer is always 7!

## ACTIVITY 2 (20 points)

LOGIC/MIND STRETCHERS
Read and solve each of the word problems below. Be prepared to explain how you arrived at your answer.

1. At last week's junior varsity basketball game, the final score was 62-59.
   The stars for our team were Jim, Steve, and Chris who all made baskets.
   One of them made five baskets, another made four baskets, and the other made three.
   Chris made one more basket than Jim.
   Combined, Steve and Chris made three times as many baskets as Jim.

   <u>HOW MANY BASKETS DID EACH PLAYER MAKE?</u>

2. The Smiths have four cats: Fluffy, Calico, Tiger, and Mittens. The cats' ages are 4, 6, 8, and 12 years, but not necessarily in that order.
   Fluffy's age times Mittens' age is equal to Calico's age times Tiger's age.
   Fluffy's age plus Tiger's age is equal to Mittens' age.

   <u>HOW OLD IS EACH CAT?</u>

3. Dave, Larry, Ray and Simon trade baseball cards. Today one of the boys brought four cards to trade; one brought five cards; one brought seven cards; and one brought ten cards.
   If Dave had brought three more cards, he'd have brought twice as many as Larry brought.
   Ray didn't bring the most cards.
   Larry didn't bring the fewest cards.

   <u>HOW MANY CARDS DID EACH BOY BRING?</u>

4. Many of us are collectors. Some of us collect stamps, coins, buttons, autographs. I have three friends, Tina, Sue, and Jean, who collect teddy bears. One has collected 14, another has 17, and the other has 23 already!
   If Sue gives 11 of her bears to Jean, Jean will have twice as many as Tina.
   If Jean gives 5 of hers to Sue, Tina will have the fewest teddy bears.

   <u>HOW MANY TEDDY BEARS DOES EACH GIRL HAVE?</u>

5. Tom, Joe, Bob, Sam, and Pete were weighing themselves before the wrestling match. Their weights were 184, 170, 163, 156, and 142 pounds.
Tom does not weigh the most.
The total of what Joe and Sam weight is equal to the total of what Tom and Pete weigh.
Joe weights 7 pounds more than Bob

### HOW MANY POUNDS DOES EACH BOY WEIGH?

6. Sara, Jennifer, Megan, and Lynn are best of friends. They are in the same math class and study together every day. Their scores on this week's math test were 78, 83, 87, and 92.
Although Megan's score wasn't the best, she did beat Jennifer by 5 points.
Jennifer and Lynn together made the same total score that Sara and Megan made.

### WHAT WAS EACH GIRL'S SCORE?

## ACTIVITY 3 (20 points)

CODES

1. VOCABULARY: Define the following words related to codes:
    - cipher
    - code
    - cryptography
    - decipher/decode
    - encipher/encode
    - key
    - null
    - plaintext

2. Choose one of the following codes to research and send a message to a classmate or teacher using the code you learned about.

| | |
|---|---|
| Spartan secret codes | Morse code |
| Pegpen cipher | High Seas Code |
| A letter within a letter | Simaphone |
| The Polybines square | Knocking Nihilists |
| Caliar's Cipher | Thomas Jefferson's Cipher |
| Zig zag writing | Cipher Disk |
| Cryptograms | The Turning Grille |
| Pig Latin | The Enigma Machine |
| Hieroglyphics | |

3. Codes have been used throughout history to send messages by spies and governments. Select a code from the list and learn about its historical significance. Would history have been changed or altered if this code had not been used? Write a paragraph describing the code and it's historical importance.

---

## BONUS (20 points)

What does SUPERENCIPHERING mean? Explain and give and example.

---

## Real Life Mysteries

PURPOSE
To investigate and explore mysteries and crimes as they have occurred in real life

SPECIAL MATERIALS
Newspapers; chart paper; markers and research resources

DIRECTIONS  (40 points)
Choose two of the activities at this station to complete. The bonus activity is optional.

### ACTIVITY 1  (20 points)

Crimes, suspense, and mysteries exist in real life situations every day. Using the newspaper, find a mystery you'd like to investigate and begin a journal documenting the 5 Ws (What, Where, When, Why, Who). Keep the journal through the investigation, trial, sentencing, etc. Turn your journal in for credit.

### ACTIVITY 2  (20 points)

Pretend you are an investigative reporter. Write an article for a newspaper to cover a crime you've heard about, seen in the movies or on TV, or have made up. Be sure to include the elements of investigative reporting.

### ACTIVITY 3  (20 points)

Create a timeline of a famous case or trial of historical significance. Research to find specific details and facts and illustrate them on a timeline.

EXAMPLE:   The assassination of John F. Kennedy

## ACTIVITY4 (20 points)

The historical, social, political, and economic aspects of the death penalty have been very controversial in the United States. Write an editorial or make a speech to your class sharing your points of view and thoughts on whether or not the death penalty should be an option for those who commit serious and violent crimes.

## BONUS (40 points)

Create a video documentary on violence and its place in the media, movies, TV, etc. Write a script to include the following: How do you feel about watching violence? Should parents be concerned? Do you agree with the idea of the "V-Chip" and prohibiting or censoring violence on TV. Share your video with your class and others in the school. This is a good group project. Interview teachers and classmates for your video.

## Fears and Phobias

PURPOSE
To learn about different kinds of fears and phobias

SPECIAL MATERIALS
List of phobias; phobia quiz; drawing paper; markers; dictionaries

DIRECTIONS  (80 points)
A phobia is defined as an intense, illogical, abnormal yet persistent fear of something. To those who don't experience this fear, it seems silly, obsessive, unrealistic. Yet for others, their lives are guided, planned, and dominated by these irrational fears.

Complete all of the activities at this station. The bonus question is optional.

## ACTIVITY1 (20 points)

Look up and define the list of phobias.

### LIST OF PHOBIAS

| | |
|---|---|
| Claustrophobia | fear of confined spaces |
| Pyrophobia | fear of fire |
| Ophidiophobia | fear of snakes |
| Acrophobia | fear of high places |
| Cynophobia | fear of dogs |
| Agoraphobia | fear of open spaces |
| Triskaidekaphobia | fear of the number 13 |
| Necrophobia | fear of death |
| Nyctophobia | fear of darkness |
| Zoophobia | fear of animals |
| Hypnophobia | fear of sleep |

| | |
|---|---|
| Sitophobia | fear of food |
| Phonophobia | fear of noise |
| Aquaphobia | fear of water |
| Ichthyophobia | fear of fish |
| Hemophobia | fear of blood |
| Astraphobia | fear of lightning |
| Aerophobia | fear of drafts |
| Ailurophobia | fear of cats |
| Algophobia | fear of pain |
| androphobia | fear of men |
| anthropophobia | fear of society |
| erotophobia | fear of love |
| gynophobia | fear of women |
| ochlophobia | fear of crowds |
| xenophobia | fear of foreigners |

## ACTIVITY 2 (20 points)

Make a drawing of five of the phobias in the list or think of a story to share that would illustrate the meanings of the phobias you chose.

## ACTIVITY 3 (20 points)

In a cooperative group, share the phobias you selected by showing the group your drawing or relating a story that illustrates the meaning of your phobia. Each person in the group should take turns and continue until all the phobias have been shared.

## ACTIVITY 4 (20 points)

Take the matching quiz on phobias. Record your score! How many of the ones that you knew did you remember because of the drawing or story that was shared in your group? (This is a great way to recall and remember vocabulary!)

**Matching Quiz on Phobias**

Name: _____     Score: _____

Match the phobia with the definition. Place the letter next to the appropriate word.

| 1. _____ | Claustrophobia | A. | fear of open spaces |
| 2. _____ | Necrophobia | B. | fear of darkness |
| 3. _____ | Cynophobia | C. | fear of high places |
| 4. _____ | Agoraphobia | D. | fear of dogs |
| 5. _____ | Triskaidekaphobia | E. | fear of water |
| 6. _____ | Nyctophobia | F. | fear of confined spaces |
| 7. _____ | Acrophobia | G. | fear of fire |
| 8. _____ | Pyrophobia | H. | fear of drafts |
| 9. _____ | Aquaphobia | I. | fear of the number 13 |
| 10. _____ | Astraphobia | J. | fear of cats |
| 11. _____ | Hypnophobia | K. | fear of animals |
| 12. _____ | Ophidiophobia | L. | fear of sleep |
| 13. _____ | Zoophobia | M. | fear of food |
| 14. _____ | Sitophobia | N. | fear of noise |
| 15. _____ | Phonophobia | O. | fear of fish |
| 16. _____ | Ichthyophobia | P. | fear of blood |
| 17. _____ | Hemophobia | Q. | fear of lightening |
| 18. _____ | Aerophobia | R. | fear of snakes |
| 19. _____ | Ailurophobia | S. | fear of death |
| 20. _____ | Algophobia | T. | fear of pain |

## BONUS (20 points)

1. Research and find other phobias not listed. Share them with the class.
2. Interview a person who suffers from a phobia. Find out why they have the fear and when it started. How does it affect their lives? Share this information with the class.

# Halloween — A Mystery Holiday

PURPOSE
To understand the historical significance of Halloween and how it evolved into today's celebration or holiday

SPECIAL MATERIALS
Art paper; markers; reference book

DIRECTIONS  (80 points)
Read the factual information presented at this station. Choose four of the activities to complete relating or applying what you've learned. You may need to use additional reference materials. The bonus is optional.

Our present-day celebration of Halloween has evolved from a Celtic festival of 2000 years ago. The Celts lived in what is now Great Britain, Ireland, and Northern France. The ancient Celtic festival honored Samhain, the Lord of Death, and it was celebrated just before winter, the season of cold, darkness, and decay.

The people would extinguish their hearth fires and then relight them from a community bonfire in which crops, animals, and possibly people had been sacrificed. Sometimes costumes made of animal heads and skins were worn.

When the Romans conquered the Celts in 43 AD, Roman festivals honoring the dead were combined with the Celtic customs. During the later years, when many people became Christians, the church established All Saint's Day on November 1.

Many early American settlers came from England and other Celtic regions. They brought their various customs with them, which evolved into present-day Halloween.

## ACTIVITY 1 (20 points)

LANGUAGE
Imagine that you are a child in a Celtic community 2000 years ago. Write a description of what happened on the Samhain festival night when you were ten. Tell what you saw, heard, smelled, and how you felt.

## ACTIVITY 2 (20 points)

MATH
Based on the fact that present day Halloween celebrations became popular in this country during the early 1800s, estimate the number of pumpkins that have been carved through the year 1989. Show your calculations. (HINT: Use averages of total people celebrating Halloween each year, and don't forget to figure in our country's population increases.)

## ACTIVITY 3 (20 points)

SOCIAL STUDIES
Write a letter to convince the pastor of your church (who recently gave a sermon saying that Halloween is evil and should be abolished) that present-day Halloween celebrations are just good clean fun.

## ACTIVITY 4 (20 points)

SCIENCE
Imagine that you are a scientist in an ancient Celtic community. Design an experiment to test a hypothesis regarding the effects of the customs (Samhain festival) on health and/or crop success or failure.

## ACTIVITY 5 (20 points)

ART
Sketch out three designs for Jack-O-Lantern faces. Decide which one is best and tell why you think so.

## BONUS (20 points)

Create a "new" Halloween that would be acceptable to everyone regardless of their religious beliefs. What customs would you keep? Which would you do away with? Create an advertisement campaign to sell your "new" holiday to the public.

## Mystery Station Class Project
### (OPTIONAL)

MYSTERY MURALS  (20 points)
Create a Mystery mural similar to the Find Waldo pictures or books. In your mural, use your team or school mascot as the hidden object. Use a topic or theme that is described by the class. A suggestion might come from Science or Social Studies content that you are currently studying. Display your mural in the hall so that other students can have fun solving your mystery.


MYSTERY GAME DAY  (20 points)
Bring in your favorite mystery game to play in class, e.g. Clue or Who Done It? For one class period, students can play their games in cooperative groups with each other.

## ANSWERS

### BERMUDA TRIANGLE

1.  see below

2.  625,000 sq. mi.

3.  more than 50

4.  Many ships and planes have disappeared with no survivors.

5.  Answers will vary. Some possibilities: huge magnetic forces, sudden tidal waves, UFO kidnappings, attacks by sea monsters, and shifting into the fourth dimension.

7.  See map — letters A-J

8.  B, C, D, F, G, H

### MINDSTRETCHERS

| | | | | |
|---|---|---|---|---|
| 1. | Jim=3 | Steve=5 | Chris=4 | |
| 2. | Fluffy=4 | Calico=6 | Tiger=8 | Mittens=12 |
| 3. | Dave=7 | Larry=5 | Ray=4 | Simon=10 |
| 4. | Tina=17 | Sue=14 | Jean=23 | |
| 5. | Tom=142 Joe=170 | Bob=163 | Sam=156 | Pete=184 |
| 6. | Sara=83 Jennifer=92 | | Megan=87 | Lynn=78 |

### LOCH NESS MONSTER

1.  If calculated from 1989 = 1424
2.  camel, giraffe, seal

# Signaling Student Success

## PIONEERS

- Westward Ho!
- Pioneer Problems
- Trailblazers
- Pioneer Prints
- Pioneer Good Luck Symbols
- Adventure!
- Pioneer Scavenger Hunt
- Space Pioneers
- Pioneer Impersonation
- Pioneering the Internet

National Middle School Association

**An Introduction to PIONEERS**

A pioneer is a person who ventures into unexplored or unclaimed territory to explore, open up, or settle a region. Another definition of a pioneer is an innovator or a person who makes discoveries. Pioneers of the past have opened our country for settlement and pioneered the inventions that drive our daily lives. Today the term *pioneer* has been extended to mean a person or group that explores new areas of thought. The pioneers of the future will lead us to life in outer space or under the seas and enhance our lives with inventions yet to be imagined.

Every subject area – whether it be math, science, social studies, language arts, the fine arts, the practical arts, or physical education – has its pioneers, past, present, and future. The activities in these learning stations will help you to meet some of these pioneers, to travel in their footsteps, to discover their innovations, and to look ahead to the pioneers of the future.

## THE GUIDING QUESTIONS:

1. Who are pioneers?

2. What characteristics do pioneers possess?

3. What contributions have pioneers made to contemporary society?

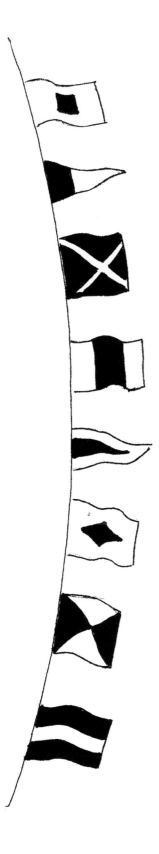

# At a glance — topics and tasks

- **View the westward movement through the eyes of early pioneers**
- **Simulate some of the difficult decisions that pioneers going west had to make**
- **Establish and maintain a nature trail in your area**
- **Experience the pioneer art of stenciling**
- **Design a pioneer barn good luck symbol**
- **Use group brainstorming tools to write and illustrate a short story**
- **Discover some pioneers – those who were first to do, to discover, or to invent something important**
- **Investigate pioneers in space technology**
- **Present a performance as a pioneer autobiography**
- **Discover the pioneers of the information highway**

# Pioneers Rubric

You may select from the following stations. The activity must be done completely, accurately, and neatly to earn full point value. The grading scale is as follows:

| A | B | C | D |
|---|---|---|---|
| **940 pts.** | **850 pts.** | **750 pts.** | **650 pts.** |

| Date Completed | Activity | Possible Points | Points Earned |
|---|---|---|---|
| _____ | Westward Ho! | 100-125 | _____ |
| _____ | Pioneer Problems | 50-100 | _____ |
| _____ | Trailblazers | 100-150 | _____ |
| _____ | Pioneer Prints | 100 | _____ |
| _____ | Pioneer Good Luck Symbols | 75 | _____ |
| _____ | Adventure! | 125 | _____ |
| _____ | Pioneer Scavenger Hunt | 120 | _____ |
| _____ | Space Pioneers | 100 | _____ |
| _____ | Pioner Impersonation | 100 | _____ |
| _____ | Pioneering the Internet | 100 | _____ |

**TOTAL POINTS** _____

**GRADE** _____

# Westward Ho!

**PURPOSE**
To view the westward movement through the eyes of early pioneers

**SPECIAL MATERIALS NEEDED**
Access to the library/media center or a collection of books at the station; blank outline map of the U.S. for each student

**DIRECTIONS** (100 points)
The people who led the movement westward were true pioneers. They were the men and women who opened up new territories and who were hunters, fur traders, farmers, ranchers, and frontier soldiers. These pioneers faced many dangers: illness, injuries, wild animals, and unfriendly Indians. Despite the dangers they were very courageous, inventive, and strong in their resolve to be free and to live their lives as they chose. Through the following activities, you will travel with the pioneers who moved our nation westward.

## ACTIVITY 1 (25 points)

You will be contributing to a class booklet called *Westward Ho*. Each person in the class will select a different pioneer to research and write about. Compose a 1-2 page biography about when and where your pioneer was born and information about their family, childhood, and pioneering experiences. Create a full-page, color illustration to accompany your report.

| | | |
|---|---|---|
| Daniel Boone | Stephen Austin | Jim Baker |
| Robert Rogers | Sam Houston | Calamity Jane |
| James Smith | Jim Bridger | Annie Oakley |
| Alexander Henry | Bill Hickok | Gen. William Wolfskill |
| George Rogers Clark | Jedediah Smith | Gen. Jim Beckwourth |
| Andrew Jackson | Kit Carson | Brigham Young |
| Meriwether Lewis | James C. Fremont | Jesse Applegate |
| William Clark | Charles Goodnight | John Colter |
| Wyatt Earp | William F. Cody | Santa Anna |
| John Colter | George W. Bush | Father Junipero Serra |
| Davy Crockett | Jacob Dodson | Marcus & Narcissa |
| James Bowie | William Travis | Whitman |

## ACTIVITY 2  (25 points)

The movement to the West was affected by the transportation routes from East to West. First, the Appalachian Mountains and then the Rockies stood in the way. So the early pioneers followed river valleys and mountain passes as they made their way west. Take one of the outline maps at this station and locate and label each of the following transportation routes to the west on it.

| | | |
|---|---|---|
| Erie Canal | Mormon Trail | California Trail |
| National Road | Santa Fe Trail | Gila Trail |
| Wilderness Road | Oregon Trail | Old Spanish Trail |

## ACTIVITY 3 (25 points)

What is a wagon train? A Conestoga wagon or prairie schooner? Dig a little to find out what pioneers might have carried west in their wagons. Write the alphabet along the left hand margin of your paper. As you discover the contents of the wagons, write them on the appropriate line. More than one word can go on each line. Finish the list that has been started for you.

A - axe
B - bed, blankets, Bible
C - coffee pot, cooking pots, candles
D -
E -
F -
G -
H -
I -
J -
K -
L -
M -
N -
O -
P -
Q -
R -
S -
T -
U -
V -
W -
X -
Y -
Z -

## ACTIVITY 4 (25 points)

Between 1841 and 1860 the following numbers of people immigrated to California from the eastern and middle western parts of the United States:

| | | |
|---|---|---|
| 1841 ... 34 | 1848 ... 400 | 1855 ... 1,100 |
| 1842 ... 0 | 1849 ... 25,000 | 1856 ... 8,000 |
| 1843 ... 38 | 1850 ... 44,000 | 1857 ... 4,000 |
| 1844 ... 53 | 1851 ... 1000 | 1858 ... 6,000 |
| 1845 ... 260 | 1852 ... 50,000 | 1859 ... 17,000 |
| 1846 ... 1,500 | 1853 ... 20,000 | 1860 ... 9,000 |
| 1847 ... 450 | 1854 ... 12,000 | |

1. How many people immigrated to California in this 21 year period?
2. Why did so many immigrate between 1849 and 1853?
3. Why did people want to immigrate to California?
4. What happened to the Donner Party in 1846? Do you think it affected immigration in 1847 and 1848? Explain.

## BONUS (25 points)

Engage in one of the following computer simulations of "westward expansion."

Oregon Trail (MECC) .................Apple, IBM, Mac
The Forty Niners (ENTREX) .................Apple, IBM
Santa Fe Trail (United Learning)..............Apple
Wagon Train 1848 (MECC) .................Mac
Wagons West (Focus MEDIA) ..............Apple

Upon completing the simulation, write a journal or diary entry about your trip west.

## Pioneer Problems

PURPOSE
To simulate some of the difficult decisions that pioneers going west had to make

SPECIAL MATERIALS NEEDED
History books related to the Donner party (i.e., *The Pioneers*, by Time Life); video - "Donner Pass: Road to Survival"

DIRECTIONS  (50 points)
The life of the American pioneers as they struggled westward was filled with many trials and tribulations. Some people survived the trails west; others were not so fortunate. One of the most famous of the western wagon trains was a group which came to be known as the Donner party. Brothers George and Jacob Donner, neighbor James Reed, their families, and hired hands set out from Illinois to California in 1846. Along the way they were joined by other pioneers. They made many mistakes along the trail, such as overloading their wagons and starting out late in the season. You will become a member of the ill-fated Donner party for these activities.

At the end of each of the following situations, you will be faced with a decision, similar to those faced by the Donner party. When you have finished, you will be asked to compare your decisions to those actually made by the leaders of this famous wagon train.

## ACTIVITY 1 (50 points)

Number your paper from 1-6, skipping four lines after each number. After reading each decision, indicate your choice next to the number. After each choice, explain your decision.

### THE DECISIONS

1. You are behind schedule and winter is fast approaching. You must reach the Sierra Nevada mountains before it snows and blocks the pass. You read in the Hastings' Guidebook that there is a new trail from Fort Bridger in Wyoming to the Sierras that is about 400 miles shorter than the standard Oregon Trail. Unfortunately Langsford Hastings, the one guide who knows the trail, has just left with another wagon train. You must decide what to do. Do you . . .

    A. *take the longer Oregon Trail,* or
    B. *try to make up time on the Hastings' shortcut?*

2.   Your wagon train crossed the Wasatch mountains but the trail was long and hard and you and your oxen are exhausted. Once on the other side of the mountains you find yourself faced with a great barren desert. The guidebook advises you that the desert crossing will take at least two days and two nights of constant hard driving. You decide to rest for a day and a half to build up your strength for the crossing. You start off across the Nevada Desert. Three days and nights later you are still in the desert, you are without water, and the oxen are at the point of collapse. You must decide what to do. Do you . . .

   A. *drive the oxen on to water, leaving your wagons and families behind*, or
   B. *keep pushing with the hope of finding water soon?*

3.   You finally make it across the desert. When you get there and take stock, you find that some of the oxen are in better shape than the others. It is suggested that the party split into two groups with those that can move faster going on ahead. You are being followed by Indians and some members of your party feel you are more at risk by splitting the group. You must decide what to do. Do you . . .

   A. *split the wagon train into two groups*, or
   B. *keep them together?*

4.   The wagon train continues to follow the course of the Humbolt River. Everyone is tired and tempers are on edge. The drivers of two of the wagons fight. James Reed tries to stop them but one of the men, John Snyder, attacks Reed with his bull whip. Reed kills Snyder in self-defense. Some members of the party want to hang Reed on the spot while others want to banish him from the wagon train leaving his family and wagon behind. If banished, he will likely starve to death or be killed by Indians. You must decide what to do. Do you . . .

   A. *kill Reed,*
   B. *banish him,* or
   C. *allow him to remain?*

5.   It is now the twentieth of October and you find yourself at the foot of the Sierra Nevada Mountains. You can see snow on the high ridges of the mountain ahead. The wagon train has been rejoined by one of the members, Charles Stanton, who went on ahead to acquire some supplies. He reports that the climb to the pass is difficult and urges the wagon train to rest for a while. He says you have three or four weeks before the pass is closed by snow. Some of the party agrees that the oxen need to be rested for the long, hard, climb. Others feel the need to keep moving to assure safe passage through the pass. You must decide what to do. Do you . . .

    A. *stop and rest,* or
    B. *continue on?*

6.   You make it to the pass only to find the snow too deep. Attempts to hike across the pass on foot fail. Stanton says that he knows the way to a valley that will protect you. He convinces some of the people to go with him. Others choose to stay in the camp at the pass. You must decide what to do. Do you . . .

    A. *go with Stanton,* or
    B. *stay in the camp?*

Select one of the books at the station. Read about the Donner Party. Go back to the six decisions you have made above. How do your decisions compare to the real ones they made? Write the real decision results on the lines you skipped. What happened to the Donner Party in the end?

---

## BONUS (50 points)

Watch the video "Donner Pass." Take on the personage of one of the characters in the video. Write a journal entry as if you were that person. Choose a situation from the video that caused you to experience a strong emotional reaction.

---

# Trailblazers

PURPOSE
To establish and maintain a nature trail in your area

SPECIAL MATERIALS NEEDED
A variety of field guides, 8 ½ X 11" white paper, poster pieces, markers or colored pencils

DIRECTIONS  (100 points)
The early pioneers and settlers in this country followed trails from place to place that had been made by the Native Americans or animals that inhabited the area. Today we have roads and super highways to travel. However, in our fast-paced, everyday world we seldom stop to enjoy the nature around us. At this station you will work as a team to design and create one section of a nature trail. As a class you will need to decide on an area either on your school grounds or close by that would make an interesting nature trail. The area should have a variety of trees and plants growing there. Obtain permission to create a nature trail in the area you have chosen. Each team of 4-5 students should select a section of the area for which they are responsible. Complete the following trailblazing activities.

## ACTIVITY 1 (25 points)

There will be some cleaning up of your section of the trail that needs to be done. Pick up any trash you find. Pull weeds if needed and pick up hazards like fallen tree limbs.

Draw a map of your section of the trail. Locate points of interest, flora, and fauna for identification.

## ACTIVITY 2 (25 points)

Use the field guides located at the station to help you identify the following items on your section of the trail:

| | | | |
|---|---|---|---|
| grasses | trees | plants | shrubs |
| mushrooms | lichens | rocks | seeds |
| insects | birds | mammals | leaves |
| fungi | mosses | landforms | snails |

## ACTIVITY 3 (10 points)

Make identification signs out of posterboard pieces for each of the things you identified in Activity Two. Have the signs laminated to make them weatherproof. Post the signs on your nature trail.

## ACTIVITY 4 (40 points)

Name your nature trail and create a brochure telling people who created it, how it was created, how long it is, what will be seen along the trail, etc. Include a map of the entire trail. Illustrate the brochure with some of the trail's flora and fauna. Reproduce your brochure to give to visitors of the trail.

## BONUS (25 points)

Send invitations to family members, community members, or other classrooms to visit your nature trail. Act as a nature guide for their visit(s). Write and memorize a script for what you want to say on your trail tour.

## BONUS (10 points)

To make sure there are some wild birds in your nature trail area, make some bird feeders to attract them. There are several kinds of bird feeders you could make. A pine-cone turned upside down, stuffed with a mixture of birdseed and peanut butter, and hung by a cord from a branch makes a good bird feeder. Likewise, suet from the supermarket hung in a plastic mesh bag or berries, raisins, and popcorn strung on heavy thread and wrapped around tree branches can also make effective bird feeders. Make one of these or any other type of bird feeder for your nature trail.

## BONUS (15 points)

Create a Trailblazer's Coloring Book for younger children visiting your nature trail. Include pictures of the flora and fauna found along your trail.

# Pioneer Prints

PURPOSE
To experience the pioneer art of stenciling

SPECIAL MATERIALS NEEDED
Books showing stencil art; file folders cut in various sizes; rulers; 12" X 18" paper; poster paint; small pointed scissors; stiff brush; tissue paper; adding machine tape

DIRECTIONS  (100 points)
The life of the pioneers was hard. There was always plenty of work to be done with crops to plant and harvest, animals to feed and raise, meals to prepare and serve, clothes to make and keep clean, and buildings to construct and maintain. There was no time for fancy decorations in the home. When people did find time for simple household decorating, it often took the form of stenciling. Sometimes the stenciling was done by a creative housewife and sometimes by a traveling barn and house painter who would do his decorating in exchange for room and board and sometimes a small fee. The parlor and the bedrooms were the most often stenciled rooms. Usually a repeating border or a whole wall pattern was used. Frequently a design might be repeated on a chair, chest, table, or headboard, and perhaps on lampshades, bedspreads, or curtains.

The designs ranged from simple (hearts) to complex (patriotic eagles.) Heart and flower designs were often used in the bedroom. The living room was often decorated with stencils of baskets or urns filled with flowers or fruits. The dining room was often decorated with pineapples (the symbol of hospitality.) These stencils were made from heavy paper which was oiled, then dried to make them sturdier. The stencil design was then cut and a thick paint was applied with a stiff brush.

Complete the following activities as directed.

## ACTIVITY 1 (10 points)

Look at the books at the station to find examples of stencil art. List the various designs you find. Star the ones you like the best.

## ACTIVITY 2 (40 points)

1. Create a design you would like to make into a stencil.
2. Draw it the size you want it to be on a piece of file-folder paper (designs smaller than four inches may be too hard to cut.)
3. Shade in the areas to be cut out. This will give you an idea of what your finished design will look like.
4. Cut out the shaded areas in the design with a small, pointed pair of scissors or a craft knife.
5. Choose a piece of paper on which to paint your design. Choose the paint color you wish to use.
6. Place your stencil firmly on the paper. Tape or hold it in place.
7. Dip the brush in the paint; then gently dab the paint over the cutouts.
8. Carefully lift the stencil from the paper. Clean the stencil.
9. Let the first design dry; then repeat the design or paint an alternating design.

## ACTIVITY 3 (25 points)

Use stencils to create wrapping paper to be used for gift wrap.

## ACTIVITY 4 (25 points)

Use small stencils and create a border for a classroom bulletin board. Measure the perimeter of the bulletin board and cut a matching length of adding machine tape. Create an alternating stencil pattern.

## Pioneer Good Luck Symbols

PURPOSE
To design a pioneer good luck barn symbol

SPECIAL MATERIALS NEEDED
8 ½ X 11" white paper, colored pencils or markers, compasses, rulers

DIRECTIONS  (75 points)
In the early seventeenth century, Mennonite and Amish pioneers settled in southern Pennsylvania. Most of the settlers were farmers. They decorated their barns with large, colorful, geometric signs featuring stars and circles. These signs were considered good luck symbols and were thought to bring them good luck and protect them from harm.

The number of points on a star is significant.

| | | |
|---|---|---|
| 4  points | . . . . . . . . | brings good luck |
| 5  points | . . . . . . . . | protects the barn from lightning |
| double 5 points | . . . . . . . . | brings good weather |
| 6  points | . . . . . . . . | brings love and happiness |
| 7  points | . . . . . . . . | protects from harm |
| 8  points | . . . . . . . . | brings good will and freedom |
| 12 points | . . . . . . . . | brings knowledge and wisdom |

## ACTIVITY 2 (25 points)

To visit a Mennonite or Amish community today is like a step back in time. Find out more about these people. Use the media center to discover the following things about their unique lifestyle:

style of dress                 crafts
foods                          celebrations/rituals
leisure activities             sources of energy
mode of transportation         family life

## ACTIVITY 2 (50 points)

Make your own Pennsylvania Dutch geometric signs. Use the figures below to guide you. Follow these steps.

1.  Place a pencil point in the center of your paper.
2.  Place your compass point on the pencil point. Use the compass to draw a large circle on the paper as shown in figure A.
3.  Draw three more circles using the same pencil point as shown in figure B.
4.  Lay your ruler from one side of the circle through the center point to the opposite side of the circle. Draw the line between the inner and outside circle as shown in figure C, line 1. Draw a second line perpendicular to the first as shown in figure C, line 2. Draw a line half way between each of these lines as shown in figure C, lines 3 and 4.
5.  Place points on the outside of the inner circle halfway between each line as shown in figure C.
6.  Use the ruler to draw lines from the top of each line to the points between the lines.
7.  Color and decorate.

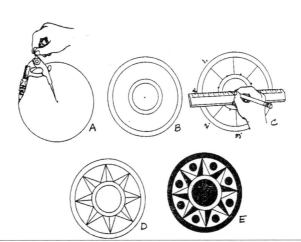

## Adventure

PURPOSE
To use group brainstorming tools to write and illustrate a short story

SPECIAL MATERIALS NEEDED
Story Grid Reproducible Page; anthologies of adventure short stories (e.g., Jack London)

DIRECTIONS  (125 points)
You and the other students at this station will be going on an adventure together as you work through the activities at this station. So, put on your action wear, grab your survival kit, and let's go! Your team is to work together to accomplish each of the following activities.

## ACTIVITY 1 (25 points)

Select one of the short stories found at the station. Take turns reading the story aloud to one another. After listening to the story, respond individually to these questions:
- What was happening in your mind? What were you thinking about?
- What was there about the story that involved you the most?
- Did the ending surprise you?
- What questions/comments come to mind?

## ACTIVITY 2 (25 points)

With your team create a mind map to get you thinking about the topic of adventures and adventurers. As you brainstorm, think of personal experiences, adventures you've read about, or seen in the movies or on TV. Take a large piece of paper and set it up similar to the mind map. Then, start brainstorming!

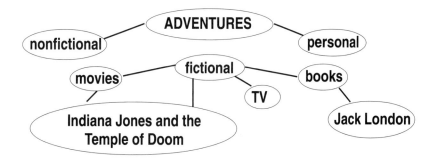

## ACTIVITY 3 (1 point per added item up to 25)

Use the reproducible page at this station entitled Story Grid. The list for each category has been started for you. As a team, add to the list. Some of the ideas may come from your mind map activity.

## ACTIVITY 4 (50 points)

Your team will now use the completed Story Grid to help you write a series of adventure stories. The grid will help give you ideas. You do not have to use all of the ideas in your stories. To begin this writing process, each team member selects a different setting and starts a story on his/her own paper. Write for ten minutes; then stop. You may want to set a timer. At the end of ten minutes, pass your paper to the teammate on your left. Read the story started by your teammate. Set the timer again for ten minutes. Add to the story you now have. Keep rotating the stories around your team, adding to each as they come to you in turn. When the story that you started gets back to you, bring the story to closure. Draw and color a full page picture to illustrate a scene in the story. Share with your teammates.

# STORY GRID

DIRECTIONS

A way to brainstorm before beginning to write a story is to fill out a story grid. Add to what has been started for you in the grid below. You earn one point for each addition you make.

| Protagonist | Antagonist | Setting | Hardship | Reactions | Ending |
|---|---|---|---|---|---|
| family | pack of wolves | wagon train | broken wheel | frightened | rescued |
| child | grizzly bear | mountains | illness | courageous | escaped |
| soldier | cattle rustler | noon | starvation | panicked | survived |
| mountain man | bank robber | Oregon Trail | blizzard | curious | died |
| Indian | gunslinger | Santa Fe | gun wound | tired | won |

## Pioneer Scavenger Hunt

PURPOSE
To discover some pioneers – those who were first to do, to discover, or to invent something important

SPECIAL MATERIALS NEEDED
Access to the library/media center; adding machine tape; 12" X 18" colored construction paper; magazines; scissors; glue sticks

DIRECTIONS  (100 points)
At this station you can work collaboratively if you wish. You will be going on a scavenger hunt. The people you are looking for are pioneers in their fields. They may have been the first to accomplish something, the person who discovered something previously unknown, or the inventor of something new.

## ACTIVITY 1 (30 points)

Complete each of the following questions with a name, country, and year.

**For example:**

Who was the first U.S. president?
<u>George Washington</u>          <u>USA</u>                    <u>1789-1797</u>

Who was the first . . .

1.   to perform a heart transplant?

2.   to map the stars?

3.   to measure the distance to the stars?

4.   to reach the North Pole?

5.   to reach the South Pole?

6.   to fly in a balloon?

7.   woman to fly solo across the world?

8.   woman to orbit the Earth?

9.   person to step on the moon?

10.   to fly nonstop across the Atlantic Ocean?

253

Who discovered . . .

11.  cells?

12.  gravity?

13.  electricity?

14.  relativity?

15.  the structure of DNA?

16.  a cure for scurvy?

17.  why rainbows happen?

18.  the battery?

19.  how the Earth revolves around the sun?

20.  how the planets move?

Who invented . . .

21.  the pendulum clock?

22.  more than 1,000 inventions?

23.  the aqua-lung?

24.  the seismograph?

25.  the barometer?

26.  the ballpoint pen?

27.  the elevator?

28.  bluejeans?

29.  the jet engine?

30.  the laser?

## ACTIVITY 2 (20 points)

1.  Find ten more items to add to the scavenger hunt. Write them on a piece of paper. Add them to the station for others to hunt. Make an answer key. Give it to the teacher.

2.  Complete ten more scavenger hunt items that have been supplied by your classmates.

## ACTIVITY 3  (25 points)

Create a timeline of the firsts, discoveries, and inventions you have just researched.

## ACTIVITY 4  (25 points)

Create a collage that includes at least 25 of the 1,093 patented inventions of Thomas Edison.

255

## Space Pioneers

PURPOSE
To investigate pioneers in space technology

SPECIAL MATERIALS NEEDED
Adding machine tape, red and blue colored pencils

DIRECTIONS (100 points)
Space travel had been an imaginary dream for so long that when the first artificial satellite was launched on October 4, 1957, the world was taken completely by surprise. That pioneer launch, Sputnik 1, was made by the USSR. Two years later a second Soviet rocket hit the moon, and in 1961 a Russian became the first person in space. The space age and the race to explore the solar system had begun. So step into your space suit, fasten down your helmet, and get ready to become a space pioneer yourself!

## ACTIVITY 1 (25 points)

Create a timeline of major events in space exploration over the five decades since Sputnik was launched. The pioneering countries have been primarily the United States and Russia. Measure and cut a five-foot length of adding machine tape. On the bottom left-hand side put a pencil dot and label it vertically "October 4, 1957 - Sputnik 1 - artificial satellite" with a red pencil. With a ruler, measure one inch and pencil in another dot. Label the dot 1960.

Measure one foot from the 1960 dot and make a new dot labeling it 1970. Measure another foot and label the dot 1980. Repeat the procedure for 1990 and the year 2000. As you discover the major events, record them on your time line using a red pencil for Russian launches and a blue pencil for launches made by the United States.

With the room still left on the timeline, predict what future space travel might occur. Would you like to be a pioneer on any future space travel? Would you like to live and work on a space station? On the back of your timeline, respond to these questions. Explain your answers.

256

## ACTIVITY 2 (25 points)

The space program has had many pioneers and supporters over the years. Use reference books or electronic reference sources to help you write a short paragraph about the part each of the following people have played in conquering space:

Werner Von Braun      John F. Kennedy      Sally Ride
Alan B. Shepherd      Christa McAuliffe    Aleksie Leonov
Yuri Gagarin          Neil Armstrong

## ACTIVITY 3 (25 points)

On April 12, 1981, a new type of space craft was launched. Its name was Columbia and it was the pioneer of the American space shuttle. Not only was Columbia the largest space craft, it used a new and unique technique for the return to Earth. Pretend you were a reporter for *The Chicago Tribune* on hand for the Columbia's touchdown in a Southern California desert. Describe the shuttle's return and explain how its landing compared to all previous manned spacecraft re-entries.

## ACTIVITY 4 (25 points)

Choose one of the following situations. To complete this activity:

1.  Pretend you are a travel agent in the year 2050. Design a travel brochure to lure passengers into taking a trip to Mars.

2.  Pretend you want to be a Mars pioneer. Write a letter and a resumé to convince NASA that you are the perfect candidate to send on the first manned mission there.

3.  Pretend you are a famous science fiction novelist. Write a two (or more)-page story that takes place on another planet.

4.  Pretend you are an architect specializing in space communities. Draw a blueprint for a space station which would support 50 space scientists for a year.

5.  Pretend you are a space engineer. Your job is to design and build a device to launch a tennis ball into orbit around the Earth. Use typical household materials to build your launcher. Draw your design. Take your launcher outside for testing. Record the distances of five launches. Make adjustments with each launch trying for improvements. Record the results.

## BONUS (5 points each)

Do you have "the right stuff"? To be a pioneer takes courage, a keen sense of observation, the ability to think quickly, and a willingness to try new ways of doing things. Try these brainteasers to see if you have what it takes.

1.  You are exploring here on Earth. You find yourself in a place where no matter which direction you turn your compass always points North. Where are you? Explain.

2.  By moving four toothpicks, can you change this pattern so that only two squares remain?

3.  The following multiplication problem uses each numeral from 0 to 9 only once (both in the problem and the answer but not in the intermediate steps).

$$\begin{array}{r} 2XX \\ \underline{X4} \\ XX0XX \end{array}$$

4.  Two men and two women sat around a square table. All but one of them were astronauts. Bob sat facing Joe. Sue and Joe sat across from astronauts. Ann sat next to Bob and Joe. Sue and Ann each sat next to two astronauts. Who was not the astronaut?

---

## Pioneer Impersonations

PURPOSE
To present a performance as a pioneer autobiography


SPECIAL MATERIALS NEEDED
Access to the library/media center; access to a video camera


DIRECTIONS  (100 points)
Choose one of the people listed below to research. Note that all of them fit our unit definition of pioneers – persons who venture into unexplored territories, who open up new opportunities for those following behind, and whose discoveries or inventions change our lives. Complete all the activities that follow. Be prepared to share your impersonation with the class.

---

## ACTIVITY

Matthew Henson
Guion Stewart Bluford, Jr.
Dr. May C. Jemison
Jackie Robinson
Thurgood Marshall
Sandra Day O'Conner
Jesse Owens
Dr. Ellen Ochva
Cesar Chavez
Leonardo da Vinci
Alexander Graham Bell
Amelia Earhart
Dale Messick
Susan B. Anthony

Wilma Rudolph
Elizabeth Blackwell
Pearl S. Buck
Jeannette Rankin
Juliette Gordon Law
Howard Jenner
Louis Pasteur
Dr. Floyd A. Hall
Franklin Ramon
   Chang-Diaz
Jonas Salk
Walt Disney
Margaret Mead
Babe Didrickson
Martin Luther King, Jr.

Jane Addams
Harriet Tubman
Henry Ford
George Washington
   Carver
Thomas Alva Edison
Meriwether Lewis
William Clark
Eli Whitney
Samuel Morse
Shirley Chisolm
Jesse Jackson
Benjamin Banneker
Garrett Morgan

KNOWLEDGE (20 points)
1.  Locate information about the person you chose to study.
2.  Discover who this person was, what this person did, why (s)he might be considered a pioneer, when and where this person lived, and how you might portray this person.

COMPREHENSION (10 points)
1.  Determine the characteristics that make this person special.
2.  Suggest how this person has impacted our lives.


APPLICATION (10 points)
1.  Plan how you will impersonate this person and what information you will share.
2.  Experiment with your plan to refine it.


ANALYSIS (10 points)
1.  Transform yourself into this person by taking on his/her physical characteristics.
2.  Select props, costume, setting, etc., that will help transform you.


SYNTHESIS (35 points)
1.  Write your script for a two- to three-minute oral or video taped presentation.
2.  Perform your presentation live for the class or present your video production.


EVALUATION (15 points)
1.  Critique your performance.
2.  Decide what you could do to improve your performance if you were to do this again.

# Pioneering the Internet

PURPOSE
To discover the pioneers of the information highway

SPECIAL MATERIALS NEEDED
Access to *Current Biography*, *The Reader's Guide to Periodic Literature*, and current magazines and newspapers

DIRECTIONS (100 points)
Complete the following activities.

## ACTIVITY 1 (25 points)

Vinton Cerf and Robert E. Kahn created the world's largest network, Internet. The Internet links more than 27,000 computer networks and over 20,000,000 users worldwide. Cerf predicts there will be over one billion networks on the Internet soon. In 1973, Cerf and Kahn were commissioned by the United States government to create a communications system with no central control point. That way if one part of the network was shut down by attack, the users could just switch to another route and keep communicating. Later the two pioneers envisioned the power of the Internet as a research tool. Then their vision expanded to e-mail.

Locate information on one of the following topics:

| | | | |
|---|---|---|---|
| Cerf and Kahn | Prodigy | Comp-U-Serve | e-mail |
| Internet | America Online | E-World | |

## ACTIVITY 2 (50 points)

Share what you learned about the topic from Activity 1 in one of the following ways:

| | | | |
|---|---|---|---|
| exhibit | pamphlet | written report | oral report |
| news story | debate | editorial | video tape |

## ACTIVITY3 (25 points)

1. Survey at least ten people from each of the following categories. Ask them if they use e-mail or the Internet. Create a survey form to discover if they use it for schoolwork, their job, communication with family and friends, research, recreation, etc.

<blockquote>classmates        teachers        family        businesses</blockquote>

2. Design a chart or graph to display your findings.

---

### PIONEERS - ANSWER KEY

Westward Ho!
1. 199,835 people
2. California gold rush
3. Land of opportunity
4. Snowed in at Donner Pass, many died

Hard Decisions
1. B     They lost time and exhausted the oxen.
2. A     They lost six travel days and almost 100 oxen.
3. A     They lost more oxen.
4. B     Reed led the rescue party back to them.
5. A     The snow fell early and blocked their passage.
6. A or B  Most of those that left died; most of those who stayed lived.

Scavenger Hunt

| | | | |
|---|---|---|---|
| 1. | Christiaan Barnard | South Africa | 1967 |
| 2. | Hipparchus | Rhodes | 134 B.C. |
| 3. | Frederich Wilhelm Bessel | Prussia | 1838 |
| 4. | Matthew Henson & Robert Peary | USA | 1909 |
| 5. | Roald Amundson | Norway | 1912 |
| 6. | Montgolfier Brothers | France | 1783 |
| 7. | Amy Johnson | England | 1930's |
| 8. | Valentina Tereshkova | Russia | 1963 |
| 9. | Neil Armstrong | USA | 1969 |
| 10. | John Alcock & Arthur Brown | Britain | 1919 |
| 11. | Robert Hooke | Britain | 1665 |
| 12. | Isaac Newton | Britain | 1642 |
| 13. | Luigi Galvani | Italy | 1780 |
| 14. | Albert Einstein | USA | 1905 |

| 15. | Francis Crick and | Britain | |
| | James Watson | USA | 1953 |
| 16. | James Lind | Scotland | 1947 |
| 17. | Isaac Newton | Britain | 1665 |
| 18. | Alesandro Volta | Italy | 1800 |
| 19. | Aristarchus | Alexandra | about 280 B.C. |
| 20. | Claudius Ptolemy | Egypt | about 200 A.D. |
| 21. | Christian Huygens | Holland | 1657 |
| 22. | Thomas Edison | USA | 1867-1931 |
| 23. | Jacques Cousteau | France | 1930's |
| 24. | Chang Heng | China | 100 A.D. |
| 25. | Evangelista Torricelli | Italy | 1643 |
| 26. | Lazeo Biro | Hungary | 1935 |
| 27. | Elisha Otis | USA | 1847 |
| 28. | Levi Strauss | USA | 1847 |
| 29. | Frank Whittle | Britain | 1929 |
| 30. | Theodore Maiman | USA | 1960 |

Space Pioneers

1.  South Pole

2.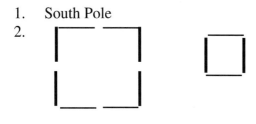

3.      297
          54
      16,038

4.  Sue

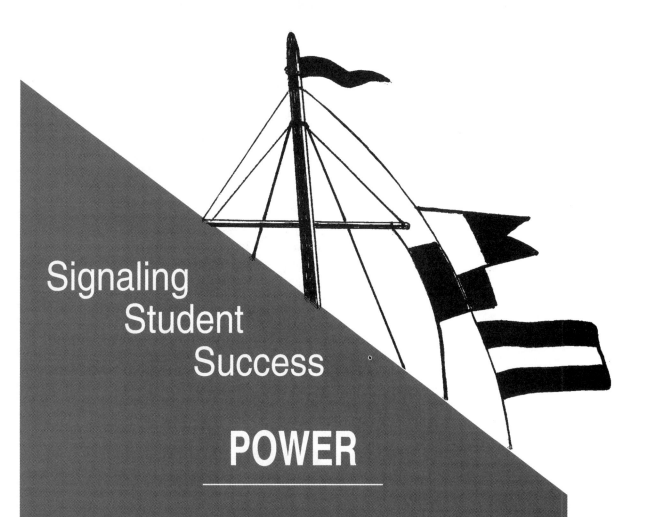

# Signaling Student Success

# POWER

- Power Plays
- Powers and Exponents
- The Power of Percentages
- Powers of Ten
- Power of Optical Illusions
- Make Friends with Your Power Dictionary
- The Power of Metaphors
- Powerful Characters in Literature
- The Powers of Government
- Powerful Messages Sent by Powerful People Over Time
- How Things Work by Power
- The Power of Work
- It's in the Wind Power
- The Power of Advertising
- Unlock Your Power Feelings

National Middle School Association

264

## An Introduction to POWER

**Although *power* is a simple five letter word that is spelled much the way it is pronounced, the actual idea of "power" is complex with many different definitions and interpretations.**

In mathematics, we refer to the power of numbers because they rule our lives in so many ways. People have social security numbers, charge account numbers, telephone numbers, and many other. Likewise, people are influenced by statistics when it comes to such issues as crime, abuse, income, divorce, school drop-outs, suicides, and television viewing habits.

In social studies, we think about the power of great leaders and nations. Many consider the power of authority to reflect intelligence, opportunity, challenge, and responsibility. People in power make decisions that start wars, lower taxes, pass laws, or sentence criminals.

In science, we rely on the more technical definitions of power that deal with the study of simple or complex machines and the transfer of energy in order to perform work. Power, in this case, is considered a part of the basic physical science principles that govern our ability to understand the world around us.

In language arts, we find excitement in the power of the written and spoken word. People are said to be empowered when they are able to read, write, speak, and communicate with others. By contrast, they are said to be powerless when lacking these tools of communication.

In short, the concept of "power" has many meanings and can be applied to any subject area or topic. We can look at power from several perspectives – intellectual, scientific, literal, or emotional. We all have the power to control our own lives in some way, shape, or form!

### THE GUIDING QUESTIONS

1. What are the literal and interpretive definitions of power?

2. How does one look at power from several different perspectives or subject areas?

3. What applications of the concept "power" can be found in the real world?

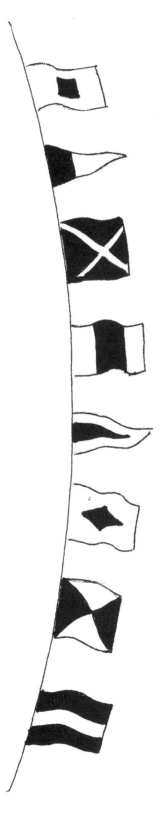

# At a glance — topics and tasks

- Show students a variety of definitions, interpretations, and applications of the concept "power."

- Review the concept of powers and exponents in mathematics and show how numbers can be used in powerful ways

- Show how decimal fractions or decimals are fractions with denominators of 10 or powers of 10

- Show students the power of optical illusions to challenge one's preconceived notions

- Encourage dictionary use as a tool for discovering the power of words and show how metaphors are used to enrich the power of language

- Help students recognize how writers use the idea of power in building their characters

- Review ways that the concept of power is used in both our Constitution and our government

- Discover the powerful messages and legacies of figures from history

- Research various power sources used to operate machines and pieces of equipment

- Examine the scientific definitions of power and translate them into formulas for discovering the relationship between energy and work

- Explore the power of the wind and its influence on weather

- Examine the power of advertising by analyzing a popular children's fad

- Encourage student expression of personal feelings about powerful ideas that are often complex and opposite in their meaning or context

266

## Power Rubric

You may select from the following stations. Activities chosen must be done completely, accurately, and neatly to earn full point value. The grading scale is as follows:

| A | B | C | D |
|---|---|---|---|
| 1580 pts. | 1440 pts. | 1300 pts. | 1170 pts. |

| Date Completed | Activity | Possible Points | Points Earned |
|---|---|---|---|
| _____ | Power Plays | 100-120 | _____ |
| _____ | Powers And Exponents | 30-40 | _____ |
| _____ | The Power Of Percentages | 120-140 | _____ |
| _____ | Powers Of Ten | 60-70 | _____ |
| _____ | Power Of Optical Illusions | 50-60 | _____ |
| _____ | Make Friends With Your Power Dictionary | 80-100 | _____ |
| _____ | The Power Of Metaphors | 50-100 | _____ |
| _____ | Powerful Characters In Literature | 80-100 | _____ |
| _____ | The Powers Of Government | 80-100 | _____ |
| _____ | Powerful Messages of Powerful People | 110-130 | _____ |
| _____ | How Things Work By Power | 50-100 | _____ |
| _____ | The Power Of Work | 60-100 | _____ |
| _____ | It's In The Wind Power | 100-130 | _____ |
| _____ | The Power of Advertising | 60-80 | _____ |
| _____ | Unlock Your Power Feelings | 30-100 | _____ |
| | | **TOTAL POINTS** | _____ |
| | | **GRADE** | _____ |

# Power Plays

PURPOSE

To show students a variety of definitions, interpretations, and applications of the concept "power" in their home, school, and community

SPECIAL MATERIALS NEEDED

Dictionary and/or thesaurus

DIRECTIONS  (100 points)

Complete each of the five required activities according to the guidelines given.

---

## ACTIVITY 1  (20 points)

Label each of these "power" definitions with one or more of the following subject areas: Math, Science, Social Studies, Language Arts, Physical Education, or The Arts.

| | |
|---|---|
| _____ | Exponents |
| _____ | Measure of the magnification of an optical instrument |
| _____ | The might of a nation, political organization, or similar group |
| _____ | An offensive maneuver in a team game |
| _____ | Greek Gods and Goddesses |
| _____ | Renaissance Movement |

---

## ACTIVITY 2  (20 points)

Briefly give an example from history, personal experience, or research to illustrate the meaning of any four of these "power-related" ideas:

1. Power of the pen
2. Power of the sword
3. Power play
4. Power politics
5. Power broker
6. Power of attorney
7. Power pack
8. Power of numbers or statistics

## ACTIVITY 3 (20 points)

In your own words, explain what you think is meant by any two of these quotations:

1. *The great secret of power is never to will to do more than you can accomplish.* — Henrik Ibsen

2. *The imbecility of men is always inviting the impudence of power.*
    — Ralph Waldo Emerson

3. *The qualities that get a man into power are not those that lead him, once established, to use power wisely.* — Lyman Bryson

4. *The only prize much cared for by the powerful is power. The prize of the general is not a bigger tent, but command.* — Oliver Wendell Holmes, Jr.

## ACTIVITY 4 (20 points)

Give an interesting or unusual example for each of the following "power" options and be able to defend your choices:
1. A powerful leader
2. A powerful book
3. A powerful movie or play
4. A powerful image
5. A powerful word
6. A powerful piece of music or art
7. A powerful sport
8. A powerful invention
9. A powerful event
10. A powerful math formula or application
11. A powerful science principle or law
12. A powerful place

## ACTIVITY 5 (20 points)

Write a good paragraph discussing some things in your personal life or experiences that make you (or have made you) feel a sense of "power" or a sense of "powerlessness."

## BONUS (20 points)

Create an international symbol to represent the concept of power.

## Powers and Exponents

PURPOSE
To review the concept of powers and exponents in the area of mathematics

SPECIAL MATERIALS NEEDED
Math textbook

DIRECTIONS  (30 points)
To find the powers of a number, multiply the number over and over by itself. The first power is the number. The second power is the product of the number multiplied once by itself. The third power is the number multiplied twice by itself, etc. There is a special way of writing the power of a number called an "exponent." It is the very small number written above and to the right side of the number.

EXAMPLE  $2^1 = 2$  $1 = 2$  $2^2 = 2$  $2 = 4$  $2^3 = 2$  $2$  $2 = 8$

### ACTIVITY  (30 points)

Create a chart to show the powers of the numbers from 1 through 9 beginning with the first power and ending with the tenth power.

### BONUS  (10 points)

Is there a zero power? Prove your answer.

## The Power of Percentages

PURPOSE
To show how numbers can be used in interesting ways to document errors and encourage accuracy when computing facts and figures

SPECIAL MATERIALS NEEDED
None

DIRECTIONS  (120 points)
Complete each of the following activities in the order given.

---

## ACTIVITY 1 (20 points)

KNOWLEDGE:          Define the concept of "percentage" in math and record the steps in converting a decimal to a percentage from memory – or from a textbook if your memory is faulty!

---

## ACTIVITY 2 (20 points)

COMPREHENSION:  In your own words, describe in some detail three or more real life situations when you would need to understand the calculation, use, and power of percentages.

---

## ACTIVITY 3 (20 points)

APPLICATION:         Interview at least five students in your math class and determine whether they find the study of percentages easy or hard to learn and why. Summarize your notes and findings in one or two good paragraphs.

---

## ACTIVITY 4 (20 points)

ANALYSIS:              Examine the percentage figures which follow and determine why 99.9 percent is not always good enough!

### *If 99.9 percent is good enough, then . . .*

- 811,000 faulty rolls of 35 mm film will be loaded this year.
- 22,000 checks will be deducted from the wrong bank accounts in the next 60 minutes
- 12 babies will be given to the wrong parents each day.
- 14,208 defective personal computers will be shipped this year.
- 2,488,200 books will be shipped in the next 12 months with the wrong cover.
- 5,517,200 cases of soft drinks produced in the next 12 months will be flatter than a bad tire.
- Two plane landings daily at O'Hare International Airport in Chicago will be unsafe.
- 18,322 pieces of mail will be mishandled in the next hour.
- 880,000 credit cards in circulation will turn out to have incorrect cardholder information on their magnetic strips.
- $9,690 will be spent today, tomorrow, next Thursday, and every day in the future on defective, often unsafe sporting equipment.
- 20,000 incorrect drug prescriptions will be written in the next 12 months.
- 114,500 mismatched pairs of shoes will be shipped this year.
- $761,900 will be spent in the next 12 months on tapes and compact discs that won't play.
- 107 incorrect medical procedures will be performed by the end of the day.
- 315 entries in Webster's Third New International Dictionary of the English Language will turn out to be misspelled.

SOURCE: Unknown

---

## ACTIVITY 5 (20 points)

SYNTHESIS:  Create a bumper sticker that encourages others to "strive for perfection" based on this set of activities.

---

## ACTIVITY 6 (20 points)

EVALUATION:  Select the five most frightening statistics for you from the list presented in the Analysis activity and defend your choices.

---

## BONUS (20 points)

What does the expression "to play the percentages" mean in the real world of business, sports, or politics? Explain.

## Powers of Ten

PURPOSE
To show how decimal fractions or decimals are fractions with denominators of 10 or powers of 10

SPECIAL MATERIALS NEEDED
Math textbook

DIRECTIONS  (60 points)
Decimal fractions or decimals are really just fractions with denominators of 10 or powers of 10.

EXAMPLE    10, 100, 1,000, 10,000, and so on

Decimal fractions are written using a decimal point.

EXAMPLE    1/10 = .1        1/100 = .01     1/1000 = .001

A fraction is written as a decimal fraction (or decimal) by eliminating the denominator and adding a decimal point as many places to the left of the numerator as there are zeroes in the denominator.

EXAMPLE    25/100 = 25 ÷ 100 (count over two places) = .25
6/10 = 6 ÷ 10 (count over one place) = .6

Applying what you know about fractions and decimals, write out a quality example for each of the following situations:

## ACTIVITY 1 (10 points)

Situation:     Changing a Fraction to a Decimal

## ACTIVITY 2 (10 points)

Situation:     Changing a Decimal to a Fraction

## ACTIVITY 3 (10 points)

Situation:     Adding Decimals

## ACTIVITY 4 (10 points)

Situation:     Subtracting Decimals

## ACTIVITY 5 (10 points)

Situation:     Multiplying Decimals

## ACTIVITY 6 (10 points)

Situation:     Dividing Decimals

## BONUS (10 points)

What reminders, rules, or cautions would you give a classmate who was learning how to multiply or divide decimals?

# Power of Optical Illusions

## PURPOSE
To show students the power of optical illusions by challenging one's preconceived notions, experiences, and perceptions of a reality.

## SPECIAL MATERIALS NEEDED
Reference books and examples of popular optical illusions

## DIRECTIONS  (50 points)
An optical illusion has the power to "make you believe what you see" even though your eyes and your mind are both playing tricks on you. Optical illusions are, by definition, situations or conditions which cause us to be deceived by a false perception or belief.

Study each of the optical illusions below and try to figure out the deception being demonstrated and/or the explanation of why "seeing is not believing."

## ACTIVITY  (50 points)

A. Which is longer, line "a" or line "b"?

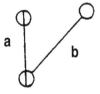

B. Do these circles sit on level ground or do they arch upwards?

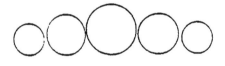

C. Is the church tower longer than the base of the church?

D. What is the matter with this triangle?

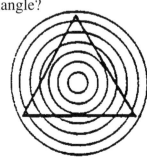

E.  Turn this graphic in a circle clockwise. Then turn it in a circle counter-clockwise. Is there a difference, besides just their direction?

## BONUS (10 points)

Write a review of any of the books on optical illusions that you find at the learning station, the school media center, or your community library.

---

ANSWERS:

A. In each figure, "a" equals "b"
B. They all sit on level ground.
C. Height is the same as the width (with tower)
D. Nothing, but your eyes follow the intersecting lines, and that makes the sides look crooked.
E. Clockwise, the distance between the lines seems to constrict. Counter-clockwise, the distances between the lines appear to expand.

## Make Friends with Your Power Dictionary

PURPOSE
To encourage use of the dictionary as a tool for discovering the power of words

SPECIAL MATERIALS NEEDED
Dictionary

DIRECTIONS  (80 points)
Complete each of the dictionary tasks outlined below.

### ACTIVITY 1 (20 points)

Write down three good reasons why it is important for you to build and use a solid vocabulary while in school.

### ACTIVITY 2 (20 points)

Did you know that there are only twelve simple words which account for one-fourth of everything spoken and written in English? These "most-used" words are: *a, and, he, I, in, it, is, of, that, the, to,* and *was.* Randomly select a full page from a novel, short story, or literature series you are reading in class and tally the number of times each of these twelve words appears on that page. Graph the results.

### ACTIVITY 3 (20 points)

Read carefully every word on "one" page of your dictionary. Record ten things that you discovered about the origin and meaning of any word entries of interest to you.

## ACTIVITY 4 (20 points)

Open the dictionary up to any page and select a word on that page with which you are not familiar. Design a king-size dictionary page for that word which includes the following information about it:

1. Its correct spelling
2. Its syllabication
3. Its pronunciation
4. Its part(s) of speech
5. Its meaning(s)
6. Its origin
7. Synonyms for the word
8. Antonyms for the word
9. Anything else about the word

## BONUS (20 points)

Make a list of the ten most powerful words you can think of in the English language. Be ready to defend your choices!

## The Power of Metaphors

PURPOSE
To show how metaphors are used to enrich the power and images of language

SPECIAL MATERIALS NEEDED
None

DIRECTIONS  (50 points)
A metaphor is a figure of speech that combines two objects or ideas that are, for the most part, different from each other but turn out to be alike in some special way. Metaphors are used in all subject areas including science, home economics/shop, math, social studies, physical education, and language arts. They are a way of explaining abstract ideas in more concrete or down-to-earth terms.

Complete each of the following phrases (which are also metaphors) according to the category of words specified. In each category, an example is done to get you started.

## ACTIVITY 1  (10 points)

METAPHORS USING HUMAN BODY PARTS

Example — wet behind the _____ (ears)

1.    _____ of a needle
2.    turn the other _____
3.    get it off your _____
4.    _____ jerk reaction
5.    _____ of the matter

## BONUS  (10 points)

Tthink of a common metaphor for each of these body parts — *tooth, foot, shoulder, back.*

## ACTIVITY 2 (10 points)

METAPHORS USING ITEMS OF CLOTHING

Example — tied to his mother's _____ strings (apron)

1. To have something up your _____
2. A feather in one's _____
3. Fits like a _____
4. Goody two-_____
5. Living on a _____

## BONUS (10 points)

Tthink of a common metaphor for each of these items of clothing — *belt, pants, bonnet, collar.*

## ACTIVITY 3 (10 points)

METAPHORS USING COLORS OF THE SPECTRUM

Example — paint the town _____ (red)

1. Once in a _____ moon
2. Every cloud has a _____ lining
3. He looks at the world through _____-colored glasses
4. The committee gave her proposal the _____ light
5. _____ journalism

## BONUS (10 points)

Think of a common metaphor for each of these colors of the spectrum — *pink, red, black, gold.*

## ACTIVITY 4 (10 points)

METAPHORS USING FOODS

Example – crying in his _____ (soup)

1. cool as a _____
2. the proof of the _____
3. flat as a _____
4. nutty as a _____
5. It's a piece of _____

## BONUS (10 points)

Think of a common metaphor for each of these types of food — *bacon, nut, egg, beans.*

## ACTIVITY 5 (10 points)

METAPHORS USING MUSICAL TERMS

Example — play second _____ (fiddle)

1. a soap _____
2. blow your own _____
3. an up _____ attitude
4. Don't give me a _____ and _____.
5. reach a fever _____

## BONUS (10 points)

Think of a common metaphor for each of these musical terms — *tune, drum, harp, bandwagon*

Try drawing some of these metaphorical expressions so that your art work reflects the literal meaning!

## Powerful Characters in Literature

PURPOSE
To help students recognize how authors and writers use the idea of power in building their characters

SPECIAL MATERIALS NEEDED
Reference books on myths, legends, fairy tales, and tall tales

DIRECTIONS (80 points)
Browse through the reference books at this center looking for characters from famous myths, legends, fairy tales, and tall tales who exhibit some type of special power in their actions, deeds, relationships, physical appearance/dress, or life style.

## ACTIVITY (80 points)

Choose a favorite mythological character, legendary character, fairy tale character, and tall tale character to write about. Describe the "power of each of these characters" in a series of four brief character sketches. Make each character sketch one good paragraph in length.

## BONUS (20 points)

Write an autobiographical tall tale using yourself as the main character who has superhuman or supernatural powers to do extraordinary things at home or at school.

## The Powers of Government

PURPOSE
To review ways that the concept of power is used in both our United States Constitution and our United States government

SPECIAL MATERIALS NEEDED
Reference books on U.S. Constitution and Government

DIRECTIONS  (80 points)
Research to find out as much information as you can about the powers of the United States Constitution and the powers of the branches of government. Use this information to complete the tasks below. Write your answers on a separate piece of paper.

## ACTIVITY 1 (10 points)

In your own words, explain how the Constitution provides for a federal system of government in which power is divided between the states and the federal government.

## ACTIVITY 2 (10 points)

In your own words, describe how power is shared through representation of the people in the House of Representatives versus the Senate.

## ACTIVITY 3 (10 points)

In your own words, summarize the meaning of "checks and balances" in our United States government.

## ACTIVITY 4 (10 points)

List the powers of the Legislative Branch.

## ACTIVITY 5 (10 points)

List the powers of the Judicial Branch.

## ACTIVITY 6 (10 points)

List the powers of the Executive Branch.

## ACTIVITY 7 (10 points)

List the powers of the President.

## ACTIVITY 8 (10 points)

List the order of power if a President is unable to serve out a term and must pass on the Presidential power to someone else.

## BONUS (20 points)

Create an editorial cartoon or locate one that represents some idea related to power.

284

## Powerful Messages of Powerful People

PURPOSE
To discover the powerful messages of figures from history who have left a legacy for us to remember

SPECIAL MATERIALS NEEDED
Reference books and access to media center

DIRECTIONS  (110 points)
The United States has produced many powerful people with many powerful messages over time. Work with a friend to research and write down what you think each of these deceased figures from American history has left behind as their legacy to our society.

## ACTIVITY  (110 points)

Athlete:    Arthur Ashe

President:    John F. Kennedy

Civil Rights Leader:    Martin Luther King, Jr.

Entertainer:    Elvis Presley

Inventor:    Eli Whitney

Author:    Jack London

Leader:    Sitting Bull

Manufacturer:    Henry Ford

Artist:    Grandma Moses

Frontiersman:    Daniel Boone

Pioneer:    Charles Lindbergh

## BONUS  (20 points)

Design a trophy, award, monument, or headstone to honor one of these individuals.

## How Things Work by Power

PURPOSE
To research how various power sources and principles are used to operate many common machines, pieces of equipment, and inventions.

SPECIAL MATERIALS NEEDED
Access to reference books and media center

DIRECTIONS  (50 points)
So often we take many fabulous inventions for granted because they have become so common and so integrated in our daily living experiences. Choose one of the common machines or pieces of equipment listed below to research and study. Discover the scientific power principles behind your choice.

## ACTIVITY (50 points)

Draw a simple diagram and write out a brief explanation about the object of your research, telling something about both its source of power and how that power makes the thing work!

Finally, work with a small group of friends and choose one of the machines or pieces of equipment to "act out" as a pantomime. See if your classmates can guess which one you are operating and demonstrating!

### POSSIBLE INVENTIONS TO RESEARCH AND STUDY

| | | |
|---|---|---|
| air conditioner | funicular | security system |
| camera | hair dryer | sewing machine |
| carousel | helicopter | ski lift |
| cash register | hydrofoil | telegraph |
| compact disc player | jet engine | telephone |
| computer | lawn mower | television |
| digital clock | microwave oven | vacuum cleaner |
| dishwasher | motorcycle | vending machine |
| electric guitar | piano | video game |
| elevator | pinball machine | video recorder |
| food processor | sailboard | X-ray machine |

## BONUS (50 points)

Find out who Rube Goldberg was and create a Rube Goldberg invention that relies on very unique power sources to do its work!

## The Power of Work

PURPOSE
To examine the scientific definitions of work and power and to translate these definitions into formulas for discovering the relationship between energy and work

SPECIAL MATERIALS NEEDED
Reference books and textbooks on work, force, and motion

DIRECTIONS  (60 points)
Do each of the following activities.

## ACTIVITY 1  (30 points)

In scientific terms, work is energy transferred both through force and motion. For work to be done, there must be force, there must be motion, and the motion must be in the direction of the force. That is to say, work is done when an object moves while there is a force acting in the direction of motion. The amount of work done is found by multiplying the force times the distance that the object moves. The mathematical formula is: $W = F \cdot d$. W means work done, F means force in the direction of motion, and d means distance moved. Solve the problem below for practice.

PROBLEM    If a student's skateboard weighs 20 pounds and the student lifts the skateboard a distance of six feet over his head, how much work is done in the lifting of the skateboard?

Now . . . make up three similar problems of your own using this formula. Provide an answer key for your solutions.

## ACTIVITY 2  (30 points)

Power, on the other hand, is the work done divided by the time it took to do it. The mathematical formula is: P = work - time. P means power used, work means work done and time means amount of time to do the work. Solve the problem below for practice.

PROBLEM:  If you and a friend take a bike trip up a hill and the bikes weigh the same and you weigh the same but it takes your friend ten minutes longer to get to the top, what power was used in the process?

Now . . . make up three similar problems of your own using this formula. Provide an answer key for your solutions.

## BONUS  (40 points)

There is much difference in the way work is done in industrialized and unindustrialized countries of the world. Compare an industry, such as farming, fishing, or manufacturing in the United States and a Third World country. Determine where work is done with less human effort and what makes this possible.

## It's in the Wind Power

PURPOSE
To explore the power of the wind and its influence on weather conditions and patterns

SPECIAL MATERIALS NEEDED
Reference books on wind and weather; assorted construction materials for making models of windmills, kites, wind socks, or pinwheels

DIRECTIONS  (100 points)
Wind is created when air flows from an area of high pressure to an area of lower pressure. The sun heats up some parts of the earth more than others. The air above these "hot spots" is warmed, too, and rises. Air flows from higher pressure areas to these low-pressure areas unless something changes the direction of the wind such as mountains, buildings, forests, and rotation of the earth.

There is a wind-rating scale called the Beaufort Scale which describes how the wind behaves at various speeds. A calm day rates a 0, while a hurricane rates a 12. The Beaufort Wind Scale is shown on a separate page.

Complete each of the "wind" activities below to determine the power of the wind on any given day or in any given setting. Record your observations and findings in a learning log.

## ACTIVITY 1  (20 points)

On a windy day, go outside and look for the following "windy" situations:

a.   The effect of wind on trees, leaves, and branches
b.   The effect of wind on people going about their work or personal business
c.   The effect of wind on the grass or flowers in the ground
d.   The effect of wind on litter lying on the ground
e.   The effect of wind on man-made objects such as swings, doors, telephone wires, clothing, flags, or signs

Record what you see, feel, hear, and smell in your learning log.

## ACTIVITY 2 (20 points)

Design a chart to record the strength or power of the wind for a two week period of time using the Beaufort Wind Scale for this purpose. Include this chart in your learning log.

## ACTIVITY 3 (20 points)

Browse through some poetry books looking for poems about the wind. Can you find a different poem that reflects each of the 12 levels of the Beaufort Wind Scale? Copy the poems that you find in your learning log and label each one with a Beaufort number from 1 to 12.

## ACTIVITY 4 (20 points)

Locate a book of Van Gogh paintings. Look at the way he uses color, line, and texture to depict the effects of wind and movement in his pictures. Write down your observations in your learning log. Try to create an original version of a Van Gogh painting using thick paint and bold streaks of color.

## ACTIVITY 5 (20 points)

Locate a pattern or design for making a windmill, wind sock, or pin wheel. Construct one of these objects and demonstrate its use.

## BONUS (30 points)

Plan a kite flying contest for students in your school. Determine the time, place, rules, entry requirements, and prizes.

## THE BEAUFORT WIND SCALE

| BEAUFORT NUMBER | KM/H | MPH | DESCRIPTION |
|---|---|---|---|
| 0 | less than 1 | | Calm: smoke rises vertically |
| 1 | 1-5 | 1-3 | Light air: not enough to move a wind vane, but shows in smoke drift |
| 2 | 6-11 | 4-7 | Light breeze: wind felt on face, leaves rustle, wind vanes moved by wind |
| 3 | 12-19 | 8-12 | Gentle breeze: leaves and small twigs in constant motion, enough to blow a light flag |
| 4 | 20-29 | 13-18 | Moderate: raises dust and loose paper; moves small branches |
| 5 | 30-39 | 19-24 | Fresh: small trees in leaf begin to sway, crested wavelets form on inland waters. |
| 6 | 40-50 | 25-31 | Strong: large branches move, umbrellas used with difficulty |
| 7 | 51-61 | 32-38 | Near gale: whole trees in motion, inconvenience in walking against the wind |
| 8 | 62-74 | 39-46 | Gale: wind breaks twigs off trees, makes walking difficult |
| 9 | 75-87 | 47-54 | Strong gale: slight damage occurs to building structures |
| 10 | 88-102 | 55-63 | Storm: trees uprooted, considerable damage |
| 11 | 103-121 | 64-72 | Violent storm: widespread damage |
| 12 | over 122 | over 73 | Hurricane |

## The Power of Advertising

PURPOSE

To examine the power of advertising through analysis of the commercialization of a popular children's fad or fantasy.

SPECIAL MATERIALS NEEDED

Display of items and ads based on a current Disney movie or children's television program

DIRECTIONS  (60 points)

Think about the many toy fads and fantasies that you have experienced growing up and that you now see other young children enjoying. Marketing of toys and related items through the media (radio, television, newspaper, magazines, billboards, promotional flyers/coupons, etc.) is big business for many toy manufacturers, and millions of dollars are spent on this task every year.

Among recent movies that immediately led to a raft of toys and other products were *Alladin*, *Pinochio*, and the *Hunchback of Notre Dame*. Select one currently "hot" image and complete each of the activities below as you investigate how the appeal of that image is translated into various toys and products.

## ACTIVITY 1  (20 points)

Visit a local toy or department store and make a list of all the items that you see there for sale built around that character or movie . Look in many different departments because you will find items in housewares, book/magazine sections, game/toy/video areas, and even in departments where they sell linens, toothpaste, and clothing.

## ACTIVITY 2  (20 points)

Study the advertising facts below and draw some conclusions as to the buying habits and values of today's consumer.

**In an average lifetime . . .**
— the average American spends 6 months looking at advertisements.
— the average American is hit with 136,692,500 advertisements and commercial messages and remembers 2,925,330 of them.
— the average American receives 18,187 pieces of direct-mail advertising.
— direct-mail advertisers destroy 112 trees, sending 1,218 pounds of junk mail to the average American.
— the average American spends 550 days listening to radio commercials.
— the average American spends 2 years, 7 months watching TV commercials.

## ACTIVITY 3 (20 points)

Pretend you have been asked to describe and explain the selected craze to a group of foreign visitors who know nothing about them. Do this by answering the 5 W's and How questions below. Do your work on a separate piece of paper.

1. Who are they?
2. When did they first become popular?
3. Where can you buy them?
4. What makes them so appealing to kids?
5. How are they marketed?
6. Why are they being "panned and banned" by parents, educators, religious leaders, and youth organizations all over the world?

## BONUS (20 points)

Compose a friendly letter to a younger child warninghim/her of how excessive application of a current fad may be dangerous to his/her health.

## Unlock Your Power Feelings

PURPOSE
To encourage student expression of personal feelings about powerful ideas that are often complex and opposite in their meaning or context


SPECIAL MATERIALS NEEDED
None


DIRECTIONS  (30 points)
Think about each of the "powerful" questions in the activities below. Notice that the ideas expressed in these questions are not simple, but very complex. The terms are also opposite in meaning which forces us to make choices in our responses to the questions and to validate or defend those choices.

Choose any three of the "powerful" questions and react to them by writing a response to each one expressing your personal feelings and sharing your personal opinions. You may want to review and/or include the multiple definitions of "power" as you learned them through your investigations and work at this learning station. Do this on a separate piece of paper.


### ACTIVITY 1  (10 points)

Question:      Which is more POWERFUL — love or hate?


### ACTIVITY 2  (10 points)

Question:      Which is more POWERFUL — success or failure?


### ACTIVITY 3  (10 points)

Question:      Which is more POWERFUL — infancy or old age?

## ACTIVITY 4 (10 points)

Question:     Which is more POWERFUL — keeping a promise or keeping a secret?

## ACTIVITY 5 (10 points)

Question:     Which is more POWERFUL— honesty or loyalty?

## ACTIVITY 6 (10 points)

Question:     Which is more POWERFUL — an open mind or an open heart?

## ACTIVITY 7 (10 points)

Question:     Which is more POWERFUL —  marriage or divorce?

## ACTIVITY 8 (10 points)

Question:     Which is more POWERFUL — a dream or a nightmare?

## BONUS (20 points)

Try creating a comic strip or cartoon to illustrate one of your "powerful" questions!

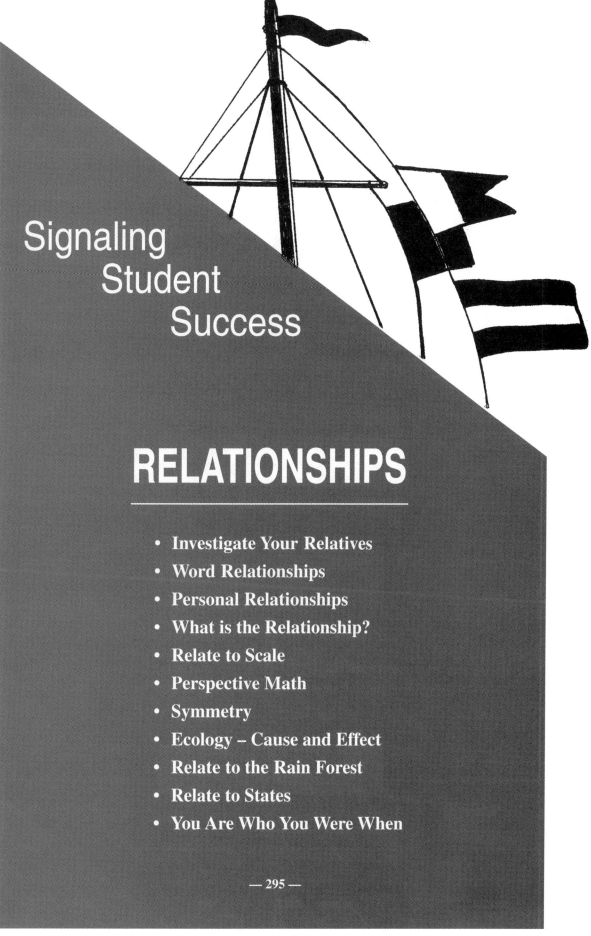

Signaling
Student
Success

# RELATIONSHIPS

- **Investigate Your Relatives**
- **Word Relationships**
- **Personal Relationships**
- **What is the Relationship?**
- **Relate to Scale**
- **Perspective Math**
- **Symmetry**
- **Ecology – Cause and Effect**
- **Relate to the Rain Forest**
- **Relate to States**
- **You Are Who You Were When**

National Middle School Association

**An Introduction to RELATIONSHIPS**

A *relationship* is a connection between or among things. "Kinship" and "affinity" are two synonyms for "relationship." A reviewer might show the relationship between a book and a movie; countries have diplomatic relationships; and one would hope to have good doctor-patient relationship.

Personally, we experience relationships with family members, neighbors, teachers, friends, and business people. Relationships in mathematics include perspective, scale, and symmetry, to name a few. We explore cause/effect relationships as we investigate ecological concerns. We even discover that analogies show relationships between words.

Here are some "related" words: relate, related, relating, relative, relativity, and relation. Look for these as you complete the learning station activities.

## THE GUIDING QUESTIONS

1. Why are family and personal relationships important?

2. How and why do relationships change?

3. What do your relatives mean to you?

4. What makes a relationship?

5. What are different kinds of relationships?

297

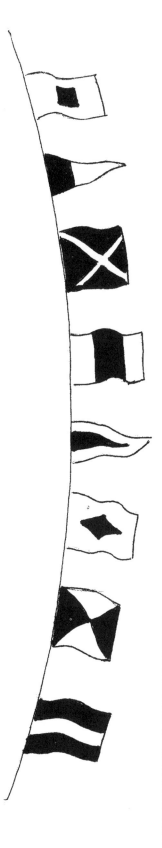

# At a glance — topics and tasks

- **Discover family relationships**
- **Complete and write analogies**
- **Read children's literature and explore various types of relationships**
- **Consider different kinds of relationships**
- **Practice using scale to show the relationship of duplication in art**
- **Investigate and experience the relationship of background and foreground in perspective drawing**
- **Explore and discover relationships in lines of symmetry**
- **Examine the relationship between cause and effect in situations related to ecology**
- **Investigate various aspects of tropical rain forests**
- **Discover the origin of state names**
- **Investigate the relationship of immigration or migration patterns of people in the United States to their appropriate time and place in history**

## Relationship Rubric

Here is a list of the learning stations from which you may choose to work to earn your points. All activities must be done completely, accurately, and neatly to earn full point value. The grading scale is as follows:

| A | B | C | D |
|---|---|---|---|
| 1034-1100 pts. | 935-1033 pts. | 825-934 pts. | 415-824 pts. |

| Date Completed | Activity | Possible Points | Points Earned |
|---|---|---|---|
| _____ | Investigate Your Relatives | 100 - 115 | _____ |
| _____ | Word Relationships | 100 - 115 | _____ |
| _____ | Personal Relation-ships | 100 | _____ |
| _____ | What is the Relation-ship? | 100 - 115 | _____ |
| _____ | Relate to Scale | 100 | _____ |
| _____ | Perspective Math | 100 - 125 | _____ |
| _____ | Symmetry | 100 - 120 | _____ |
| _____ | Ecology   Cause and Effect | 100 - 115 | _____ |
| _____ | Relate to the Rain Forest | 100 | _____ |
| _____ | Relate to States | 100 - 120 | _____ |
| _____ | You Are Who You Were When | 100 - 125 | _____ |

**TOTAL POINTS** _____

**GRADE** _____

## Investigate Your Relatives

PURPOSE
To discover family relationships

SPECIAL MATERIALS NEEDED
Dictionary

DIRECTIONS  (100 points)
Complete the activities below.

---

### ACTIVITY 1 (5 points)

Define these family terms:

| | |
|---|---|
| sibling | half-sister |
| in-law | stepfather |
| nephew | great-grandparent |
| niece | foster brother |
| | cousin |

---

### ACTIVITY 2 (10 points)

Explain the meaning of these two quotations:

*Fate chooses our relatives; we choose our friends.* — J. DeLille
*It is a melancholy truth that even great men have poor relations.*— Charles Dickens

---

### ACTIVITY 3 (15 points)

Select a favorite relative you would like to interview. Who is it and what is this person's relation to you? Prepare a set of 10 interview questions you would like to ask this individual.

## ACTIVITY 4 (20 points)

Determine these relationships to you:
   a. your mother's brother
   b. your father's sister
   c. your grandfather's brother
   d. your sister's husband
   e. your brother's child
   f. your mother's mother

Discover how your parents, guardians, or grandparents met. Illustrate the meeting using some media.

## ACTIVITY 5 (25 points)

Plan a family reunion. Decide on the date (day of the week and month of the year) and time of day; create the invitation; plan the menu. Decide on the activities and the category for a special prize. List the names of the relatives you will invite.

## ACTIVITY 6 (25 points)

Complete each of these starter statements and justify each of your responses.

The relative I most admire is . . . because . . .

The one thing I'd like to change about my family is . . . because . . .

I would like to be just like my . . . because . . .

I wish my . . . would . . . because . . .

I'll never understand why my . . . says/does . . .

## BONUS (15 points)

Interview the favorite relative from Activity 3 and present the information you learned.

## Word Relationships

PURPOSE
To complete and write analogies

SPECIAL MATERIALS NEEDED
None

DIRECTIONS (100 points)
Read the information below and follow all directions.

## ACTIVITY 1 (70 points)

Analogies show relationships between two things. In the following sets of analogies, you must discover the relationship between the first two words in order to determine the same relationship for words three and four (your answer).

Here are some examples of word relationships:

| | |
|---|---|
| SYNONYMS | automobile is to car |
| ANTONYMS | tall is to short |
| CATEGORIES | instrument is to clarinet |
| PART/WHOLE | mouth is to face |

Consider these types of relationships as you complete the following analogies. Use notebook paper for your answers. Note the use of the colon (:) in each analogy.

**Example:** automobile : car :: blimp : dirigible

1. hotel : inn :: house : _____
2. leaf : tree :: blade : _____
3. fruit : jelly :: milk : _____
4. physician : doctor :: educator : _____
5. burger : sandwich :: rose : _____
6. crown : hat :: boot : _____
7. store : shop :: cafe : _____
8. sit : stand :: ride : _____
9. night : day :: mom : _____

10. enter : exit      ::    up : _____
11. red : danger      ::    yellow : _____
12. stop : go      ::    black : _____
13. act : stage      ::    cook : _____
14. Columbus : Ohio      ::    Sacramento : _____
15. pound : Britain      ::    drachma : _____
16. Mustang : Ford      ::    Corvette : _____
17. Tallahassee : Florida      ::    Springfield : _____
18. Nile : Africa      ::    Amazon : _____
19. yen : Japan      ::    lira : _____
20. descend : canyon      ::    ascend : _____
21. plant : seed      ::    harvest : _____
22. cherish : value      ::    loathe : _____
23. airplane : hangar      ::    automobile : _____
24. hand : arm      ::    foot : _____
25. run : track      ::    swim : _____
26. visualize : see      ::    vocalize : _____
27. daisy : flower      ::    oak : _____
28. bear : cub      ::    cow : _____
29. student : teacher      ::    player : _____
30. diver : sea      ::    climber : _____
31. brush : artist      ::    instrument : _____
32. car : road      ::    train : _____
33. paternal : father      ::    maternal : _____
34. book : read      ::    song : _____
35. clock : time      ::    thermometer : _____

## ACTIVITY 2 (30 points)

Create ten more original analogies. Write them using the colon (:). Identify each one as to type:

| | | | |
|---|---|---|---|
| a. | synonyms | c. | categories |
| b. | antonyms | d. | part/whole |
| | | e. | other |

**Example:** a. peer : colleague    ::    magazine : periodical

## BONUS (15 points)

Define the following terms and give an example of each.

Symbiotic Relationship      Etymology
Sibling Rivalry      Fraternal
     Theory of Relativity

# Personal Relationships

PURPOSE
To read children's literature as a means of exploring various types of relationships

SPECIAL MATERIALS NEEDED
2-3 copies of each of these titles:

*The Pain and the Great One*, Judy Blume
*The Giving Tree*, Shel Silverstein
*Together*, George Ella Lyon
*Love You Forever*, Robert Munsch
*My Mother's Getting Married*, Jean Drescher
*A Letter From Mom, A Letter From Dad*, David Novak
Others - teacher's choice

Posterboard; markers

DIRECTIONS (100 points)
Select four of the books to read; then complete the activities below.

## ACTIVITY 1 (5 points)

List the titles and authors of the four books you choose to read. Identify the main character(s) in each.

## ACTIVITY 2 (10 points)

Explain the title of each story in two or three sentences for each book.

## ACTIVITY 3 (15 points)

Differentiate between reality and fantasy in all four books.

## ACTIVITY 4 (20 points)

Compare and contrast the stories focusing on the relationships in each.

## ACTIVITY 5 (25 points)

Design a poster advertising one of the books. Include title, author, brief summary, and colorful illustrations. Be sure to pay attention to the relationships in the story.

OR

In two or three well-developed paragraphs, rewrite the ending of one of the stories.

## ACTIVITY 6 (25 points)

Decide which story you liked the best. Justify your choice with three reasons.

# What Is the Relationship?

PURPOSE
To consider different kinds of relationships

SPECIAL MATERIALS NEEDED
Plain white paper; black pens; markers; magazines; scissors; glue sticks

DIRECTIONS  (100 points)
Think carefully about the relationships suggested below and write at least one paragraph for each one selected.

## ACTIVITY 1 (80 points)

Select ten relationships from the list that follows. Explain in detail the relationship between . . .

a coach and the team
leisure time and enjoyment
punctuation and writing or speaking
an older sister and a younger brother
studying, practicing, and success
you and your pet
dress/clothing and behavior
music and emotions
volunteer work and satisfaction
you and your best friend

diet and fitness
teamwork and success
a cashier and a customer
an employer and an employee
your attitude and your behavior
courage and heroic acts
holiday dinners and family stories
an outline and a research report
latitude and longitude
a photograph and a memory

## ACTIVITY 2 (20 points)

Discover four different pictures that represent four different kinds of relationships. Label each picture and describe what you think is happening. Use a different piece of plain paper for each.

## BONUS  (15 points)

Draw an eight-frame comic strip depicting a relationship between siblings or best friends. Use the white paper and black pens at this station.

## Relate to Scale

PURPOSE
To practice using scale to show the relationship of duplication in art

SPECIAL MATERIALS NEEDED
Magazines; scissors; 1/4" graph paper transparency (one per person); 1" graph paper (one per person)

DIRECTIONS (100 points)
One way to show relationships of size in art is by using graph paper of varying dimensions and replicating a design or picture square by square. Try your hand at duplicating a picture in a larger size. Complete the following activity.

## ACTIVITY (100 points)

The vase of flowers has been reproduced and enlarged by replicating the same lines in the larger squares (Figure B) that you see in the smaller squares (Figure A).

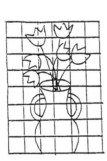
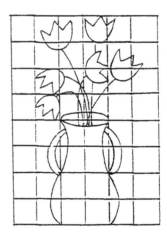

Figure A                    Figure B

To try this technique, cut out a picture from a magazine. (It should not be any larger than 1/4 of the page.) Place the transparency graph on top of the picture. Take a piece of one inch graph paper and try to replicate the magazine picture, one square at a time.

## Perspective Math

PURPOSE
To investigate and experience the relationship of background and foreground in perspective drawing

SPECIAL MATERIALS NEEDED
Books on perspective drawing; drawing paper; pencils; rulers; scissors; access to reference books; magazines; 12 X 18 construction paper; water base markers; glue sticks

DIRECTIONS  (100 points)
Art uses mathematics to show the relationship between background and foreground in a picture. Artists draw objects as they appear to the eye: smaller in the background, larger in the foreground. They use a procedure called PERSPECTIVE to achieve a realistic look. Perspective makes distant objects look smaller and is achieved by drawing parallel lines that meet at a vanishing point.

## ACTIVITY 1 (50 points)

Notice how the parallel lines in the following picture make the foreground look closer and the background look farther away.

As the result of the study of perspective, a new branch of mathematics called projective geometry was founded by a Frenchman named Girard Desargues. Do some research on Desargues and/or projective geometry. Find ten facts on the topic and create a magazine report (see directions on next page).

## MAGAZINE REPORT DIRECTIONS

1. Make a list of the ten most important facts or key ideas and restate them into a set of ten sentences.
2. Fold three pieces of 12" X 18" construction paper in half to make a booklet.
3. Starting with the inside front cover, carefully print one sentence on each page.
4. Search through magazines for illustrations to go with each idea (or draw your own). Paste them in the booklet.
5. Design a creative title page for the front of the booklet and tell about the author (you) on the back.

## ACTIVITY 2 (50 points)

In the example below, figure ABDE is the same shape as figure GHJK, but it is smaller. Draw something in figure ABDE and duplicate it in figure GHJK. What is the relationship?

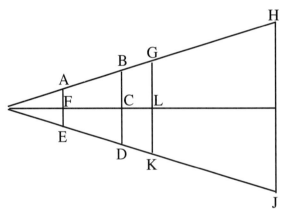

## BONUS (25 points)

Try your hand at perspective drawing. Study the art books at the station to get a "feel" for it. Use parallel lines and one or more vanishing points. Consider drawing one of the following:

    a. a train coming toward you
    b. a room inside a house
    c. an external view of a house
    d. a country lane with a distant farm
    e. an abstract design of three dimensional geometric shapes

---

## Symmetry

PURPOSE
To explore and discover relationships in lines of symmetry

SPECIAL MATERIALS NEEDED
Construction paper; scissors; rulers; compass; magazines; drawing paper; colored pencils

DIRECTIONS  (100 points)
The dictionary defines symmetry as a similar form or arrangement on either side of a dividing line. In other words, when something is divided in half, both halves are the same. Not all things are symmetrical when divided in half. Sometimes a figure or an item has no line of symmetry; sometimes there is only one line of symmetry; and sometimes there are two or more lines of symmetry. In the following activities, you will make some "symmetric" discoveries.

---

## ACTIVITY 1 (50 points)

1.  Measure and cut a 6" by 9" piece of construction paper.
2.  Fold the paper in half.
3.  Draw an irregular design on one half, cut through both thicknesses (do not cut the fold) and open it up. For example:

 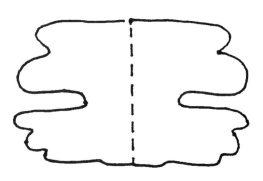

What do you notice about the halves? The fold is called the line of symmetry.

4.  Try folding your cut out another way so that both halves are symmetrical. Can you do it?
5.  Measure and cut a 6" square piece of construction paper.
6.  Fold the square in half, side to side, then open it back up. Are the two halves symmetrical?

310

7. Fold the same square in half, top to bottom. Are the two halves symmetrical?
8. Now fold on the diagonal. Is it symmetrical?
9. Predict what will happen if you fold on the other diagonal. Test your hypothesis. The irregular design had only one line of symmetry. How many lines of symmetry did the square have? How many lines of symmetry does a circle have? Set up an experiment to test your hypothesis.
    a. State your hypothesis.
    b. Perform an experiment to test your hypothesis.
    c. Analyze the results.
    d. State your conclusions.

---

## ACTIVITY 2 (50 points)

A. Use the letters of the alphabet to answer the following questions.

# A B C D E F G H I J K L M N O P Q R S T U V W X Y Z

1. Which letter(s) have no lines of symmetry?
2. Which letter(s) have one line of symmetry?
3. Which letter(s) have two lines of symmetry?

B. Name at least five examples of symmetry in nature.
C. Name at least five examples of symmetry in construction.
D. Name at least five examples of geometric shapes that are symmetrical.

---

## BONUS (20 points)

Look through the magazines for a good picture of a person's head (front view). Find one as large as possible. Cut the picture out. Fold the picture in half on its line of symmetry. Cut on the fold. Take a piece of drawing paper and fold it in half. Open it back up. Paste the half picture on the drawing paper along the fold as shown.

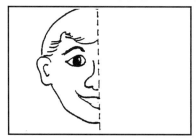

Draw the other half of the face so that it is symmetrical.
**Note:** If you have access to a digital camera, have the teacher or classmate take your picture; then print it out to use in the activity instead of a magazine picture.

## Ecology — Cause and Effect

PURPOSE
To examine the relationship between cause and effect in situations related to ecology and to take action to minimize the negative impact on our environment

SPECIAL MATERIALS NEEDED
Access to reference materials on ecology

DIRECTIONS  (100 points)
Complete each of the following activities as directed.

## ACTIVITY 1 (70 points)

For each of the following facts, consider some possible effects and suggest some possible solutions. Use reference books as needed.

A.     *Fact* – The current worldwide carbon dioxide releases from burning fossil fuels (oil, coal, gasoline) total 22 billion tons per year.


*Possible Effects*


*Possible Solutions*


*Fact* – Flying in an airplane generates a half-pound of carbon dioxide per passenger per mile.


*Possible Effects*


*Possible Solutions*

*Fact* – As of the 1990 Census, there were almost six billion people on earth. That figure is expected to double in 60 years.


*Possible Effects*


*Possible Solutions*


*Fact* – Each year, the earth's population increases by 85 million people.


*Possible Effects*


*Possible Solutions*


*Fact* – In just one year, the United States buries enough metals to build two million cars.


*Possible Effects*


*Possible Solutions*


*Fact* – In just one year, the United States buries enough wood to construct one million homes.


*Possible Effects*


*Possible Solutions*

*Fact* – In one year, the United States dumps enough aluminum to build 500,000 mobile homes.

*Possible Effects*

*Possible Solutions*

*Fact* – It costs $20 billion a year to process our garbage.

*Possible Effects*

*Possible Solutions*

*Fact* – Styrofoam takes thousands of years to decompose, yet the United States makes 25 billion styrofoam containers each year, most of which end up in landfills.

*Possible Effects*

*Possible Solutions*

*Fact* – Nineteen trillion gallons of waste are dumped directly into streams, rivers, and oceans each year.

*Possible Effects*

*Possible Solutions*

314

*Fact* – Despite the 1972 Clean Water Act, factories and cities in the United States continue to dump five trillion gallons of toxic waste into coastal waters every year.

*Possible Effects*

*Possible Solutions*

*Fact* – More than 1,000 children in the world die every hour from diarrhea caused by polluted water.

*Possible Effects*

*Possible Solutions*

---

## ACTIVITY 2 (30 points)

Respond to three of the following four quotations. What meaning does each have for you?

*If you don't buy recycled products, you're not recycling.* — Will Steger

*Think globally, act locally.* — Buckminster Fuller

*Conservation dos not mean the locking up of our resources, nor a hindrance to real progress in any direction. It means only wise, careful use.* — Mary Huston Gregory

*Our wildlife resources are among our most valuable assets, and there can be no higher public duty than to aid in their preservation.* — Charles Lathrop Pack

## BONUS (15 points)

Take action against pollution or for conservation in one of the following ways:

Create a public service announcement for your school news program.

      OR

Design a postage stamp for the post office.

      OR

Invent a slogan and make computer banners to display in your school.

      OR

Write a letter to your local member of Congress.

      OR

Create a poster to display in a store window.

      OR

Compose a song, rap, or poem, and perform it for your class.

      OR

Plan a Conservation Awareness Day for your school.

## Relate to the Rain Forest

PURPOSE
To investigate various aspects of tropical rain forests

SPECIAL MATERIALS NEEDED
Access to reference materials, CD-ROM, and the media center; plain white paper; posterboard and markers

DIRECTIONS  (100 points)
Select and complete one activity from five of the seven intelligences below. Each of the five will be worth 20 points – total 100.

All of the following activities are related to rain forests. Here are some interesting facts:

1. Rain forests account for only 7% of the earth's land surface but contain 50% of the earth's trees and more than 10 million species of plants and animals.
2. 45 million chopsticks made from rain forest hardwoods are imported by Japan every month.
3. In Brazil alone, an area the size of the state of Nebraska, 76,000 square miles of rain forest are destroyed each year.
4. Publishing the Sunday edition of the *New York Times* consumes 10,000 trees each week.

## ACTIVITY  (100 points — 20 each X 5)

1. Verbal/Linguistic Intelligence

    a. Write an editorial stating your opinion of the destruction of rain forests. Support your opinion with factual information.

    b. Create five slogans to be used on a poster protesting the destruction of rain forests.

2. Logical/Mathematical Intelligence

    a. Discover and categorize facts and information relating to the causes, effects, and possible solutions for rain forest destruction.

    b. Design a chart depicting the different species of animal and plant life in the three largest tropical rain forests – the American, the African, and the Asian.

3. Bodily/Kinesthetic Intelligence

    a. Use the CD-ROM to research tropical rain forests. Discover: a definition; location in the world; temperature; rainfall; plant and animal life; types of destruction; and suggestions for solutions.

    b. Plan a simulation which will enable your class to learn more about tropical rain forests. What will you do? How long will this simulation last? What will your class do as a result of this experience?

4. Visual/Spatial Intelligence

    a. Design a billboard to make the public aware of the destruction of tropical rain forests.

    b. Illustrate or draw a scene from a tropical rain forest.

5. Musical/Rhythmic Intelligence

    a. Use a well-known melody to help you write the words to a song about the beauty of a tropical rain forest.

    b. Create a poem or rap related to the effects of the destruction of tropical rain forests.

6. Interpersonal Intelligence

    a. Plan a family vacation to a tropical rain forest area as an "ecotourist." Determine where you will go, how you will get there, and how long you will stay. Why did you choose this area?

    b. With a partner, investigate the depletion of rain forests because of the worldwide demand for lumber. For what is the lumber needed? What are the effects on the rain forest? What is your opinion about this? Who is FOR this policy and who is AGAINST it? Why?

7. Intrapersonal Intelligence

    a. Pretend you are a visitor to a tropical rain forest. Write five daily journal entries describing what you see, what you do, and your personal reactions to your experiences. Where are you?

    b. Discover the many ways that a jungle differs from a tropical rain forest. Which would you prefer to visit? Why?

## Relate to States

**PURPOSE**
To discover the origin of state names

**SPECIAL MATERIALS NEEDED**
Access to media center or several reference materials in the classroom

**DIRECTIONS** (100 points)
Complete the instructions with each activity.

## ACTIVITY 1 (70 points)

Find the origin of the following state names.

Example: Alabama – from a tribe of the Creek Confederacy
New York – honors the English Duke of York
Texas – Caddo word for "friendly tribe"

1. Mississippi
2. Arizona
3. West Virginia
4. Michigan
5. Missouri
6. Arkansas
7. Massachusetts
8. Montana
9. Washington
10. California
11. Maine

12. Virginia
13. Nevada
14. Connecticut
15. Kentucky
16. Vermont
17. New Jersey
18. Delaware
19. Utah
20. Tennessee
21. Kansas
22. Rhode Island
23. District of Columbia

24. New Mexico
25. South Dakota
26. Pennsylvania
27. Georgia
28. Iowa
29. Oregon
30. Indiana
31. North Carolina
32. Hawaii
33. Idaho
34. North Dakota
35. Illinois

## ACTIVITY 2 (20 points)

Discover the state name for the following origins:

>    Example:   Honors Louis XIV of France — Louisiana
>              Chippewa word for "grassy place" — Wisconsin
>              Honors Queen Henrietta Marie — Maryland

1. Spanish word for "red"
2. Honors King Charles I
3. Omaha name for Platte River, "broad river"
4. Delaware word meaning "mountains and valleys alternating"
5. Named for English county of Hampshire
6. Sioux word for "sky-tinted water"
7. Spanish word meaning "feast of flowers"
8. Iroquois word for "beautiful river"
9. Choctaw word for "red people"
10. Russian version of Aleut word meaning "great land"

## ACTIVITY 3 (10 points)

Using all of the information gathered in the previous two activities, classify the origins of our states' names. Be specific and explain your classifications.

## BONUS (20 points)

Select ten capital cities to research to discover the origin of each name. Can you draw any conclusions as you did in Activity 3?

320

## You Are Who You Were When

PURPOSE
To investigate the relationship of immigration or migration patterns of people in the United States to their appropriate time and place in history

SPECIAL MATERIALS NEEDED
World map for each student; reference book(s) on surnames; library books on immigration/migration

DIRECTIONS  (100 points)
All of us, or our ancestors, have either emigrated to this country from somewhere else (unless you are a Native American) and/or we have migrated from another part of the country to where we now live. Complete the following activities to find the relationship of your immigration to personal or historical events.

## ACTIVITY 1 (20 points)

1. Consider your personal experiences with moving. Ask yourself or your family the following questions:

    a. Have you ever moved from one country to another? one state to another? one town to another? one part of town to another?

    b. What reasons did you or your family have for moving? a better job? a better way of life? safety? Relate your reasons to the first set of questions.

2. Interview your parents and/or grandparents to find out where your roots lie. On the world map, trace your roots (as many as you could find). Draw a line from where you live now to places you have lived previously and to places where your ancestors lived.

    a. Determine the reason for your family's immigration/migration.

    b. Identify the hardships along the way.

OR

Determine information about your genetic history.

OR

Trace the origins of your first and/or last name.

## ACTIVITY 2 (20 points)

Discover the relationship of your origin (native country or region of the United States) to each of the following:

a. favorite music style (i.e., country, reggae, jazz, bluegrass, urban rap, etc.)
b. favorite foods
c. art/architecture
d. dance
e. sport
f. customs and traditions
g. phrases, slang, and dialect
h. other

## ACTIVITY 3 (20 points)

1. Research to discover the waves of immigration/migration in the United States and their relationship(s) to major world or United States events. Set up a chart like the one below and enter the data as you find it. Here is a start.

| DATE | ETHNIC GROUP(S) | EVENT |
|------|-----------------|-------|
| 1848 | German | Revolution in Germany |
| 1970 | Vietnamese | Vietnam War |
| 1800s | Native Americans | Indian Removal Act |
| 1846 | Irish | Ireland Potato Famine of |
| 1870s | African Americans | United States Civil War |

2. Use the information you gathered in part 1 to create a time line of "Waves of Immigration/Migration."

## ACTIVITY 4 (20 points)

The Statue of Liberty stands as a symbol of freedom and opportunity for immigrants to this country.

a. Where is the Statue of Liberty located?
b. How did she get there?
c. What words are inscribed on her?
d. What do you think they mean?
e. How would you feel if you were an immigrant and just saw her for the first time?
f. Does America continue to open her arms to immigrants today? Should we? Why or why not?

## ACTIVITY 5 (20 points)

1.  Discover the ethnic make-up of your school and community.

    a.  Many schools keep records on the ethnic make-up of the school population. Investigate to try to find your school's make-up.

    b.  Your local school board should have the data for all the schools in your district.

    c.  Your local city and county planning departments keep figures on area population by race and ethnicity.

    d.  The phone book is a great source of information on ethnic names. Use a reference book on surnames to help you recognize ethnic names.

2.  Create a graphic representation of your findings.

## BONUS (25 points)

The videos listed below show the cause/effect relationships of forced immigration or migration. Select one to view and complete the following questions/statements.

IMMIGRATION
*An American Tail*
*Roots: The Triumph of an American Family (Parts 1 and 2)*
*Hester Street*
*The Way of the Willow*
*Manong*
America Series (Allistar Cooke)
    —*The Huddled Masses*

MIGRATION
*The Grapes of Wrath*
*The Trail of Tears*
America Series (Allistar Cooke)
    —*Gone West*
    —*Domesticating a Wilderness*
    —*Money on the Land*

1.  How does the title relate to the content of the video?

2.  Determine the kinds of relationships presented in the video.

3.  Which relationships did you relate to most and for what reason?

# RELATIONSHIPS - ANSWER KEY

**Investigate Your Relatives**

ACTIVITY 4

a. uncle
b. aunt
c. great uncle
d. brother-in-law
e. niece or nephew
f. grandmother

**Word Relationships**

ACTIVITY 1

1. home, abode
2. grass, saw
3. cheese
4. teacher
5. flower, bush
6. shoe
7. restaurant
8. walk
9. sun
10. down
11. caution
12. white
13. kitchen
14. California
15. Greece
16. Chevrolet
17. Illinois
18. South America
19. Italy
20. mountain
21. crops
22. hate
23. garage
24. leg
25. pool, lake, ocean
26. speak, sing
27. tree
28. calf
29. coach
30. mountain
31. musician
32. track
33. mother
34. sing
35. temperature

**Symmetry**

ACTIVITY 1
3. They are the same; they are symmetrical
4. no
6. yes
7. yes
8. yes
9. Will be symmetrical. It is symmetrical.
   4 lines
   Infinite

ACTIVITY 2
- A. 1.     F, G, J, L, N, P, Q, R, S, Z
     2.     A, B, C, D, E, K, M, T, U, V, W, Y
     3.     H, I, O, X
- B. Possible answers: snowflake, butterfly, flowers, starfish, shells, human body
- C. Possible answers: United States capital, capital dome, bridge, church steeple, Monticello
- D. Possible answers: square, rectangle, equilateral triangle, circle, oral, hexagon


**Ecology – Cause and Effect**

ACTIVITY 1 (suggested answers)
- A. Possible Effects – acid rain, lung disease, asthma, heart disease, cancer, fish kills, global warming, raised sea levels, shifting rainfall patterns, ozone depletion
  Possible Solutions – slow population growth, develop and use alternative fuels (natural gas, solar energy, wind energy, hydropower)
- B. Possible Effects – energy overuse, human illness and disease, famine, global warming
  Possible Solutions – slow population growth, ecology education programs
- C. Possible Effects – contamination of drinking water, air pollution, costly landfill clean-ups
  Possible Solutions – recycle and reuse
- D. Possible Effects - animal kills, chlorofluorocarbons reduce ozone layer, increased disease, skin cancer, cataracts, crop destruction, climate changes
  Possible Solutions - replace styrofoam with biodegradable packaging, recycle plastic
- E. Possible Effects – contamination of plant and animal life, hepatitis, malaria, typhoid, cancer, birth defects
  Possible Solutions - sewage treatment, enforcement of 1972 Clean Water Act, chemical recycling


**Relate to States**

ACTIVITY 1
1. Chippewa word for "great river"
2. Spanish version of Pima word meaning "little spring place"
3. Honors "Virgin Queen" Elizabeth I
4. Chippewa word for "great water"
5. Named after tribe of Missouri Indians, "town of large canoes"
6. French version of "Kansas," a Sioux word meaning "south wind people"

7.  Algonquin word for "large mountain place"
8.  Spanish word meaning "mountainous"
9.  Honors George Washington
10. Mythical island paradise in Spanish literature
11. From "The Main," used to distinguish the mainland from the offshore islands
12. Honors "Virgin Queen" Elizabeth I
13. Spanish word meaning "snow-clad"
14. Algonquin word meaning "beside the long river"
15. Iroquois word meaning "meadowland"
16. From the French words for "green mountain"
17. Named for island of Jersey in English Channel
18. Honors Lord De La Warr, an early governor of Virginia
19. Refers to Ute tribe, meaning "people of the mountains"
20. Name of Cherokee villages on the Little Tennessee River
21. Sioux word meaning "south wind people"
22. Named for Greek island of Rhodes
23. Honors Columbus
24. Named for Aztec war god "Mexitil"
25. Sioux word meaning "friend" or "ally"
26. Honors Admiral William Penn, father of the founder of the colony
27. Honors King George II
28. Sioux word meaning "beautiful land"
29. Native American word meaning "beautiful water"
30. Land of the Indians
31. Honors King Charles I
32. Polynesian word for "homeland"
33. Shoshone word for "salmon tribe" or "light on the mountains"
34. Sioux word meaning "friend" or "ally"
35. Algonquin word meaning "men" or "warriors"

## ACTIVITY 2

1.  Colorado
2.  South Carolina
3.  Nebraska
4.  Wyoming
5.  New Hampshire
6.  Minnesota
7.  Florida
8.  Ohio
9.  Oklahoma
10. Alaska

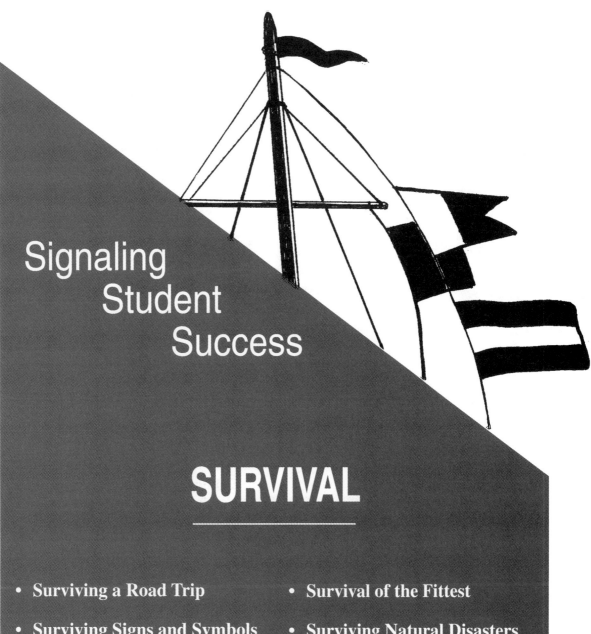

# Signaling
## Student
### Success

# SURVIVAL

- Surviving a Road Trip

- Surviving Signs and Symbols

- Daily Survival

- Surviving Teen Health Issues

- Surviving the Scourge
  of Illiteracy

- Survival of the Fittest

- Surviving Natural Disasters

- Survival Handbook

- Surviving the Wild

- Surviving
  Household Expenses

National Middle School Association

**An Introduction to SURVIVAL**

**The topic of *survival* is one which we all face every day. The dictionary defines survival as the act of existing or living in spite of adversity. Therefore, we can approach the topic of survival in the context of life or death issues and events, or we can view it as dealing with the skills needed to succeed with daily living.**

In science, we become aware that in the face of natural disasters or life-threatening experiences, survival can mean the difference between life and death. Preparedness in the face of killer storms or medical emergencies can help us meet disaster head on. By studying the relationship of the animal and human kingdoms to their environments, we see the fine line we all walk in regards to our own survival.

In social studies, we recognize people and places in the world and our mutual interdependence as we work to survive each day. Issues of transportation, universal symbols, and environmental decisions provide further evidence for the importance of nurturing relationships.

In mathematics, we find that there are skills considered necessary for survival in a complex world. The ability to compute and interpret data help to dictate our quality of life. Skills like money management and those needed to hold a job lead to a more productive and successful existence.

In language arts, we confront the issue of illiteracy that threatens our very survival. The ability to communicate is paramount for survival today.

In short, the many dimensions of "survival" can be applied to any area or topic. These learning stations focus on both routine survival skills and the more dramatic events in our lives.

## THE GUIDING QUESTIONS

1. What survival challenges do people and animals face?

2. What actions do people take for survival?

3. What qualities do survivors possess?

4. How can we help one another survive?

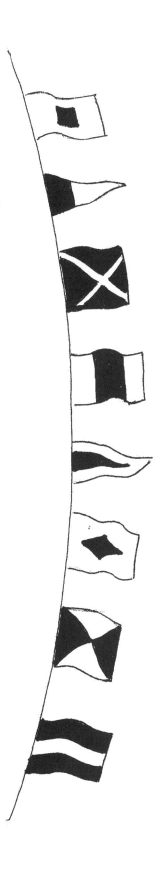

# At a glance — topics and tasks

- Experience the survival skill of planning and budgeting for a major road trip. Map skills and math skills will lead student road warriors through America's highways and byways
- Discover the survival messages of road signs and symbols for pedestrians, bike riders, and future drivers
- Become aware of eating habits that affect the survival of good health and fitness
- Provide students with the opportunity to address health issues of interest to themselves
- Engage in a social action experience helping our nation to survive the scourge of illiteracy
- Provide an opportunity for students to work cooperatively in order to explore survival relationships among animals, people, and the environment
- Discover what causes killer storms and disasters and determine how one prepares to survive these natural disasters
- Collaborate with others to publish a survival handbook on a topic of student choice
- Experience a survival situation through a video enactment
- Investigate the survival skill of dealing with household expenses

# Survival Rubric

Select from the following stations. Activities chosen must be done completely, accurately, and neatly in order to earn full point value. The grading scale is as follows:

| A | B | C | D |
|---|---|---|---|
| 940 pts. | 850 pts. | 750 pts. | 650 pts. |

| Date Completed | Activity | Possible Points | Points Earned |
|---|---|---|---|
| _____ | Surviving A Road Trip | 100 | _____ |
| _____ | Surviving Signs And Symbols | 100 | _____ |
| _____ | Daily Survival | 100 | _____ |
| _____ | Surviving Teen Health Issues | 100 | _____ |
| _____ | Surviving The Scourge Of Illiteracy | 100 | _____ |
| _____ | Survival Of The Fittest | 100 | _____ |
| _____ | Surviving Natural Disasters | 100 | _____ |
| _____ | Survival Handbook | 100 | _____ |
| _____ | Surviving The Wild | 100 | _____ |
| _____ | Surviving Household Expenses | 100 | _____ |

**TOTAL POINTS** _____

**GRADE** _____

## Surviving a Road Trip

PURPOSE
To experience the survival skill of planning and budgeting for a major road trip. Map skills and math skills will lead you student road warriors through America's highways and byways.

SPECIAL MATERIALS NEEDED
U.S. Interstate Highway map for each person; string; calculator

DIRECTIONS (100 points)
You will plan a major road trip to a location of your choice. A well-planned trip can be fun and relaxing. On the other hand, a poorly planned trip can be disastrous. Following are the decisions to be made with specific guidelines attached. Write down the major decision headings listed below on your paper. State your decision for each one. Figure the costs for each heading. Show your figures and explain your reasoning. You may use a calculator and you may estimate costs by rounding off numbers. Finally, figure the total cost for the trip.

### ACTIVITY 1 (20 points)

**Where will you go?** (Consider anywhere in the continental United States and Alaska that is a minimum of 1,500 miles from home. You must visit at least one national park.)

How long will you take to reach your final destination? How many miles do you plan to travel each day? You may take side trips, but must figure them into your calculations. What do you plan to see and do?

### ACTIVITY 2 (20 points)

**Who will go with you?** (Consider taking 1-4 people besides yourself.)
**How much time do you have?** (Consider 2-4 weeks.)

Plan a daily itinerary. Include how many miles you will cover (figure 50 - 60 miles per hour), where you will go, what you will see, and where you will spend the night.

ACTIVITY 3 (20 points)

**How much gas and how much will it cost?** (Remember it depends on the total distance.)

Calculate your total mileage from home to your final destination and back. Figure in any side trips you would make. Figure your gas mileage @ 27 miles per gallon for highway travel and 19 miles per gallon for city travel. Gas will cost $1.29 per gallon.

ACTIVITY 4 (20 points)

**How many meals?** (Plan for 2-3 per day per person.)

Meals may be purchased in restaurants @ $3.00 for breakfast, $6.00 for lunch, and $12.00 for dinner. Be sure to add 6% tax and leave a 15% tip.

OR

You can shop at supermarkets along the way and eat picnic style.

| | |
|---|---|
| bread ..................... | $1.39 a loaf |
| lunch meat ........... | $3.99 a pound (about 12 slices) |
| cheese ................ | $2.99 a pound (about 12 slices) |
| fruit ...................... | $ .99 a pound (about 4 pieces) |
| juice/sodas .......... | $ .30 each |
| others .................. | you supply the figures |

OR

You can mix and match, sometimes picnicking, sometimes eating in restaurants.

ACTIVITY 5 (20 points)

**What will your lodging costs be?** (Remember it depends on the number of rooms.)

You can stay in motels @ $59.00 plus 10% tax per night along the highways. In big cities or at resorts, hotels cost $139.00 plus 10% tax per night OR you may stay in camp grounds @ $25.00 per night OR you may combine motels and campgrounds.

BONUS

**Additional costs**

If you plan to visit attractions with entrance fees, you need to figure those in. Find out what such additional fees would be per person. Calculate your total costs.

# Surviving Signs & Symbols

PURPOSE
To discover the survival messages of road signs and the symbols for student pedestrians, bike riders, and future drivers

SPECIAL MATERIALS NEEDED
Copy of state driver's license handbook for each student

DIRECTIONS  (100 points)
Select any combination of activities to total 100 points. As you choose each question, keep a running total of your points.

## ACTIVITY

KNOWLEDGE (5 points each)
Draw the road sign that matches each of the following descriptions:

1. This five-sided sign means you are near a school. Watch for children.
2. You must not make a right hand turn at this intersection.
3. You cannot make a complete turn to go in the opposite direction where this sign is displayed. No U-turn.
4. Two-Way Traffic Ahead. The one-way road ends ahead. You will then be facing oncoming traffic.
5. Slow down and give vehicles crossing your path the right-of-way. If the way is clear, you may move forward slowly without stopping..
6. Pedestrian crossing. Watch for people crossing the street. Slow down or stop if necessary.
7. 50 miles per hour is the top speed you can travel in this area.
8. Stop sign ahead. When you come to this sign, slow down to be ready to stop at the stop sign.

COMPREHENSION (10 points each)

1. Predict which of the road signs in the driver's handbook are international road signs. Check your predictions.
2. Explain who must wear seat belts when riding in a car. Who is held responsible?
3. Describe the effects of alcohol and drugs on driving.

334

APPLICATION (15 points each)
1. Compute the years, months, and days before you will be eligible by law to drive a car alone.
2. Examine the situations that will result in a revoked driver's license. Which one(s) surprised you the most? Explain.
3. Differentiate between a license to drive a moped and a license to drive a car. Show their differences and similarities on a Venn diagram.

ANALYSIS (20 points each)
1. Categorize the signs by color and by shape. Explain.
2. Colors of road signs are used to signify certain situations. What do the following colors signify? Give examples of each.

yellow      green      black      blue      red      orange

3. Shapes of signs are also significant. What do the following shapes signify? Give examples of each.

diamond                octagon                inverted triangle
pentagon               circle                 vertical rectangle
horizontal rectangle

SYNTHESIS (25 points)
Draw a full page map of your route from school to home. Label the streets. Watch for every traffic or street sign along your route. Locate each sign on your map. Create a key to identify the signs on your map.

EVALUATION (25 points)
Interview someone who works for your state's highway patrol. It should be someone who has access to statistics on traffic accidents. Using statistics from the last five years, what conclusions can you draw? Justify your answer.

BONUS (15 points)

Try your hand at answering the student-designed driver's test questions located at the station.

Use the driver's handbook. Develop 10 multiple choice questions that might appear on the driver's test. Write the questions and four (A-D) multiple choice answers. Include an answer key. Add your questions to the station for others to try.

## Daily Survival

PURPOSE
To become aware of eating habits that affect the survival of good health and fitness

SPECIAL MATERIALS NEEDED
An assortment of recipe books; fat gram counters (from the grocery store checkout counter)

DIRECTIONS  (100 points)
Americans as a group have become more health conscious. You see them at the supermarket reading the labels on food packages. One of the ingredients they are looking for is fat. Fat is a necessary nutrient but many of us consume too much of it. The result can lead to heart disease and other serious ailments. The average adult female needs 20-40 grams per day; the average adult male 30 to 60 grams. Complete any four activities below. You may do the remaining activity as bonus points.

## ACTIVITY 1 (25 points)

Try to remember everything you ate in the last twenty-four hours.
Consider meals, snacks, and drinks. List them.

Now look for each item in the fat gram counter book. Check the front of the book for a list of categories. You may have to break up the item into its component parts. For example, to find the fat grams in a peanut butter and jelly sandwich look under:

| | |
|---|---|
| Two slices bread (breads)............................... | 1.8 fat grams |
| peanut butter (nuts)........................................ | 8.0 fat grams |
| jelly (miscellaneous)....................................... | 0.0 fat grams |

Total the number of fat grams you consumed in the last 24 hours.
Did you fall within the appropriate daily range (females 70-73, males 90-93)?

## ACTIVITY 2 (25 points)

List your favorite meal at MacDonald's, Wendy's, or any other fast food restaurant. Figure out the fat grams for your meal. What was your total? Were you surprised? Does this mean you should never eat at fast food places? What can you do to plan ahead for such a meal?

336

## ACTIVITY 3  (25 points)

Glance through the fat gram counter. Make a list of 10-15 items that you like that are very high in fat grams and a list of 10-15 items that you like that are very low in fat grams.

## ACTIVITY 4  (25 points)

Look through the recipe book. Find a recipe for a favorite food. Try to calculate the fat grams in that recipe. Be sure to look closely at the amounts in the recipe book and the fat gram counter. Where necessary multiply or divide. Once you calculate the total fat grams in the recipe, divide by the number of servings to establish the fat grams per serving.

Are there any substitutes you could make in the recipe to bring down the fat gram total?

## ACTIVITY 5  (25 points)

Watching what we eat is only part of a good health plan. Exercise is also important. Plan a well rounded daily nutrition/exercise plan for yourself. Follow it for two weeks and see what happens. Describe the plan and the results.

## Surviving Teen Health Issues

PURPOSE
To provide students with the opportunity to address health issues of interest to themselves

SPECIAL MATERIALS NEEDED
Books/pamphlets/magazines concerning teen health issues; almanacs; 12" x 18" paper; samples of surveys

DIRECTIONS (100 points)
Complete any five activities as directed. If you wish, do one or both of the remaining activities for bonus points.

## ACTIVITY 1

VERBAL/LINGUISTIC (20 points)
Write an article for a team or school newsletter summarizing the results of your health survey or write a script and videotape a health issues segment for your school news program.

## ACTIVITY 2

LOGICAL/MATHEMATICAL (20 points)

1. Design a health survey to find out the major TEEN health concerns of: other teens — parents — teachers. Be sure to secure appropriate approval of the instrument before distributing it.

2. Predict the results of your health survey; then conduct the survey and evaluate your predictions.

## ACTIVITY 3

VISUAL/SPATIAL (20 points)
Create a mind map or some other visual representation of teen age health issues. Begin with issues you are familiar with; then fill in your mind map with others from research. To start the map put a three inch diameter circle in the center of a 12 x 18 piece of paper. Label the circle TEEN HEALTH ISSUES. Next, draw lines radiat-

ing out from the center circle. Draw a smaller circle at the end of each line. In each circle write a health issue (for example; diseases, eating disorders, addictions, hygiene, etc.) Radiating from each of these circles, write words or draw symbols identifying examples in each category.

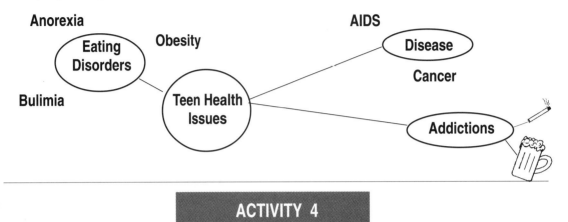

## ACTIVITY 4

BODILY KINESTHETIC (20 points)
Create a physical exercise or dance routine as part of your Personal Health Plan. Demonstrate it for your classmates.

## ACTIVITY 5

MUSICAL/RHYTHMIC (20 points)
Choose a popular song. Create new lyrics for the song using the health theme. If you like, teach the song to your class.

## ACTIVITY 6

INTERPERSONAL (20 points)
Share the results of your survey with other students at the Surviving Teen Health Issues Station. Together brainstorm guidelines for healthy living.

## ACTIVITY 7

INTRAPERSONAL (20 points)
Think about what you have learned about teen health issues so far. List the issues most important to you personally. Design a Personal Health Plan. Write up your plan and set goals for accomplishment.

## Surviving the Scourge of Illiteracy

PURPOSE
To engage in a social action experience helping our nation to survive the scourge of illiteracy

SPECIAL MATERIALS NEEDED
*Readers' Guide to Periodical Literature*; access to the media center; magazines; newspapers

DIRECTIONS (100 points)
Complete the first four activities. Consider completing one or more of the bonus activities.

## ACTIVITY 1 (25 points)

National literacy should be everyone's business. It is time the entire community gets involved. Adults aren't the only ones who can change things. Kids can too, and so can you. To discover just what the depth of the problem is, you need to do some research. Go to your library/media center and look up literacy in the Readers' Guide to Periodic Literature. Read several of the cited articles concerning the issue of literacy. Take notes. Also look in newspapers and almanacs. Identify recent statistics. Make a chart of your findings. Discover the impact illiteracy has on the following factors:

| | | | |
|---|---|---|---|
| job opportunities | income | health | welfare |
| quality of life | families | abuse | poverty |

## ACTIVITY 2 (25 points)

Literacy is a problem both inside of school and out. To combat illiteracy we need to learn to read and then read often. Some schools have grade level recommended reading lists. If your school does, you and your classmates might make recommendations for additions to keep the list current. If your school does not have a reading list, work with your classmates to build one. Be sure to include some of the old classics, Newbery and other award winners, as well as your specific favorites. Here are some ideas to pursue:

1. Create a reading list for your grade level.
2. Develop a reading list for younger students.
3. Compile an annotated bibliography of specific subject area books.

340

## ACTIVITY 3  (25 points)

Work with a partner to create a "Literate" Household Checklist. Your list should include 8-10 recommendations. Assess your household against the list. Establish a plan to upgrade your household if it is needed. Work with your classmates to get the things you need to make your homes, and the homes of others, literate places in which to live.

## ACTIVITY4  (25 points)

Work with service clubs and businesses in your community to support literacy activities. Some things you can do together might be to:

1.  Collect donations for literacy "care" packages and distribute them throughout the community.
2.  Support read-ins or read-a-thons with prizes to individuals and classes who read the most.
3. . Provide bookmarks or buttons.
4.  Start a birthday book club at school (parents donate a book to the school library in celebration of their child's birthday).
5.  Sponsor a book fair.
6.  Organize a paperback book exchange to recycle books.
7.  Write literacy tips for parents through school and local newspapers.
8.  Celebrate literacy month with school-wide celebrations.

What else can you add? Select a project and write a letter to a service club or business and ask for their help. Then JUST DO IT!

## BONUS ACTIVITY  (10 points)

An appropriate slogan to help combat illiteracy might be "EACH ONE TEACH ONE."
You might be able to come up with a better slogan for peer tutoring. Pair up with another student your age or younger and be a reading "buddy." Select a buddy with the approval of your teacher and plan a time to read together. Design a program and put it into action. You will need to consider the following:

1.  Name of reading buddy.
2.  Day and time of meetings.
3.  Place of meeting.
4.  Reading selection.

## BONUS ACTIVITY (15 points)

Build a classroom library or add to the one you already have. Bring in reading materials (books, magazines, etc.) when you are finished with them. Devise a checkout system to circulate the publications. To encourage others to read your contributions you might consider:

| | |
|---|---|
| presenting a short book talk | making a puzzle |
| creating an audio tape | inventing a game |
| designing a mobile | creating a commercial (video) |

## BONUS ACTIVITY (10 points)

Read to a younger child (family member, neighbor, or friend) on a regular basis. If possible take the child to the library so (s)he can make the selections. Set goals for yourself and keep track of the time spent together. If you belong to a service club (Builder's Club, National Junior Honor Society, etc.) keep track of your hours for service points. If you do not belong to a service group, perhaps you can arrange for extra credit points from your teacher.

## Survival of the Fittest

PURPOSE
To provide an opportunity for students to work cooperatively in order to explore
survival relationships among animals, people, and the environment

SPECIAL MATERIALS NEEDED
Cooperative groups of five students; access to library/media center; sample "Just
So" stories; large world maps; *National Geographic* magazines to cut up

DIRECTIONS  (100 points)
Complete the following activities.

## ACTIVITY 1 (25 points)

Discover how the structure of an animal's body can 1) help the animal obtain food,
2) survive temperature extremes, 3) escape enemies, and 4) raise young. Each person in the group is to choose one of the biomes listed below. Then, you are to select
two or more of the animals in the biome to research and find answers for the four
questions listed here. Share and compare each of your findings.

| **Polar Regions** | **Deserts** | **Mountains** |
|---|---|---|
| polar bear | camel | ibex |
| harp seal | jack rabbit | chamois |
| arctic hare | coyote | Rocky Mountain goat |
| musk oxen | roadrunner | bighorn sheep |
| caribou | kit fox | klipsspringer |

| **Rain Forests** | **Savannas** |
|---|---|
| orangutan | giraffe |
| spider monkey | cheetah |
| macaw | African elephant |
| three-toed sloth | ostrich |
| colugo | aardvark |

## ACTIVITY 2 (25 points)

Extinction is usually a natural process. However, people have put many plant and animal populations in serious danger of extinction. By clearing land for cities and farms, by polluting the air, and by dumping waste chemicals into rivers and lakes, people can make habitats unfit for living things. Consider the effects of acid rain, global warming, chemical dumping, and deforestation on the environment. Do some research as needed.

Think about this quote from Buckminister Fuller, "Think globally, act locally." In your group discuss what you think this means and brainstorm 15-20 actions you could take to make a difference. Personally select one or more to take action on. Set a goal, write it down, and do it.

## ACTIVITY 3 (25 points)

Throughout the world hundreds of animals are living on the brink of extinction. The list included here is just a beginning. Choose an animal and discover why it is endangered and ways it might be helped. Once you have made a selection, divide up your group research responsibilities according to these resource/research options:

Member one .................... card catalog/nonfiction collection
Member two .................... *Reader's Guide to Periodic Literature*
Member three ................. Newspaper index and/or vertical file
Member four .................... Reference section
Member five .................... Electronic reference tools

Write up your findings and share with one another.

### ENDANGERED ANIMALS

| | | | |
|---|---|---|---|
| caribou | blue whale | golden parakeet | red wolf |
| chimpanzee | margay | cheetah | jaguar |
| zebra | American | tapir | pronghorn |
| jaguarundi | crocodile | chinchilla | blue whale |
| ocelot | bald eagle | wood bison | masked |
| gray bat | gibbon | dugong | bobwhite |
| Florida panther | gorilla | Indiana bat | orangutan |
| hooded crane | panda | African gorilla | yak |
| gazelle | prairies dog | peregrine falcon | grizzly bear |
| rhinoceros | kit fox | leopard | manatee |
| wallaby | brown pelican | tiger | whooping crane |
| bobcat | African elephant | key deer | |
| American alligator | California condor | Hawaiian hawk | |

## ACTIVITY 4 (25 points)

Choose one:

1. Make an information mobile depicting endangered wildlife. Design a rubric to assess your mobile.

OR

2. Locate the endangered animals listed at this Center on a large world map. You may want to add illustrations or magazine pictures of the endangered species. What conclusions can you draw from this graphic display? Show your map in the classroom or media center. Create a rubric to assess your display.

OR

3. Choose a contemporary man versus wildlife issue to debate (such as the loggers of the American northwest versus the spotted owl.) Two of the group members should take the side of the loggers and two should take the side of the environmentalists wishing to protect the spotted owl. Gather data to support your side of the argument. The fifth person should research debate rules and etiquette, supply the information to the two teams, and organize and manage the debate. Debate your issue in front of the class. Design a rubric for the class to judge the debate.

OR

4. Write fables or "Just So" stories to explain why an animal is endangered or extinct. Use factual information or make up your own. Judge your product against a rubric you have designed.

# Surviving Natural Disasters

## PURPOSE
To discover what causes killer storms and disasters and to determine how one prepares for survival of these natural disasters

## SPECIAL MATERIALS NEEDED
Access to library/media center

## DIRECTIONS  (100 points)
Select one task from each level of Bloom's Taxonomy below. The evaluation level is for bonus points only.

---

## ACTIVITY

### KNOWLEDGE (20 points)
1. Select one of the following types of killer storms or disasters to research.

   | | | |
   |---|---|---|
   | tornado | hurricane | volcano eruption |
   | flood | blizzard | earthquake |
   | sand storm | wildfire | landslide |

2. Identify a specific killer storm or disaster (i.e. Hurricane Andrew, San Francisco Earthquake) to investigate.

3. Locate evacuation routes from your classroom as well as your home in case of a disaster or emergency. Draw a map or write out directions for others to follow.

---

### COMPREHENSION (20 points)
1. Explain what causes the type of storm/disaster you selected.

2. Describe what might happen to the following when such a storm or disaster occurs:

   | | | |
   |---|---|---|
   | humans | animals | plants |
   | buildings | land | water |
   | possessions | food | transportation |

3. Predict the environmental impact of a killer storm or disaster on your community.

APPLICATION (25 points)
1. Predict possible health problems caused by such a storm or disaster.

2. Discuss the impact on the elderly and young children.

3. Plan and conduct a food and clothing drive.

-----

ANALYSIS (20 points)
1. Determine what preparation of food, water, and supplies people should make to use in the event of a disaster.

2. Point out the economic impact of a killer storm or disaster on your community.

3. Use probability and prediction to forecast a killer storm or disaster.

-----

SYNTHESIS (25 points)
1. Create a safety brochure designed to prepare people for disaster survival.

2. Design a storm safety poster. Post it in your school or community.

3. Write a news story as if you were a journalist witnessing the disaster. Be sure to include a headline and byline.

-----

EVALUATION (20 points)
1. In the face of disaster there are many unsung heroes. If you could give an award to a hero or heroes from a recent disaster, what would the award be and who would receive it? Explain.

2. Consider the boy scout motto, "Be prepared." Assess whether this is a motto by which you want to live. Justify your answer.

3. Recommend 8-10 disaster survival tips that you think are important for people in your community. Choose the one you think is most important and tell why.

## Survival Handbook

PURPOSE
To collaborate with others to publish a "survival" handbook on a topic of student choice

SPECIAL MATERIALS NEEDED
Computer (if available); construction paper; markers; video camera/tape; sample survival manuals (from automobile clubs, park and recreation services, libraries, etc.)

DIRECTIONS (100 points)
As a group, select one of the topics below of special interest to you. If you have an idea for a topic that is not listed, ask your teacher's approval before beginning. Follow these steps to complete your handbook.

## ACTIVITY

TOPICS
New Student Handbook
Friendship Handbook
Getting Along in the Family Handbook
Peer Pressure Handbook
School Bus Safety Handbook
Household Safety Handbook
Home Alone Safety Handbook
Baby Sitter Handbook
Other

STEP ONE (10 points)
A. Choose your topic.
B. Consider your intended audience, such as a child, peer, adult, etc.
C. Decide on the format your handbook will take. Consider computer generated with illustrations, handwritten with original illustrations, video with staged setting, etc.

STEP TWO (20 points)
A. Brainstorm a list of tips that the readers /viewers of your handbook will need to know or do in order to survive the situation you have selected. You may want to do some research first.
B. Decide on the order in which you will present your tips.

STEP THREE  (20 points)
A.  Write a draft or video script of your handbook.
B.  Include an introduction and clearly stated purpose.
C.  Create any illustrations, diagrams, maps or charts that will enhance your handbook or video.

STEP FOUR  (20 points)
A.  Edit your survival handbook. Check for errors in sequencing, spelling, and grammar.
B.  Show the handbook to your teacher before completing the final draft.

STEP FIVE  (20 points)
A.  Publish your handbook.
B.  Design a creative, colorful cover. The cover should include the title of your handbook, the authors' names, and an illustration. If you produced a video handbook, create an original video case using the same guidelines.
C.  Decide on the method you will use to share your handbook with its intended audience.

STEP SIX  (20 points)
As a group use the following rubric to evaluate your final product.

|  | Little Evidence | Some Evidence | Strong Evidence |
|---|---|---|---|
| 1. Creative cover | 1 | 2 | 3 |
| 2. Cooperative effort | 1 | 2 | 3 |
| 3. Completeness (all steps evident) | 1 | 2 | 3 |
| 4. Form (spelling, grammar, punctuation, sentence structure) | 1 | 2 | 3 |
| 5. Attractively published presentation | 1 | 2 | 3 |
| 6. Originality expressed | 1 | 2 | 3 |

## Surviving the Wild

PURPOSE
To experience a survival situation through a video enactment

SPECIAL MATERIALS NEEDED
TV, VCR, Video — *A Cry in the Wild, Call of the Wild,* or *My Side of the Mountain*

DIRECTIONS (100 points)
This activity is designed to take four class periods to complete. All responses are to be written in your response journal or on your own paper. Write responses in complete sentences. Rephrase the question. Each response is worth ten points.

## ACTIVITY

### DAY ONE

*BEFORE WATCHING, RESPOND TO THE FOLLOWING:*

1. Look at the video cassette cover. On what book was this video based? Are you familiar with the book or the video? What do you remember?
2. What guesses can you make about this video? Does the title give you any clues?

- *WATCH THE VIDEO FOR THIRTY MINUTES. AFTER WATCHING, RESPOND TO THE FOLLOWING:*

3. From viewing the video so far, what feelings (excitement, fear, anger, joy, anticipation, etc.) have you experienced? Why?

### DAY TWO

- *BEFORE WATCHING, RESPOND TO THE FOLLOWING:*

4. Predict what you think will happen in the video today. Explain.
5. Tell what you hope will happen. Why?

- *WATCH THE VIDEO FOR THIRTY MINUTES. AFTER WATCHING, RESPOND TO THE FOLLOWING:*

6. How do you feel about what is happening in the story?
7. What has surprised you the most?

## DAY THREE

- *BEFORE WATCHING, RESPOND TO THE FOLLOWING:*

8.  Predict what you think will happen next.

- *WATCH THE REST OF THE VIDEO. AFTER WATCHING, RESPOND TO THE FOLLOWING:*

9.  What effect does the music have on you? Do you think it adds to the telling of the story? Explain.
10. Compare yourself to the main character. Tell five ways you are similar and five ways you are different.

---

## BONUS (50 points)

Read the book on which the video was based. Compare the book to the video. Use a Venn Diagram or other graphic organizer to make your comparison.

---

## Surviving Household Expenses

PURPOSE
To investigate the survival skill of dealing with household expenses

SPECIAL MATERIALS NEEDED
None

DIRECTIONS  (100 points)
Select any combination of activities to total 100 points. Use the attached one-month check registry on the following pages to complete the tasks below. For your information, this check registry belongs to a family of three. Both parents are public school teachers and have a child in college.

## ACTIVITY 1

KNOWLEDGE (5 points each)
1.  Identify the different kinds or categories of expenses found in the check registry. List them.
2.  Tabulate the total amount of expenses for each of these categories.

## ACTIVITY 2

COMPREHENSION (10 points each)
1.  Estimate the monthly salary necessary for this family to live comfortably and still pay their expenses.
2.  Determine the monthly expenses not represented in the check registry. List them.

## ACTIVITY 3

APPLICATION (15 points each)
1.  Assuming that these bills are representative for an average month, estimate the yearly expenses in each category.
2.  Keep a record of your personal expenses for one week. Then predict all of your own personal expenses for next month. Plan for the sources of your income and prepare a budget.

## ACTIVITY 4

ANALYSIS (20 points each)
1. Infer what kinds of unexpected expenses could occur to throw a budget off balance.
2. Outline the steps to follow in making an expense budget.

## ACTIVITY 5

SYNTHESIS (25 points each)
1. Create a skit to show the importance of creating an expense budget. Give your characters humorous names (i.e. Bonnie Budget, Debtor Dan). Present the skit to your class or Design an original poster for your classroom entitled "Don't Drown in a Sea of Debts."
2. Imagine what life would be like if everything were free. What unusual effects would this have?

## ACTIVITY 6

EVALUATION (25 points each)
1. Argue the pros and cons of using charge cards on a regular basis. Justify your answer.
2. Recommend a solution to a person who finds himself in debt. Defend its validity.

# CHECK REGISTER LISTING
## 1/1/95 THROUGH 1/31/95

| Date | Number | Transaction | Payment | Deposit | Balance |
|------|--------|-------------|---------|---------|---------|
| 1/1/95 | | Deposit | | 1150.00 | 2412.42 |
| 1/2/95 | 2260 | Express Shoe Repair | 32.10 | | 2380.32 |
| 1/3/95 | 2261 | Son's college room and utilities | 376.00 | | 2004.32 |
| 1/3/95 | | Honor cash | 40.00 | | 1964.32 |
| 1/3/95 | | Deposit | | 160.50 | 2124.82 |
| 1/3/95 | 2262 | Barnett - Jeep auto loan | 258.76 | | 1866.06 |
| 1/4/95 | 2263 | NBD Mortgage | 800.00 | | 1066.06 |
| 1/4/95 | 2264 | Vision contact lenses | 51.36 | | 1014.70 |
| 1/4/95 | 2265 | Optima credit card | 25.00 | | 989.70 |
| 1/4/95 | 2266 | State Farm Auto Insurance | 98.45 | | 891.25 |
| 1/4/95 | 2267 | Parisian clothing | 106.58 | | 784.67 |
| 1/4/95 | 2268 | Son's groceries | 50.00 | | 734.67 |
| 1/4/95 | 2270 | FSU college books | 300.00 | | 434.67 |
| 1/4/95 | 2271 | American Cancer Society charity | 20.00 | | 414.67 |
| 1/4/95 | 2272 | Burdines clothing credit card | 50.00 | | 364.67 |
| 1/4/95 | 2273 | Comcast cable TV recreation | 23.55 | | 341.12 |
| 1/4/95 | 2274 | Cellular One car telephone | 27.09 | | 314.03 |
| 1/4/95 | 2275 | Epiphany Cathedral charity | 15.00 | | 299.03 |
| 1/4/95 | 2276 | HFC credit card | 25.00 | | 274.03 |
| 1/4/95 | | Presto groceries | 85.20 | | 188.83 |
| 1/8/95 | 2277 | Panton's auto svc | 310.34 | | -121.51 |
| 1/8/95 | | Honor cash | 50.00 | | -171.51 |
| 1/8/95 | | Deposit | | 500.00 | 328.49 |
| 1/11/95 | | Presto groceries | 93.07 | | 235.42 |
| 1/12/95 | | Honor cash | 80.00 | | 155.42 |
| 1/13/95 | 2279 | Target store, misc. | 25.00 | | 130.42 |
| 1/15/95 | | Deposit salary | | 2400.00 | 2530.42 |
| 1/15/95 | | MONY Life Ins. | 153.75 | | 2376.67 |
| 1/15/95 | | Nationwide Health Insurance (son) | 149.20 | | 2227.47 |
| 1/15/95 | 2280 | BlueCross/Shield Health Insurance | 240.00 | | 1987.47 |
| 1/15/95 | 2281 | Reader's Digest entertainment | 43.15 | | 1944.32 |

354

| Date | Number | Transaction | Payment | Deposit | Balance |
|---|---|---|---|---|---|
| 1/15/95 | 2282 | Dr. Fritsch Medical | 26.00 | | 1918.32 |
| 1/15/95 | 2283 | GMAC auto (car payment) | 352.73 | | 1565.59 |
| 1/15/95 | 2284 | GTE telephone | 115.97 | | 1449.62 |
| 1/15/95 | 2285 | Presto groceries | 24.30 | | 1425.32 |
| 1/15/95 | 2286 | FPL Electric | 94.44 | | 1330.88 |
| 1/15/95 | 2287 | First Card credit card | 50.00 | | 1280.88 |
| 1/15/95 | 2288 | Son, food | 50.00 | | 1230.88 |
| 1/15/95 | 2289 | Citgo Oil, Auto fuel | 112.39 | | 1118.49 |
| 1/15/95 | 2290 | Timelife Entertainment | 23.65 | | 1904.84 |
| 1/15/95 | 2291 | Dr. Berryman, dentist | 100.00 | | 994.84 |
| 1/15/95 | 2292 | Barnett Visa credit card | 100.00 | | 894.84 |
| 1/15/95 | 2293 | Publisher's Clearing House entertainment | 18.70 | | 876.14 |
| 1/15/95 | 2294 | Timelife t entertainment | 20.65 | | 855.49 |
| 1/15/95 | 2295 | Book of the Month Club, entertainment | 35.00 | | 820.49 |
| 1/15/95 | 2296 | Walgreens Drugstore medicine | 13.45 | | 807.04 |
| 1/15/95 | 2297 | March of Dimes charity | 25.00 | | 782.04 |
| 1/15/95 | 2298 | State Farm auto insurance | 162.82 | | 619.22 |
| 1/15/95 | 2299 | Epiphany Cathedral charity | 20.00 | | 599.22 |
| 1/16/95 | | Deposit salary | | 692.36 | 1291.58 |
| 1/17/95 | 2300 | FSU Tuition | 800.00 | | 491.58 |
| 1/26/95 | | Charge for honor | 2.50 | | 489.08 |
| 1/26/95 | | Service charge | 12.00 | | 477.08 |
| 1/26/95 | 2301 | Post Office stamps | 32.00 | | 445.08 |
| 1/26/95 | 2302 | USF tuition, teacher certification | 326.73 | | 118.35 |
| 1/27/95 | | Mobil auto fuel | 20.00 | | 98.35 |
| 1/27/95 | 2303 | Aqua Soft Utilities: water | 68.62 | | 29.73 |
| 1/28/95 | | Deposit salary | | 2712.17 | 2741.90 |
| 1/28/95 | 2304 | Presto groceries | 63.34 | | 2688.29 |

# NATIONAL MIDDLE SCHOOL ASSOCIATION

National Middle School Association was established in 1973 to serve as a voice for professionals and others interested in the education of young adolescents. The Association has grown rapidly and now enrolls members in all fifty states, the Canadian provinces, and forty-two other nations. In addition, fifty-three state, regional, and provincial middle school associations are official affiliates of NMSA.

NMSA is the only association dedicated exclusively to the education, development, and growth of young adolescents. Membership is open to all. While middle level teachers and administrators make up the bulk of the membership, central office personnel, college and university faculty, state department officials, other professionals, parents, and lay citizens are also actively involved in supporting our single mission – improving the educational experiences of 10-15 year olds. This open and diverse membership is a particular strength of NMSA.

The Association provides a variety of services, conferences, and materials in fulfilling its mission. In addition to *Middle School Journal*, the movement's premier professional journal, the Association publishes *Research in Middle Level Education Quarterly*, a wealth of books and monographs, videos, a general newsletter, an urban education newspaper, and occasional papers. The Association's highly acclaimed annual conference, which has drawn over 10,000 registrants in recent years, is held in the fall.

For information about NMSA and its many services contact the Headquarters at 2600 Corporate Exchange Drive, Suite 370, Columbus, Ohio 43231, TELEPHONE 800-528-NMSA, FAX 614-895-4750.